90's Showstoppers

15800 N.W. 48th Avenue, Miami, Florida 33014

Design: Jeannette Aquino, Frank Milone
Editor: Carol Cuellar

CONTENTS

ALL 4 LOVE....60
ALL I HAVE....64
ALL I WANT....70
ALWAYS AND FOREVER....77
BREATHLESS....210
CAN'T FORGET YOU....80
CAN'T STOP THIS THING WE STARTED....88
COME TO MY WINDOW....232
THE COMFORT ZONE....93
COMING OUT OF THE DARK....44
CUTS BOTH WAYS....98
THE DANCE....35
A FACE IN THE CROWD....102
FAIRY TALES....108
FOREVER'S AS FAR AS I'LL GO....38
FROM A DISTANCE....4
GEORGIA ON MY MIND....105
GET OVER IT....178
HERE AND NOW....16
HERE I AM....227
HERE I AM (Come And Take Me)....112
HERE WE ARE....54
HOLD ON....116
HOW 'BOUT US....130
HOW CAN I EASE THE PAIN....126
HOW MANY WAYS....278
I APOLOGIZE....360
I CAN LOVE YOU LIKE THAT....80
I CAN'T MAKE YOU LOVE ME....12
I CAN'T WAIT ANOTHER MINUTE....135
(EVERYTHING I DO) I DO IT FOR YOU....20
I DON'T HAVE THE HEART....41
I DON'T WANNA CRY....140
IF TOMORROW NEVER COMES....145
IF YOU GO....348
INTO THE GREAT WIDE OPEN....148
IT'S A SHAME (MY SISTER)....152
IT'S SO HARD TO SAY GOODBYE TO YESTERDAY....32
I'LL SEE YOU IN MY DREAMS....158
I'LL TAKE YOU THERE....162
LEARNING TO FLY....173
LIGHT MY FIRE....184

LIVE AND LET DIE 187
LIVE FOR LOVING YOU 190
LOVE AT FIRST SIGHT 195
LOVE SNEAKIN' UP ON YOU 356
MASTERPIECE 25
MAKE IT LIKE IT WAS 216
MENTAL PICTURE 155
MERCY, MERCY ME (The Ecology)/I WANT YOU 205
MISSING YOU 120
MORE THAN WORDS 8
MUSTANG SALLY 220
MY GIRL 340
OYE MI CANTO 236
PLACES THAT BELONG TO YOU 49
ROAM 242
ROCKIN' YEARS 246
SEAL OUR FATE 252
SECRET 168
THE SECRET GARDEN 256
SHE'S MY BABY 249
SHOW ME THE WAY 28
SIGNS 267
SOME PEOPLE'S LIVES 200
SOUL INSPIRATION 270
TALK TO ME 275
TELL ME WHAT YOU WANT ME TO DO 282
THESE THREE WORDS 288
THINK TWICE 224
THIS OLD HEART OF MINE 294
TOUCH ME ALL NIGHT LONG 298
TRUE COMPANION 303
TRY A LITTLE TENDERNESS 308
U CAN'T TOUCH THIS 312
UNTIL YOU COME BACK TO ME (That's What I'm Gonna Do) 315
WALKING IN MEMPHIS 318
THE WAY SHE LOVES ME 264
THE WAY YOU DO THE THINGS YOU DO 328
WHAT BECOMES OF THE BROKEN HEARTED 331
WHEN SOMETHING IS WRONG WITH MY BABY 334
WHEN THE NIGHT COMES 352
A WORLD OF OUR OWN 344
YER SO BAD 337
YOU'RE THE VOICE 365

FROM A DISTANCE

Lyrics and Music by
JULIE GOLD

G D/G G Cmaj7 D Em
flight. From a dis-tance there is har - mo-ny, and it
cresc. mf
C G/B G/D D C G/B C G/B To Coda
ech-oes through the land. It's the voice of hope, it's the voice of peace. It's the
dim. mp
C D 1. G D/G C/G G
voice of ev - ery man.
C G/B D D.S. 2. G D/G G G/B Bridge: G/C C6 D
2. From a man. God is watch-ing us. God is
cresc. mf
D7/G G D/F♯ Em Em7 Am7 C/D D G
watch-ing us. God is watch-ing us from a dis - tance.
dim. mp

G
G/B
C
D
Em7
G/B
C
G/B
Am
Em/G
D/F♯
D
D.S. 𝄋 al Coda
G
D/F♯
C/E
G/D
cresc.
C
Am
Em
D
Em
D/F♯
N.C.
mf
3. From a
mp
Coda
C
D7
D/E
Em
D/E
Em
Bm/D
heart of ev - ery man. It's the
cresc.
mf
C
G/B
C
G/B
C
D7
3
hope of hopes, it's the love of loves. This is the song of ev - ery

Verse 2:
From a distance, we all have enough,
And no one is in need.
There are no guns, no bombs, no diseases,
No hungry mouths to feed.
From a distance, we are instruments
Marching in a common band;
Playing songs of hope, playing songs of peace,
They're the songs of every man.
(To Bridge:)

Verse 3:
From a distance, you look like my friend
Even though we are at war.
From a distance I just cannot comprehend
What all this fighting is for.
From a distance there is harmony
And it echos through the land.
It's the hope of hopes, it's the love of loves.
It's the heart of every man.

MORE THAN WORDS

Lyrics and Music by
BETTENCOURT, CHERONE

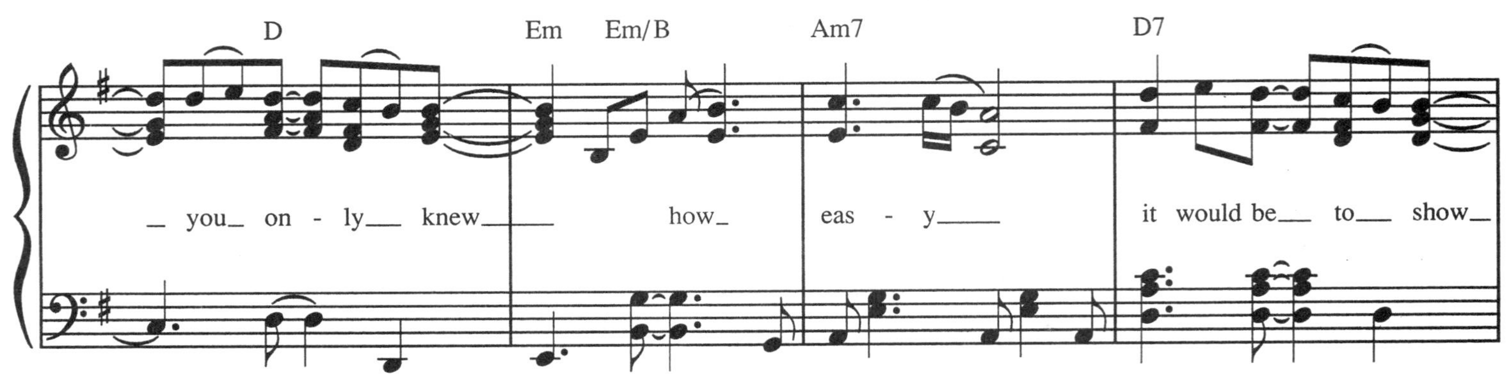

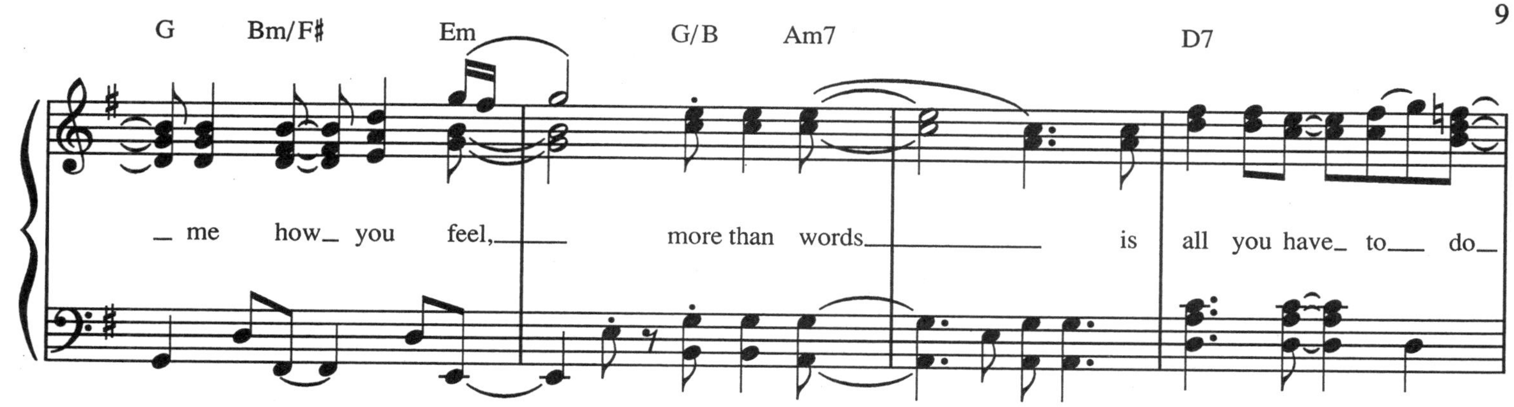
G Bm/F# Em G/B Am7 D7
me how you feel, more than words is all you have to do

G7 G7/B C Cm G Em7
to make it real. Then, you would - n't have to say that you love

G/B Em7 G/B Am7 D7 G G/B
me, 'cause I'd al - read - y know. What

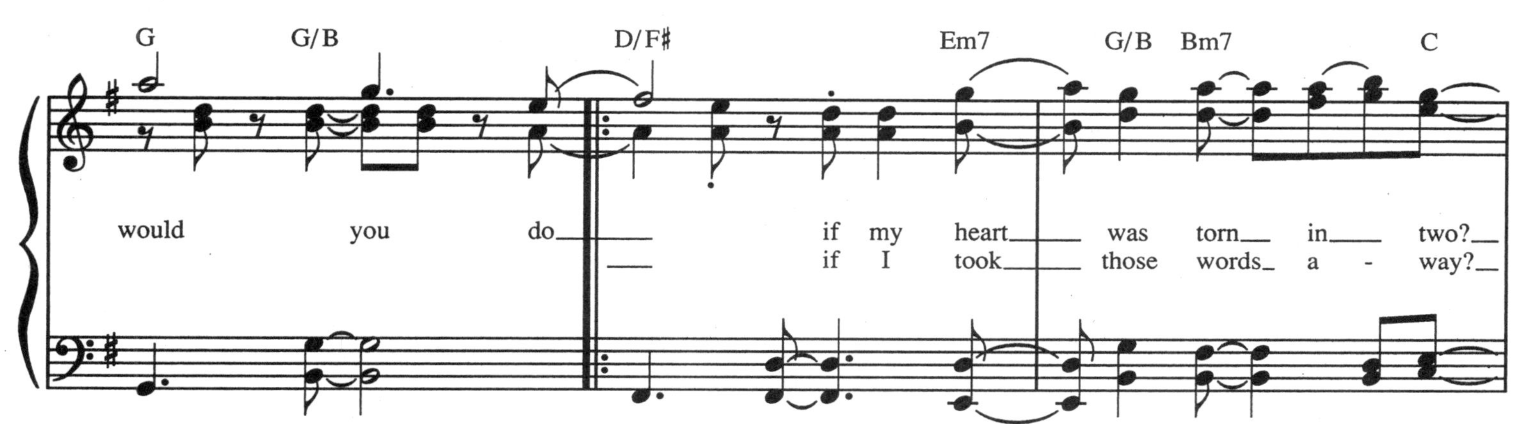
G G/B D/F# Em7 G/B Bm7 C
would you do if my heart was torn in two?
if I took those words a - way?

1. 3.
G/B Am7
D7
G
More than words to show you feel that your love for me is real.
Then, you could - n't make things new just by say -

2.
To Next Strain
4.
G/B
G
G/B
D7
D7
What would you say - in' "I love you."
- in' "I love you."

G
G/B
C(9)
G/B
Am7
G/B
C
(La di da da di da di dai dai da.

1.
D.S. 𝄋
D
D7
G
G/B
C(9)
Am7
D7
) More than words.
La di da da di da.)

2. 3. 4. D D7 | 5. D G/B | G

—) More_ than_ words._ | —) More_ than_ | words.______

D/F♯ | G/F | E

— | Ooh,______

Am7 | D | G

rit. | *(Guitar Cadenza)* | *a tempo*

– Ooh.______ | More than_ | words.______

C G/B | Gm/B♭ Am7 | G

rit.

Verse 2:
Now that I have tried to talk to you
And make you understand.
All you have to do is close your eyes
And just reach out your hands.
And touch me, hold me close, don't ever let me go.
More than words is all I ever needed you to show.
Then you wouldn't have to say
That you love me 'cause I'd already know.
(To Chorus:)

I CAN'T MAKE YOU LOVE ME

Lyrics and Music by
MIKE REID and ALLEN SHAMBLIN

Em7 Am7 C Em7 C
Gm7 Cm7 E♭ Gm7 E♭
in-side my head.
Lay down with me,
tell me no lies.
G/B
B♭/D
1.
Em7 Am7
Gm7 Cm7
Just hold me close,
don't pa - tron-ize.
Don't pa - tron-
To Next Strain
2.
G/D D G/B Em7 Am7
B♭/F F B♭/D Gm7 Cm7
-ize me.
"Cause I can't
give up this fight.
cresc. poco a poco
G/D D G/B
B♭/F F B♭/D
And I will give up this fight.
'Cause I can't
cresc. poco a poco

Chorus:
C G C G
E♭ B♭ E♭ B♭
make you love me if you don't. You can't make your heart feel
mf
G/B C Em7 G/C
B♭/C E♭ Gm7 B♭/E♭
some-thing it won't. Here in the dark in
D/F♯ Em7 G/C
F/A Gm7 B♭/E♭
these fi - nal ho - urs, I will lay down my heart and
D/F♯ Em7 Am7 G/D D
F/A Gm7 Cm7 B♭/F F
I'll feel the pow - er. But you won't no, you won't. 'Cause I can't

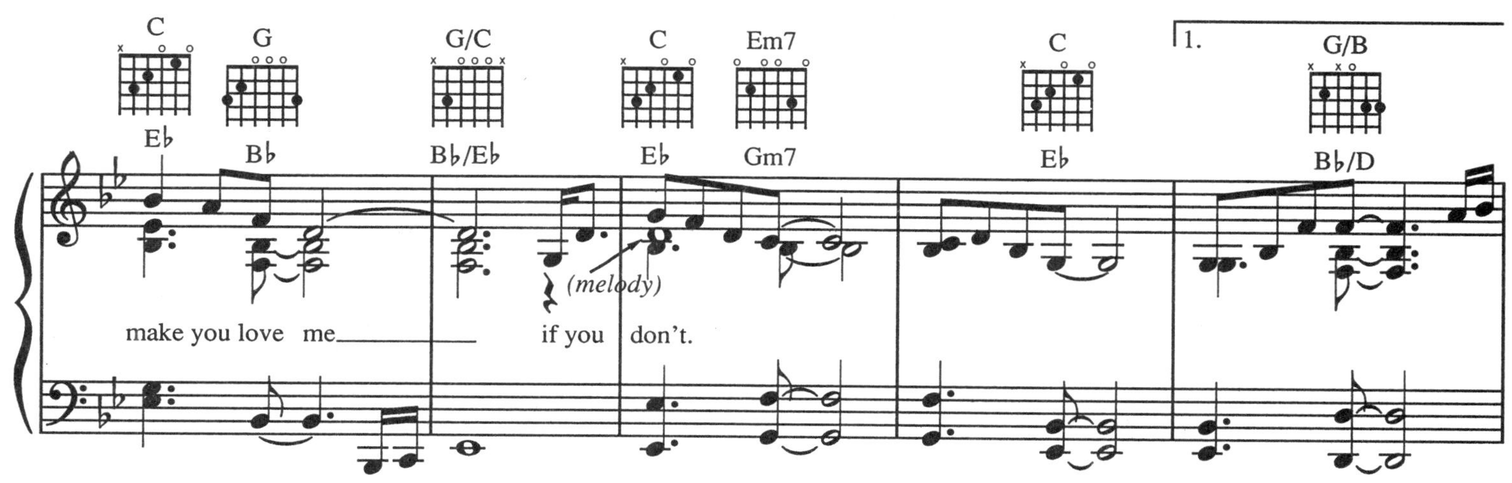

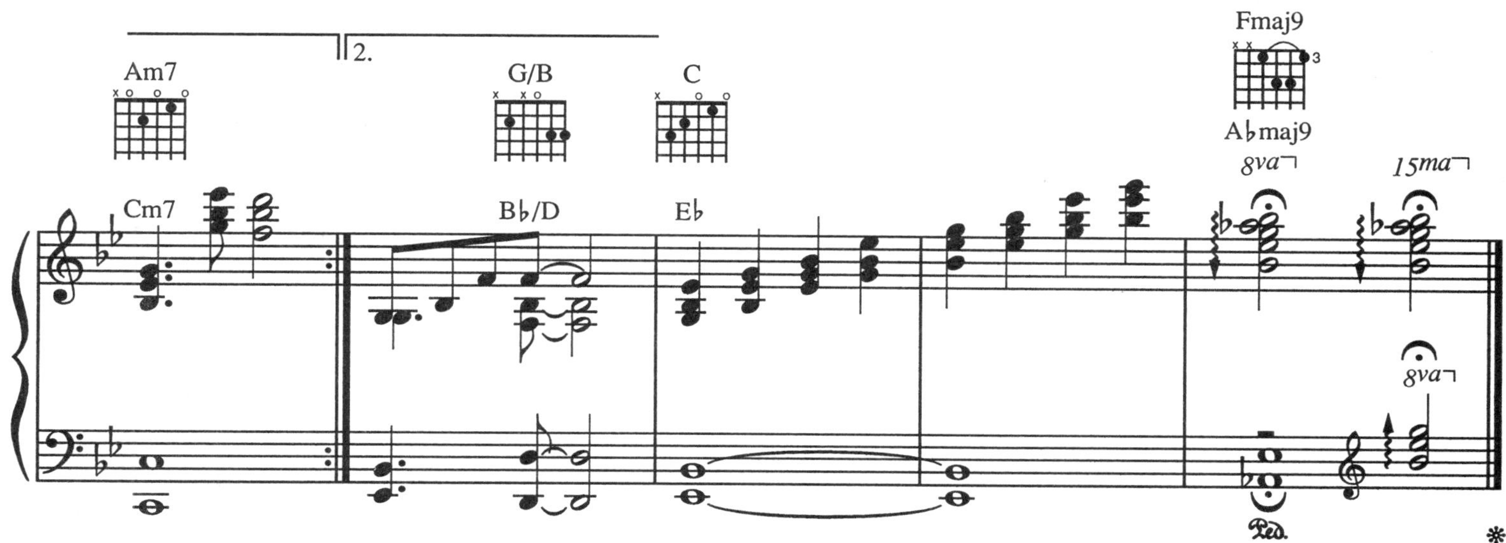

Verse 2:
I'll close my eyes, then I won't see
The love you don't feel when you're holdin' me.
Mornin' will come and I'll do what's right.
Just give me till then to give up this fight.
And I will give up this fight.
(To Chorus:)

HERE AND NOW

Words and Music by
TERRY STEELE and
DAVID ELLIOTT

1.
C G2/B D♯dim7 Em G2/B C(2) C/D
Holding you close through the night, I need you.

2. 3.
Chorus:
F♯m7(♭5) A/B Bm7 Cmaj7 D/C D/F♯
cresc. Here and now, I promise to love faithfully.
mf

G Bm7 C(2) F♯m7(♭5) A/B Bm7 Cmaj7
Faithfully. You're all I need. Here and now,

D/C D/F♯ G Bm7
I vow to be one with thee. You and me.

Cmaj9
To Coda
1.
C(2)
C/D
G
G(2)/B
Your love is all I need.

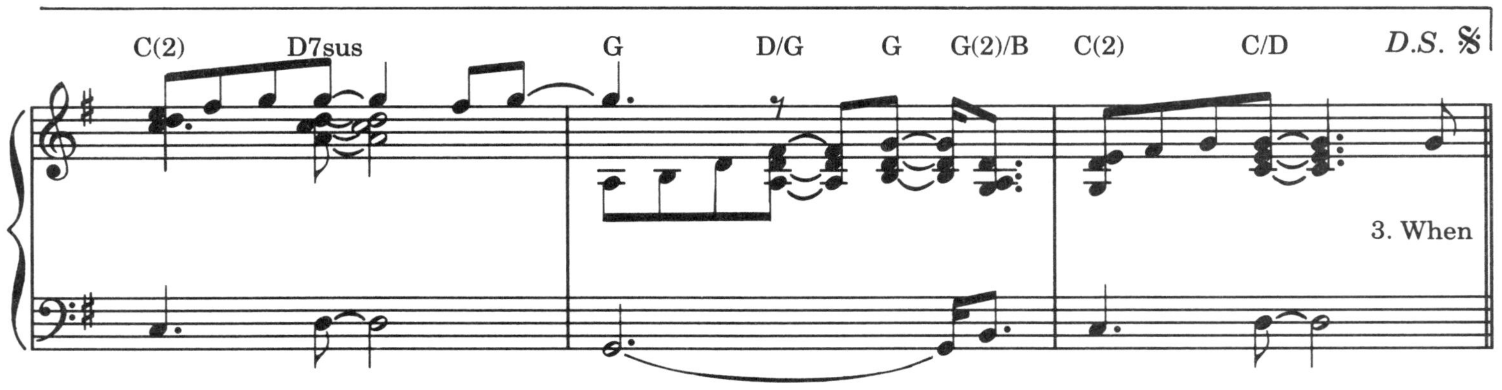
C(2)
D7sus
G
D/G
G
G(2)/B
C(2)
C/D
D.S.
3. When

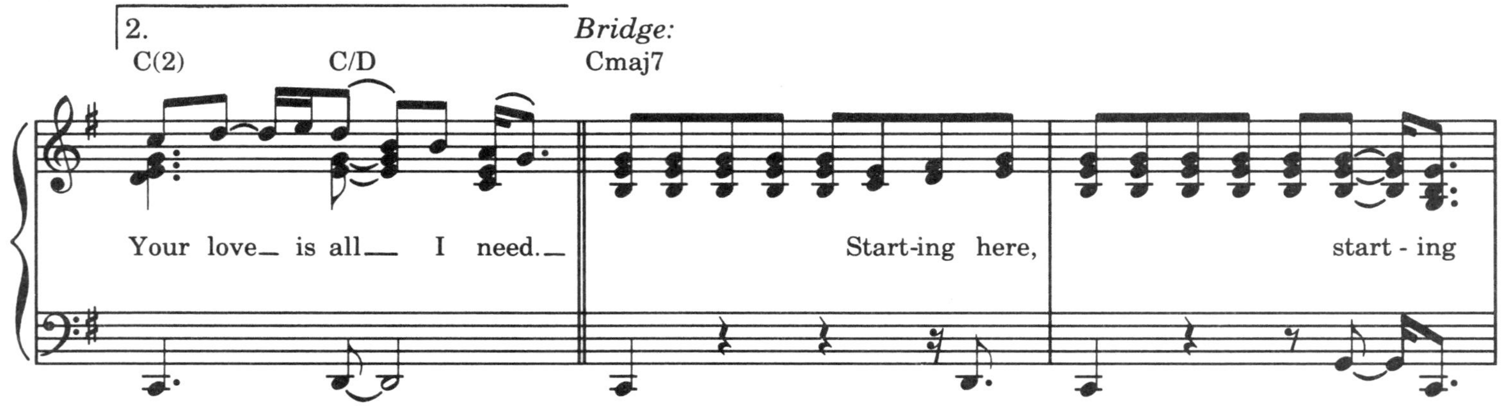
2.
C(2)
C/D
Bridge:
Cmaj7
Your love is all I need.
Start-ing here,
start - ing

D/C
C/D
G
D/G
now,
I be - lieve in love.
Start - ing here,
cresc.
f

Verse 2:
I look in your eyes and there I see
What happiness really means.
The love that we share makes life so sweet,
Together we'll always be.
This pledge of love feels so right,
And ooh, I need you.
To Chorus:

Verse 3:
When I look in your eyes, there I see
All that a love should really be.
And I need you more and more each day,
Nothing can take your love away.
More than I dare to dream,
I need you.
To Chorus:

(EVERYTHING I DO) I DO IT FOR YOU

Lyrics and Music by
BRYAN ADAMS, R.J. LANGE
and M. KAMEN

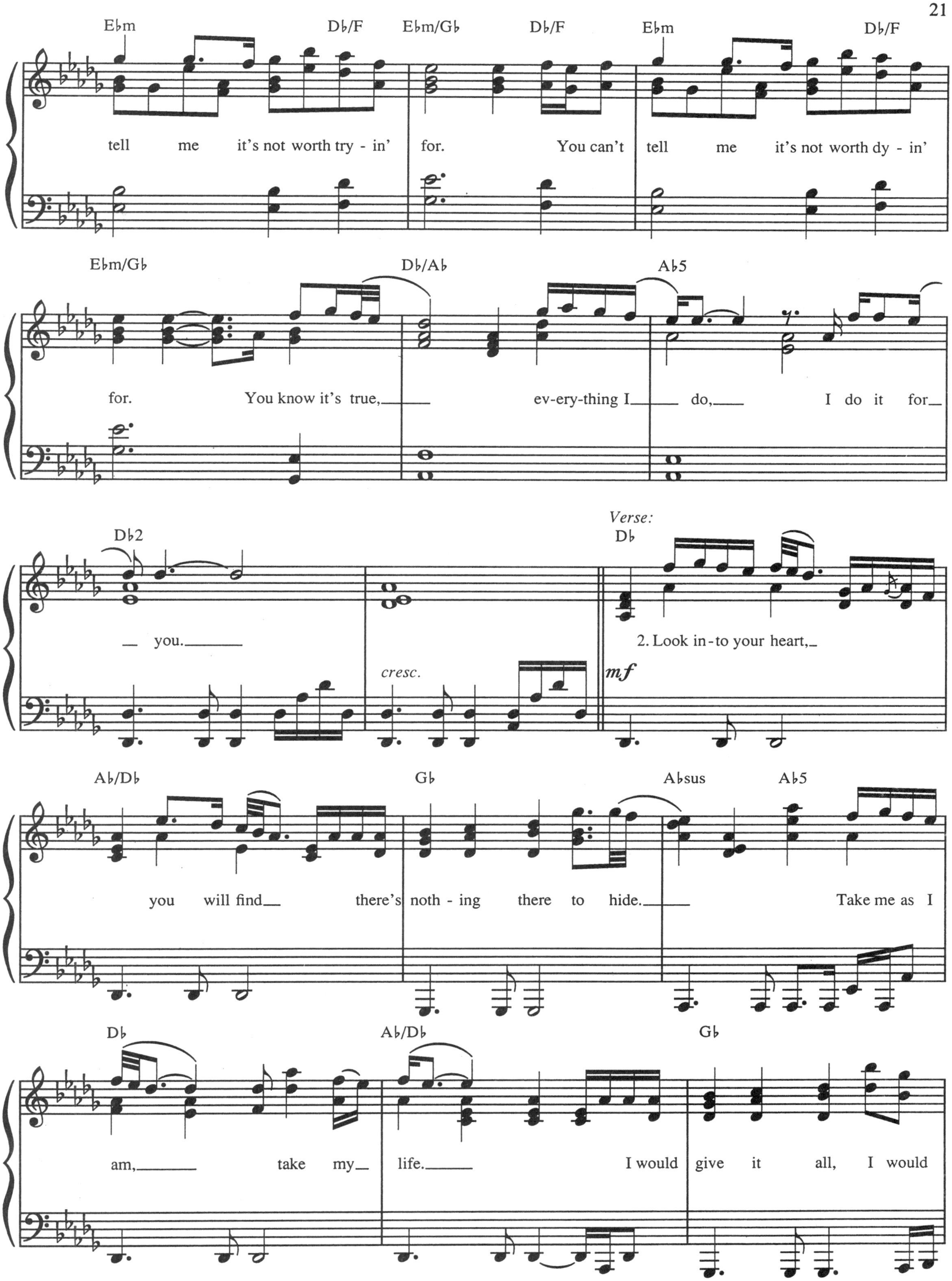

E♭m D♭/F E♭m/G♭ D♭/F E♭m D♭/F

tell me it's not worth try - in' for. You can't tell me it's not worth dy - in'

E♭m/G♭ D♭/A♭ A♭5

for. You know it's true, ev-ery-thing I do, I do it for

D♭2

Verse:

D♭

you. *cresc.* 2. Look in-to your heart, **mf**

A♭/D♭ G♭ A♭sus A♭5

you will find there's noth - ing there to hide. Take me as I

D♭ A♭/D♭ G♭

am, take my life. I would give it all, I would

Db
Ab
Ebm
Db
Ebm
Db/Eb
sac - ri - fice. Don't
tell me it's not worth fight-ing
for. I can't

Ebm
Db
Ebm
Db
help it, there's noth-ing I want
more. You know it's true,
ev-ery-thing I

Ab5
Db
Dbsus
Db
do, I do it for you.
There's
cresc.

Cb
Fb
Cb
no love like
your love, and no
oth - er could give
f

G♭
D♭
A♭
more love. There's
no - where unless
you're there, all the

E♭
A♭
time, all the
way, yeah.
dim.
mf

G♭
D♭
D♭sus
(instrumental solo . . .

1.
2.
D♭
D♭
E♭m
Oh, you can't
tell me it's not worth try - in'
. . . end solo)

Ab
Ebm
Ab
Gb/Ab
for. I can't help it, there's noth-ing I want more. Yeah, I would
cresc.
f
Db
Ab
Gb
fight for you, I'd lie for you, walk the wire for you, yeah, I'd
Gbm
Db/Ab
die for you. You know it's true, ev-ery-thing I
dim.
mp
Absus
Ab
Gb
Gb6
Db
do, oh, I do it for you.
rit.
dim.
p

MASTERPIECE

Words and Music by
KENNY NOLAN

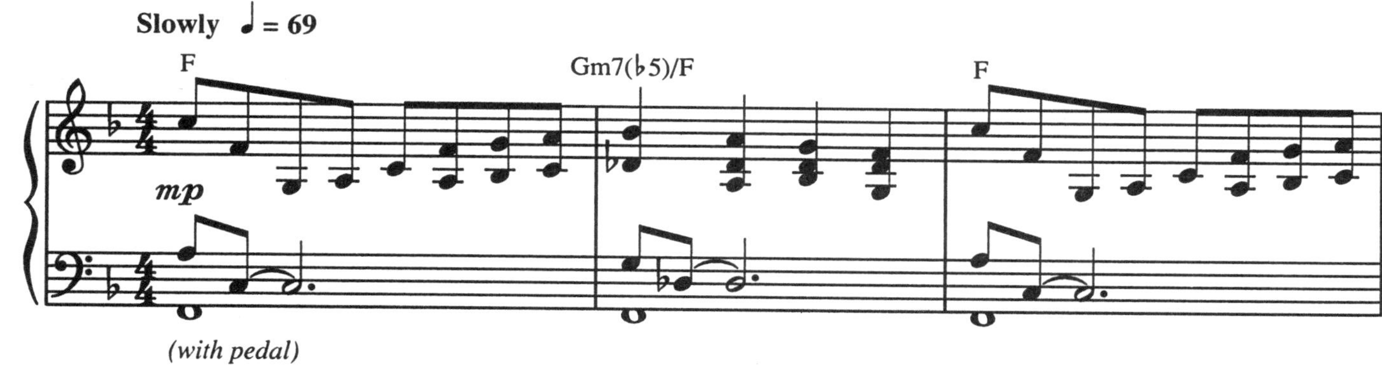

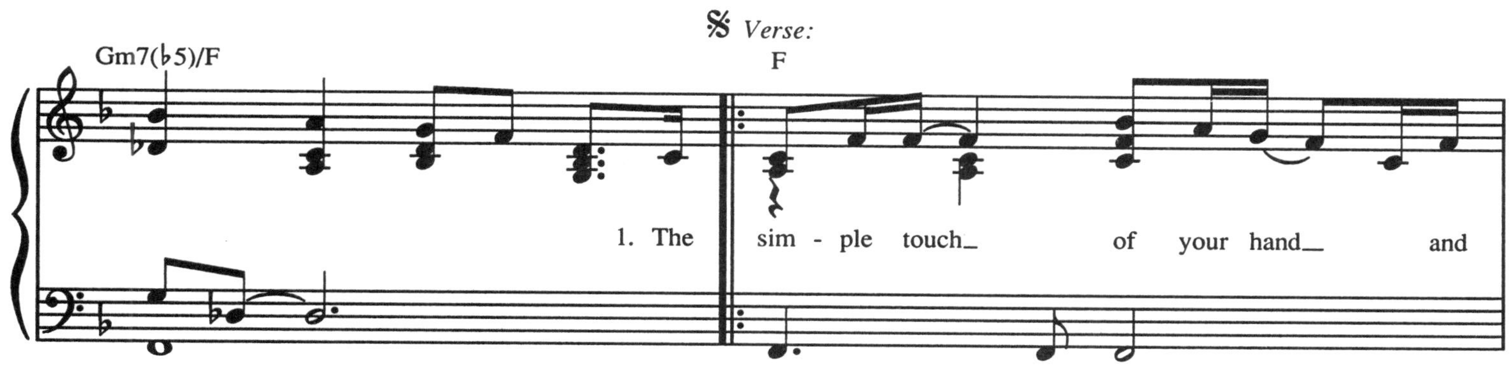

B♭(2)
B♭m6
F
oth - er love has known and now I
thank you, girl. (Thank you, girl.)
1.3.
B♭/C
Thank you, girl. (Thank you, girl.) 2. The
2.4.
B♭/C
D♭/E♭
E♭/F
now I know, ooh
cresc.
Chorus:
D♭maj7
Cm7
E♭/F
I've found a mas - ter - piece in you, a work of art it's
mf
B♭m7
D♭maj7/E♭
D♭/E♭
E♭/F
D♭maj7
true. And I trea-sure you, my love. Ooh, I've found a mas-ter-piece in
Cm7
B♭m7
1.
B♭/C
D.S.
you, a work of art it's true. And I trea-sure you. 3. Some -
dim.

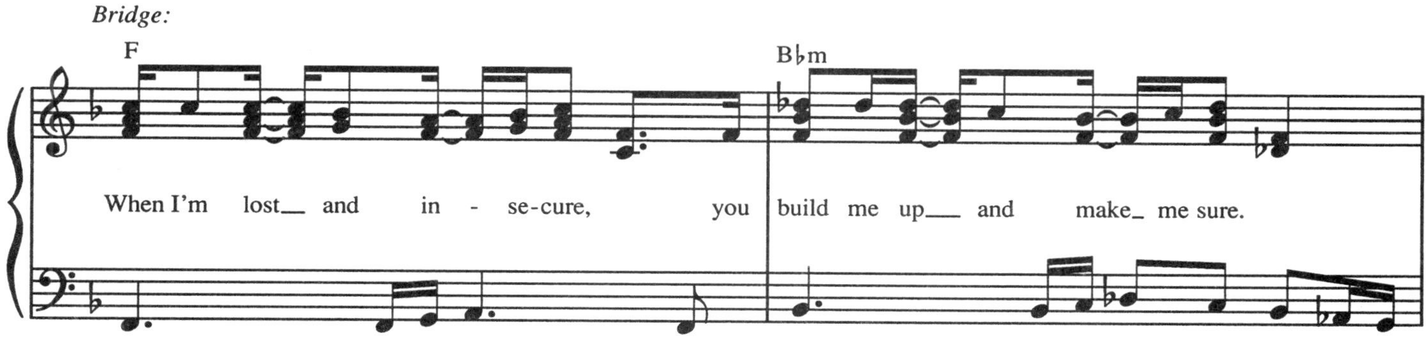

Verse 2:
The countless ways you've touched my heart
Is more than I can say.
The beauty that you've shown to me takes my breath away.
A picture perfect painting, that's what our love is.
And yes I need you so, and now I know . . .
(To Chorus:)

Verse 3:
Sometimes I wonder what I'd be had I not found you.
A lost and lonely soul,
This world could show me nothing new.
But now my life's a canvas, painted with your love.
And it will always be, and now I see . . .

Verse 4:
The two of us together, thru time will never part.
This fairy tale we're sharing is real inside our hearts.
Let it be forever, never let it end.
This promise I do make,
Heaven is ours to take.
(To Chorus:)

SHOW ME THE WAY

Lyrics and Music by
DENNIS DE YOUNG

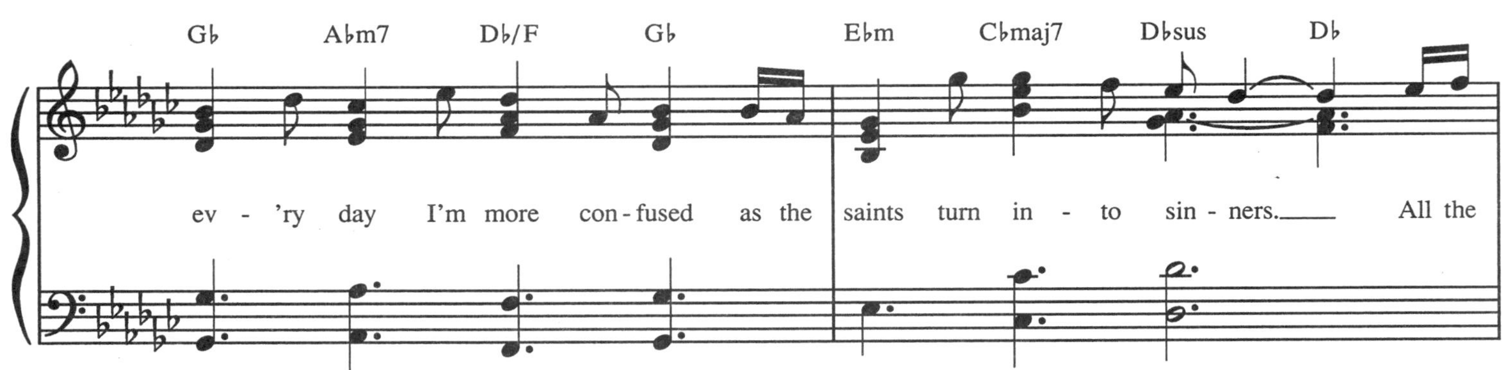

Gb Abm7 Db/F Ebm Cb Dbsus Db
feel this emp - ty place in - side; so a - fraid that I've lost my faith. Show me the
mf
Chorus:
Gb Db Cb Gb Db Cb
way, show me the way. Take me to - / Bring me to -
f
To Coda
Gb Db/F Ebm7 Gb/Db Abm7 Dbsus Db
night to the riv - er and wash my il - lu - sions a - way.
night to the moun - tain and take my con - fu - sion a - way.
Please show me the
Gb Cb/Gb Db/Gb Cb/Gb
1. D.S. 2.
Gb Cb/Gb Db/Gb Cb/Gb Gb Cb/Gb Db/Gb Cb
way. 2. And
Bridge:
Bb Ebm
and if I see a light, should I be - lieve? Tell me, how will I

Ab7
Abm7
Dbsus
Db
Dbsus
Db
A
B/A
Amaj7
B/A
know?
D.S.S. al Coda
A
B/A
A
B/A
Amaj7
B/A
Db
Cb/Db
Db
Cb/Db
Show me the
Coda
Gb
Db
Cb
way,
show me the
Gb
Db
Cb
way.
Take me to -
Gb
Db/F
Ebm7
Gb/Db
night to the riv - er and wash my il - lu - sions a -
Abm7
Dbsus
Db
way.
Show me the
Gb
Db
Cb
way,
show me the
Gb
Db
Cb
way.
Give me the

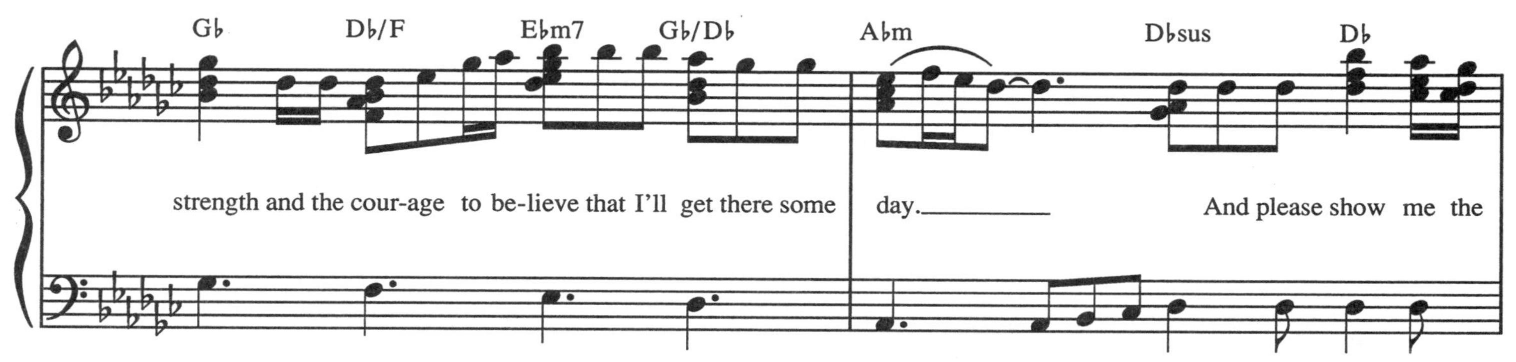
G♭ D♭/F E♭m7 G♭/D♭ A♭m D♭sus D♭
strength and the cour-age to be-lieve that I'll get there some day.
And please show me the

G♭ C♭/G♭ D♭/G♭ C♭/G♭ G♭ C♭/G♭ D♭/G♭ C♭/G♭ G♭ C♭/G♭ G♭ D♭/G♭
way.
mf
mp Slower
G A♭m7 D♭/F G♭ E♭m C♭maj7 D♭sus D♭
p
Ev - 'ry night I say a pray'r in the hopes that there's a heav-en.

Verse 2:
And as I slowly drift to sleep
For a moment dreams are sacred.
I close my eyes and know there's peace
In a world so filled with hatred.
Then I wake up each morning and turn on the news
To find we've so far to go.
And I keep on hoping for a sign
So afraid I just won't know.
(To Chorus:)

IT'S SO HARD TO SAY GOODBYE TO YESTERDAY

Words and Music by
FREDDIE PERREN and CHRISTINE YARIAN

Bsus
A6
Am6
1.
E(2)
N.C.
to yes - ter - day.
2. I don't
2.
E(2)
N.C.
And I'll
f
E
G#7(♭9)
G#7
take with me the
mem - o - ries to
C#m
C#m/B
1.
A
Am
E(2)
be my sun - shine af-ter the
rain. It's so
hard to say good-bye
Bsus
A6
Am6
N.C.
to yes - ter - day.
And I'll

Verse 2:
I don't know where this road is going to lead.
All I know is where we've been and what we've been through.
If we get to see tomorrow, I hope it's worth all the pain.
It's so hard to say goodbye to yesterday.
(To Chorus:)

THE DANCE

Words and Music by
TONY ARATA

C
D
was right.
How could I have known
that you'd ev - er
would fall.
Hey, who's to say?
You know I might
cresc.
Em
D/F♯
Chorus:
C
say good - bye?
have changed it all.
And now,
I'm glad I did - n't know
mf
D
Bm7
C
D
the way it all would end,
the way it all would go.
Our lives
C
D
Bm7
are bet-ter left to chance.
I could have missed the pain,
but I'd have had to miss
C
D
1.
G
C/G G
C/G
G
D/G C/G G
D.S. 𝄋
the
dance.
2. Hold-ing you,
dim.
mp

2.
G
C
dance. Yes, my life, it's bet-ter left to chance. I could have missed the pain,
Bm7
C
D
N.C.
but I'd have had to miss the dance.
rit.
a tempo
mp
Em
C
Dsus
D
8va
Em7(4)
Repeat ad lib. and fade

FOREVER'S AS FAR AS I'LL GO

Words and Music by
MIKE REID

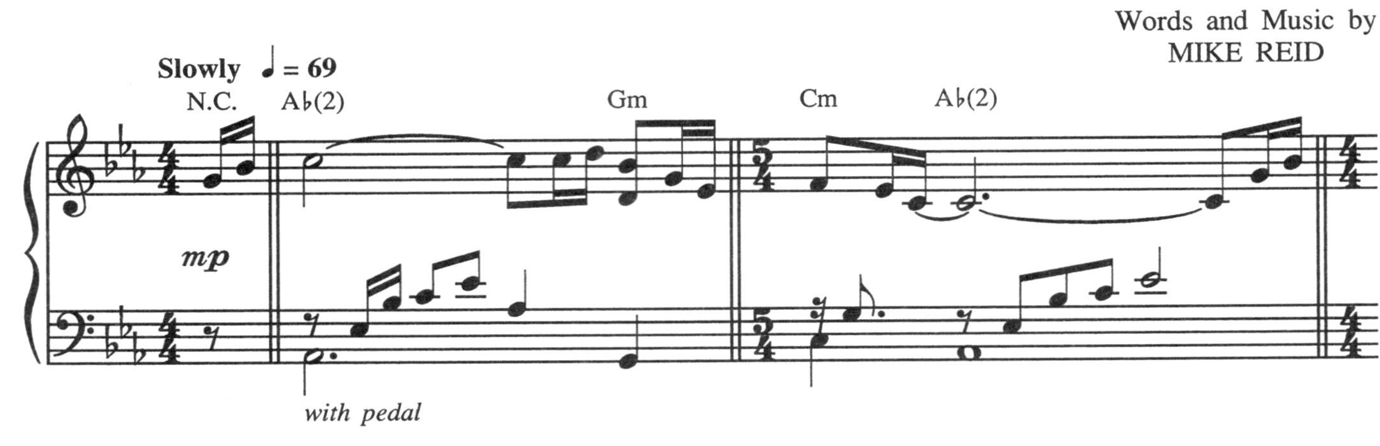

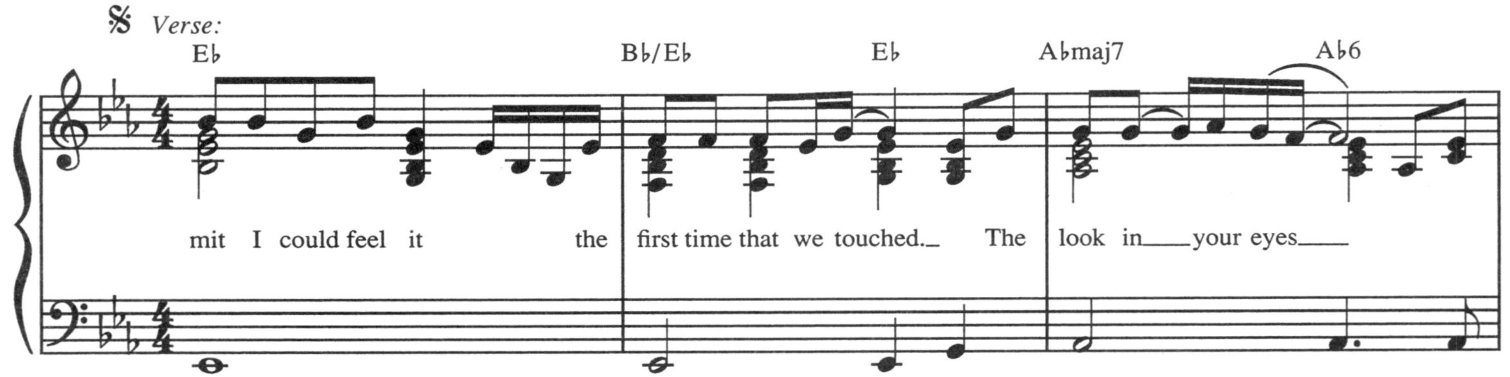

Ab6
Ab
Abmaj7/Bb
Bb
Ab/Bb
Bb
Eb/G
It's best that you know_
where you stand_ with me.
I will
cresc.
mf

Chorus:
Ab
Eb
Eb(2)/G
Ab
give you_ my heart
faith - ful_ and true,_
and all the
love it can hold

Gm
Gm7
Cm7
Gm7
Ab(2) Ab
that's all I can do._
But I've thought a - bout
how
long I'll_ love you,

Eb/Ab
Fm(11)
Eb/G
Ab(2)
Ab/Bb
and it's on - ly fair
that you know,
for
- ev - er's_ as far_ as_ I_

Verse 2:
When there's age around my eyes and gray in your hair,
And it only takes a touch to recall the love we've shared.
I won't take for granted that you know my love is true.
Each night in your arms, I will whisper to you...
(To Chorus:)

I DON'T HAVE THE HEART

Words and Music by
JUDI FRIEDMAN and
ALLAN RICH

A/G
G(2)
Em7
D(2)/F♯
fi-nal-ly found.
bout you.
ev - ery - thing you've
I'm trying to say
want - ed
this
and
as
E7/G♯
Asus
A/C♯
D A/C♯ Bm F♯m/A
need-ed
gent-ly
in
as I
me.
can
cresc.
I don't have the
'cause I don't have the
mf
Chorus:
G(2)
D/F♯ G
A(2)/C♯
G/B
A/C♯
heart to hurt you, it's the last thing I want to do
To Coda
D
D/F♯ A/E B/D F♯m/A G(2)
D/F♯ G
A(2)/C♯
But I don't have the heart to love you
1.
D.S.
G2/B
G
D(2)
Gm/B♭
A7sus A7
not the way you want me to.

2.
D(2)
Em7
Bridge:
F#7sus
You're so trust - ing and
F#7
F#7sus
F#7
Bm7
Em7(♭5)/B♭
o - pen,
hop - ing that love will start.
But
D.S.S. 𝄋𝄋 al Coda
D/A
A7sus
A7
D/A
A7sus
A7
D A/C# Bm F#m/A
I don't have the heart.
I don't have the heart.
I don't have the
Coda
A(2)/C#
G/B
A/C#
D
E B/D# C#m G#/B
you, not the way that you want me to. I don't have the
cresc.
f
Repeat ad. lib. and fade
Amaj7
B(2)/D#
A(2)/C#
B(2)/D#
E
E/G# B/F# C#m/E G#/B
heart.
Instrumental solo. . .
I don't have the

COMING OUT OF THE DARK

Words and Music by
GLORIA ESTEFAN, EMILIO ESTEFAN, JR.
and JON SECADA

Gospel rock ♩ = 66
N.C.
mp
with pedal
Verse:
(E(2))
N.C.
(D/E)
(E(2))
1. Why be a - fraid if I'm not a - lone? Life is nev - er
2. Start-ing a - gain is part of the plan, and I'll be so much
D/E
E
eas - y, the rest is un - known. And up till now for
strong - er hold - ing your hand. Step by step I'll

(D2/E)
(F♯m/A)
D/E (E/G♯) (F♯m) (E) E
me it's been hands a - gainst_ stone.
make it through,_ I_ know I can.
I spend each and ev-ery
It may not make it
D/E E/D A/C♯ Amaj7 A/B
mo - ment_ search - ing_ for what to be-lieve.
eas - i - er, but I have felt_ you near all the way.
Com-ing out of the
Chorus:
E E7 A/E Am6/E
dark I fin-'lly see the light, now, and it's shin - ing on me.

E
C#m7
A(2)
A/B
Com-ing out of the
E
E7
1.
A/E
Am6/E
dark,
I know the love that saved
me,
you're
shar - ing with me.
E
D2/E
E

D.S. 𝄋
2.
To Next Strain
3.4.etc.
D2/E
N.C.
A/E
A/B
A/E
Am6/E
me,___ you're shar-ing with me.___
me___you're shar - ing, you're shar-
(For-
Repeat ad lib. and fade
E
C♯m7
A(2)
A/B
- ing with me,
shar - ing with me,___
shar-ing with me,___
shar-ing with me.
Bridge:
A
E/G♯
F♯m7
E/G♯
F♯m/A
Amaj7/B
___ For-ev - er___
stand on the rock of your love.___
ev - er and ev - er,
stand on___ the___ rock.
For -

A
E/G♯
F♯m7
A/B
B♭7(♭5)
Ev - er,
ev - er,
ooh.
Can't no-bod - y stop me! Watch me!
ev - er
and ev - er,
ooh.
For-
A
E/G♯
F♯m7 E/G♯
F♯m/A Amaj7/B
Ev - er
and ev - er
stand on the rock of your love
ev - er
and ev - er,
stand on the rock of your love.
E
E/D
A/C♯
A
A/B
D.S.S.
is all it takes
no mat-ter what we face.
Com-ing out of the

Inspired by the Columbia Pictures' Feature Film "THE PRINCE OF TIDES"

PLACES THAT BELONG TO YOU

Lyrics by
ALAN and MARILYN BERGMAN

Music by
JAMES NEWTON HOWARD

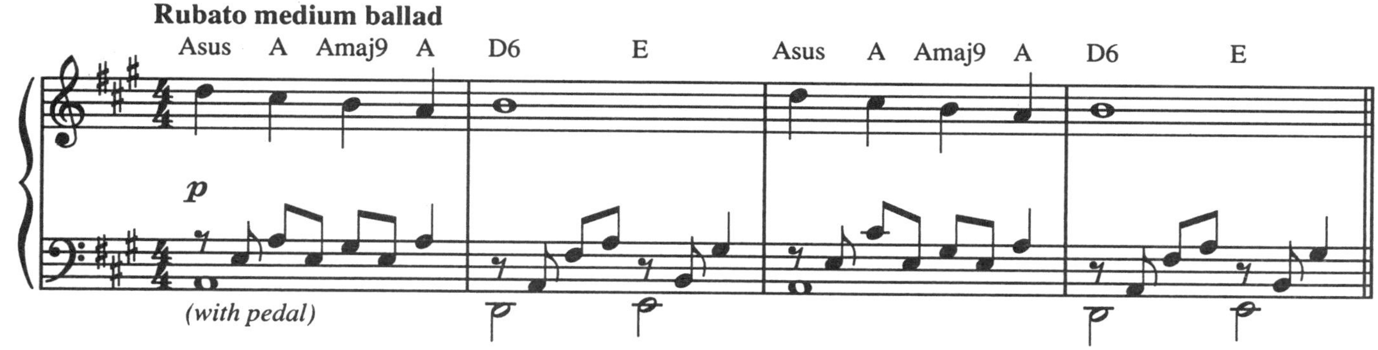

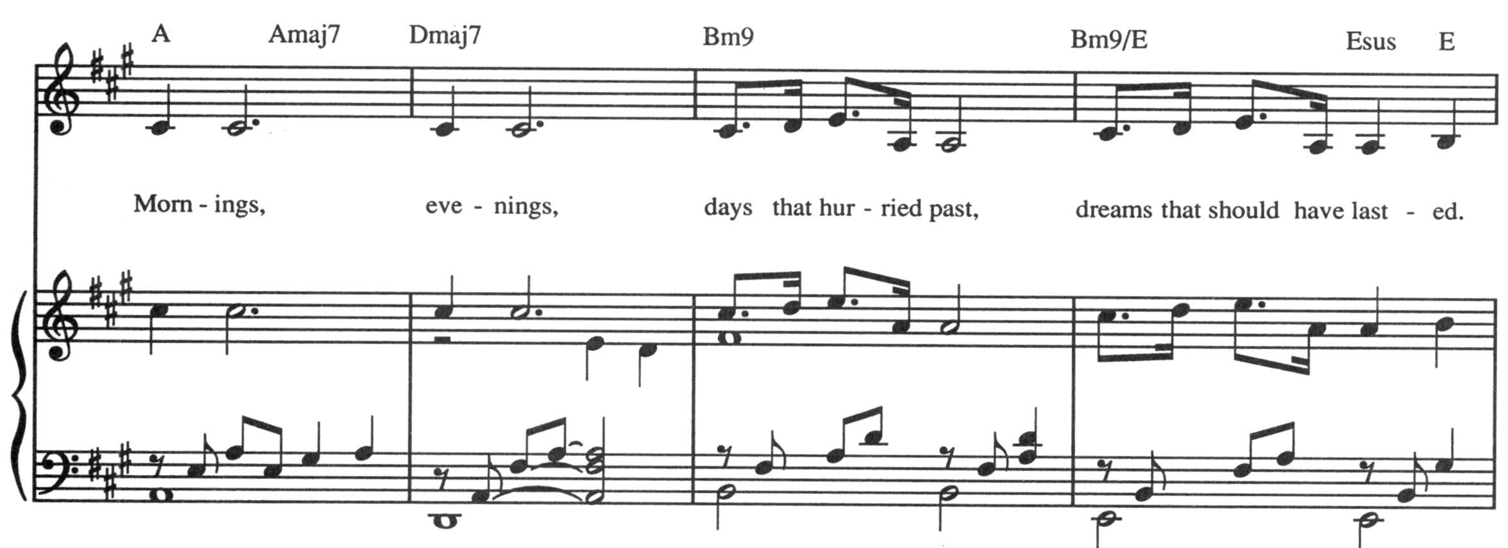

Dmaj7
F#maj7
Em7(add4)
A
A/G
F#m7
Bm7
Some - how I'll nev - er let go of the mem - 'ries.
mp
Em7
Asus
Bm7(add2)
A(add2)
G
D(add9)/F#
Some-thing al - ways seems to re - mind me of how it was, of
Em7
G/A
F#/A#
Bm(add2)
Esus4 2
E
A
Amaj7
what it was, when it was all there was. Laugh - ter,
p

Dmaj7
Bm9
Bm9/E
Esus
E
A
Amaj7
love songs,
foot-steps that I hear
make me think you're near me.
Po - ems,
cresc. poco a poco
Dmaj7
Bm9
Em9
A7sus
A
Dmaj7
F♯m7
pic - tures,
let - ters nev - er mailed,
boats that nev - er sailed. Re - mem - ber that
mf
Cmaj9
Am9
F♯m7
Bm
Em7
Asus
ev - en though we can't be to - geth - er,
we're more for hav-ing loved one an -

Bm(add2)
A(add2)
G
D(add9)/F♯
Cmaj9
Dsus4/2
D♯dim
-oth - er. We shared the sky, we learned to fly.
Emaj7
G♯m7
Dmaj9
Bm9
G♯m7
C♯m7
F♯m7
B5
B7sus
Some-day when some-one else-'s arms are a-round us, when time has put some dis-tance be-
f
C♯m(add2)
B(add2)
A
E(sus2)/G♯
F♯m7
E(sus2)/G♯
-tween us, the years will kind-ly show how mem-'ries come and go. They

Amaj7
A/B
G#5/B#
C#(add2)
E/F#
F#
ebb and flow like the tides.
dim.
B
Bmaj7
Emaj7
C#m9
C#m9/F#
E/F# F#
There are quiet places in my heart ever since we parted.
mp
Gentle, tender, traces of a song, places that belong to
B(add2) B Bmaj7
F#7sus F# B(add2)
you.
dim.
p

HERE WE ARE

Words and Music by
GLORIA ESTEFAN

Slowly ♩ = 66

F♯m9 B7

mp

F♯m9 B7

F♯m9 B7

F♯m9 B7

1. Here___ we

E
Emaj7
A/E
are face to face. We for - get time and
A2/E
E
place. Hold me now; don't let
Emaj7
A/E
go though it hurts, we both know.
A/B
B
Amaj7
The time we spend to - geth - er's gon - na fly.
G♯m7
Amaj7
and ev - ery - thing you do to me is gon - na feel so right.

G♯m7
C♯m
C♯m/B
Amaj7
Ba - by, when you're
lov - ing me
I feel like I could cry,
G♯m7
F♯m9
F♯m7/B
'cause there's
noth - ing I can do
1.
F♯m9
to keep from lov - ing you.
B7
F♯m9
F♯m7/B
2.
E2
2. Here we
There's noth - ing I can
cresc.

Bridge:
Am9
B7
Emaj7
do; I'm help - less in your arms. Oh ba - by, what you
f
Cmaj7
Amaj9/B
Cmaj7
G/B
do; I'm in love, this is it. There's no turn - ing back this time.
Am7
Am7/D
No, no, no. 3. Here we
G
Gmaj7
C/G
are once a - gain. But this time we're on - ly friends.
C2/G
G
Gmaj7
Fun - ny world; some - times lies be - come the

C/G
C2/G
C/D
D
game when love's the prize.
And though no
Am7/D
Bm7/D
one knows what's go - ing on in - side,
all the love I feel
Cmaj7/D
Bm7/D
C/D
G7
for you is some - thing I should hide.
When I have you close
Cmaj7
Bm7
to me the feel - ing's so sub - lime
that there's
Am7
Am/D
noth - ing I can do
to keep from lov - ing you.
mf

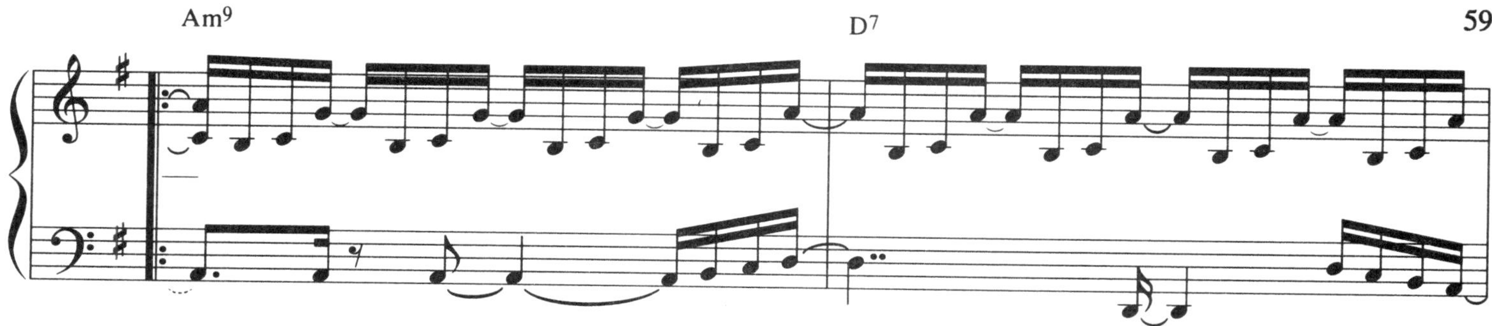

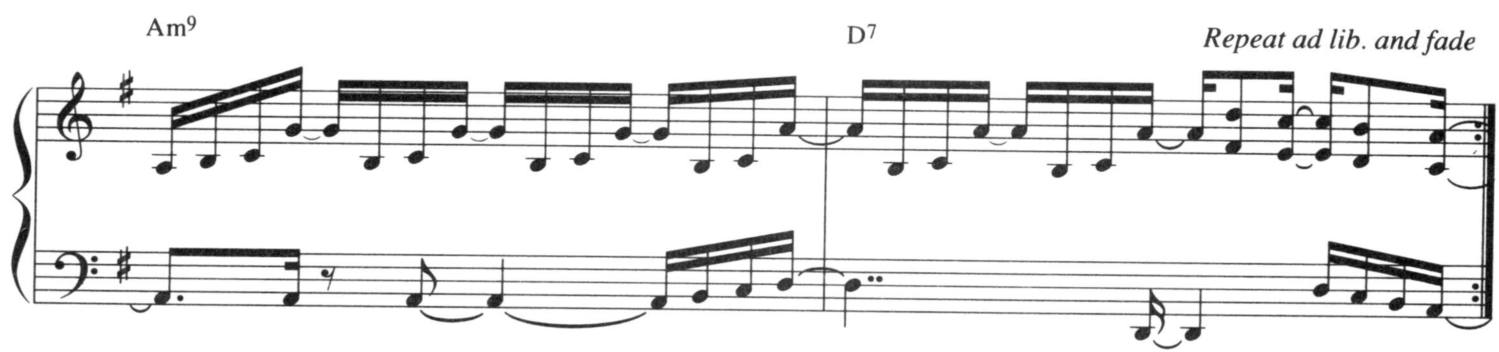

Verse 2:

Here we are all alone;
Trembling hearts, beating strong;
Reaching out, a breathless kiss
I never thought could feel like this.
I want to stop the time from passing by.
I want to close my eyes and feel
Your lips are touching mine.
Baby, when you're close to me,
I want you more each time.
And there's nothing I can do
To keep from loving you.

(To Bridge:)

ALL 4 LOVE

Lyric and Music by
COLOR ME BADD and
HOWARD THOMPSON

D G D G

ask Him ev - ery day that you'll 4 - ev - er B mine.____
wan - na take care of U, girl, I'll serve____ you well.____

D G D G

I wan - na hold your hand____ 2 show U I'll be there.____
I will B there 4 ya, 2 catch U when U fall.____

D G D G

I like 2 do_____ the things_____ that let U know I care.
I'll hold U in_____ my arms,_____ that's where U be - long.

1.
To Next Strain
2.
N.C.
D
G
you're so beau - ti - ful.
you're so beau - ti - ful...
beau - ti - ful...
yeah!
Chorus:
Oh, girl, I think I love ya.
I'm al - ways think - ing of ya.
I want ya to know I do it
all 4 love.
I love it when we're to - geth - er.
Girl, I need you 4 - ev - er,
and I want U 2 know I do it
D.S.
all 4 love.

3. 4. etc.
Repeat ad lib. and fade
N.C.
D G
D G
all 4 love.
all,
Spoken: Yo! Come here, sweetheart.
The distance B-tween us,
all,
I want U 2 know something, alright.
an ocean of tears.

1.
2.
D G
all, all, all, all, all,
See, every day N my life without U would
See, all the things I do 4 U
all.
B like a hundred years.
all.
are 4 love.
Dig it.

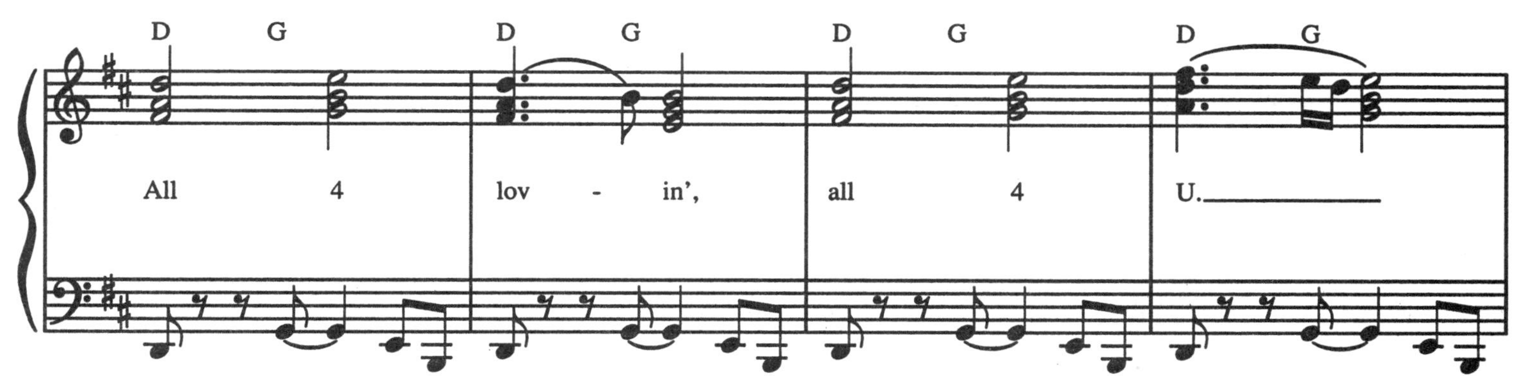
D G
All 4 lov - in', all 4 U.

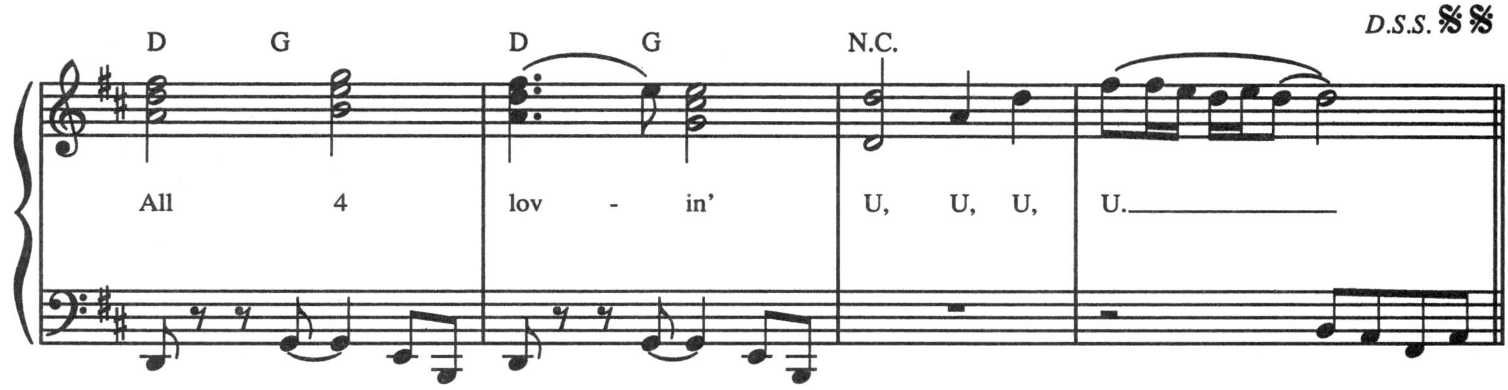
D.S.S.
D G
N.C.
All 4 lov - in' U, U, U, U.

ALL I HAVE

Words and Music by
BETH NIELSEN CHAPMAN
and ERIC KAZ

G(2)
G
G/A
A7
D
D/F♯
Trust - ing you is
Right here with you is where my life
Gmaj7
A(2)
F♯m7
Bm7
Cmaj7
eas - y. 'cause I be - lieve in you.
has come to - geth - er, and where love has filled my heart.
Em7
G/A
A7
F♯m7
Bm7
Cmaj7
3
Em7
A7sus A7
There is noth - ing I would miss as long as we're in love like this.
You know I'd go an - y - where as long as I have you to care.
All
cresc.

Chorus:
F#m7
Bm7
G
A7
F#m7
Bm7
I have is all I need, and it all comes down to you
mf
Em7
A7
F#m7
Bm7
Em7
D/F#
and me. How far a - way this world be - comes in the har-
Gmaj9
1.
Gmaj7/A
A
- bor - of each oth - er's arms.
dim.

2.
D
D/F♯
Gmaj9
A7sus
Gmaj7/A
A
— 2. I oth - er's arms.
mp
Bridge:
D
E7/G♯
F♯/A♯
Bm
E/G♯
— Ooh, and with the love you bring, I nev - er want for
A
Em7(4)
D/F♯
G(2)
A7sus
A7
an - y-thing. I found what I've been search-ing for in you.

Gm7
Cm7
A♭
B♭7
All I have is all I need, and it all
f
Gm7
Cm7
Fm7
B♭7
comes down to you and me. How far
Gm7
Cm7
Fm7
E♭/G
a - way this world be - comes in the har -

1.
A♭maj9
A♭maj7/B♭
B♭
E♭
- bor of each oth - er's arms.
2.
A♭maj9
A♭maj7/B♭ B♭
E♭
E♭(2)/G
- bor of each oth - er's arms.
dim.
mp
A♭2
B♭
Gm7
Cm7
A♭
A♭maj7/B♭ B♭
E♭
poco rit. e dim
p

From the Paramount Motion Picture "All I Want For Christmas"

ALL I WANT

Words and Music by
DAVID FOSTER and
LINDA THOMPSON

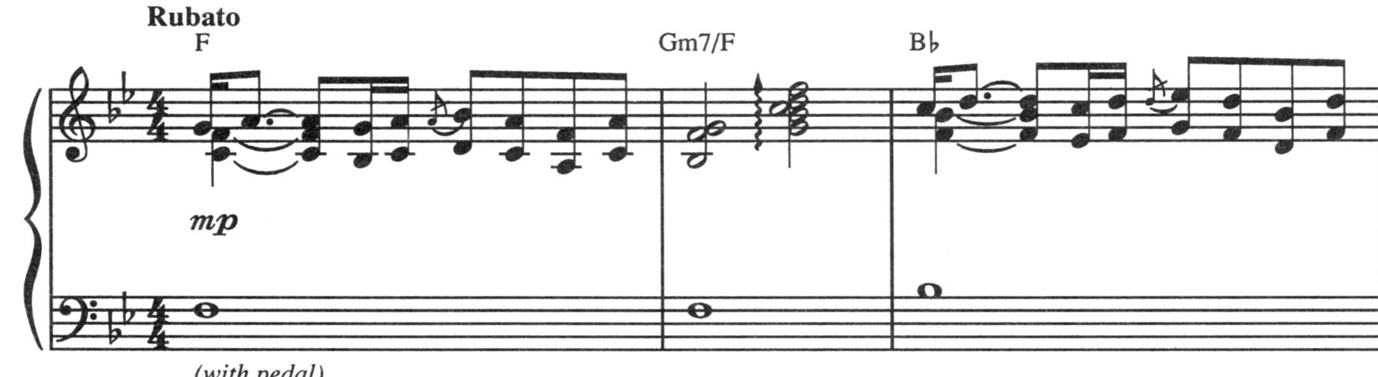

Fmaj7/A F/A D7/F♯ Gm F E♭maj7 Dm7
— Is it too much to ask? Can dreams still come true? Don't look
Cm7 Gm7
down on me with com-pro-mise. You could see the world from my point of view.
Chorus:
A♭maj7 E♭/F B♭/C F C/E Dm C
It's all up to you. All I want is the prom-ise you'll stay.

B♭/C
F
B♭maj7
C
All I want is one more yes-ter-day.
Now,
Dm
Dm(♯7)
Dm7
I don't mean to o-ver-sim-pli-fy, but I cross my heart and
G9
B♭/C
Am/C
E♭/F
Dm/F
E♭/F
hope to die.
Hey . . .
All I want
Verse:
B♭
F/A
D7/F♯
is ev-ery-thing I lost, no mat-ter what the cost,

Gm F E♭maj7 Dm7 E♭/F B♭

— 'cause I've al-read - y paid.___ All I want___ is a mem-o - ry___ or two___

Fmaj7/A F/A D7/F♯ Gm F/G Gm Dm7

— like the ones I had___ with you.___ I can't let it go.___ Don't look

Cm7 Gm7

down on me___ with com-pro-mise. You___ could see the world from my point of view.___

A♭maj7 E♭/F B♭/C *Chorus:* F C/E Dm C

___ It's all up to you.___ All I want___ is the prom-ise you'll___ stay.___

cresc. ***mf***

B♭/C
F
B♭maj7
C
A7/C♯
All I want is one more yes-ter-day.
Now
Dm
Dm(♯7)
Dm7
I don't mean to o-ver sim-pli-fy,
but I
cross my heart and
G9
Gm7
Am7
B♭maj7
hope to die.
All I want, I must con-fess,
is to - geth-er-ness with
B♭/C
Am/C
B♭/C
Am/C
B♭/C
just a lit-tle ten - der - ness.
Just a lit-tle ten -

Am/C
Bridge:
B♭/C
Am/C
- der - ness.
B♭/C
Am/C
B♭/C
Am/C
And the
E♭maj7
C7sus
C7
N.C.
young-est hearts must pay the price.
All I want
cresc.
f
Chorus:
G
D/F♯
Em
D
C/D
is the prom - ise you'll stay.
All I want

G
Cmaj7
D
B7/D♯
is one more yes - ter - day.
Now,
Em
Em(♯7)
Em7
I don't mean to o - ver sim - pli - fy,
but I
cross my heart and
A9
Am7
Bm7
Cmaj7
hope to die.
All I want,
I must con - fess,
is to - geth - er - ness
with
C/D
Bm/D
C/D
Repeat ad lib. and fade
just a lit - tle
ten - der - ness.
With just a lit - tle
ten - der - ness.

ALWAYS AND FOREVER

Bm9
Gmaj7
mor-row will still be the same, 'cause we've got a
lone-ly phone me and take a sec-ond to
Dmaj7
Em7
Em7/A
A7
Dmaj7
life of love that won't ev-er change. And
give to me that mag-ic you make, and
ev - 'ry
Gmaj7
D
Em7
Em7/A
day love me your own spe - cial way. Melt all my heart a -
Dmaj7
F♯ m7
Gmaj7
D
way with a smile. Take time to

Em7
F♯m7
Gmaj7
tell me you real-ly care and feel sad to-
and we'll share to-
Em7
Em7/A
Dmaj7
F♯m7
1. Em7
D
mor-row to-geth-er.
mor-row to-geth-er.
I'll al-ways
Em7
A9
N.C.
Dmaj7
2. Gmaj7
D
Em7
A9
love you.
There'll al-ways be
I'll al-ways love you.
8vb
loco
Dmaj7
Vocal Improvisation on Repeats
G9
Em7/A
A7
Repeat and Fade
mf
Lov-ing you (Al-ways for-ev-er, I love you.)

I CAN LOVE YOU LIKE THAT

Words and Music by
STEVE DIAMOND, MARIBETH DERRY
and JENNIFER KIMBALL

G7sus
Em7
F
Ju - li - et.
it comes to you. You
All this time that you've been wait - ing,
dream of love that's ev - er - last - ing, well
Em7
F
G7sus
you don't have to wait no more.
ba - by, o - pen up your eyes.
cresc.
mf
I can love you like that.
Chorus:
C
Em
F
I would make you my world, move heav - en and earth if you were my girl.
G7sus
C
Em7
I will give you my heart, be all that you need, show you you're ev -

F
B♭
-'ry - thing that's pre-cious to me.
If you give me a chance,
G7sus
1.
C
F
G7sus
I can love you like that.
2. I
2.
C
Bridge:
Gm7
You want
ten-der - ness, I've got ten -
Dm7
C
- der - ness and I see through to the heart of you. If you

Gm7 Dm7 F

want a man___ who un - der - stands,___ you don't have to look ver - y far.___

Gsus G

___ I can love you. I,___ I can love you like that.___

Chorus:

C Em F

___ I would make you my world,___ move heav - en and earth___ if you were my girl.___

G7sus C Em7

___ I will give you my heart,___ be all that you need,___ show you you're ev -

Repeat ad lib. and fade

F G7sus

- 'ry - thing that's pre - cious to me.___ I can love you like that.___

CAN'T FORGET YOU

Words and Music by
JORGE CASAS, CLAY OSTWALD
and JON SECADA

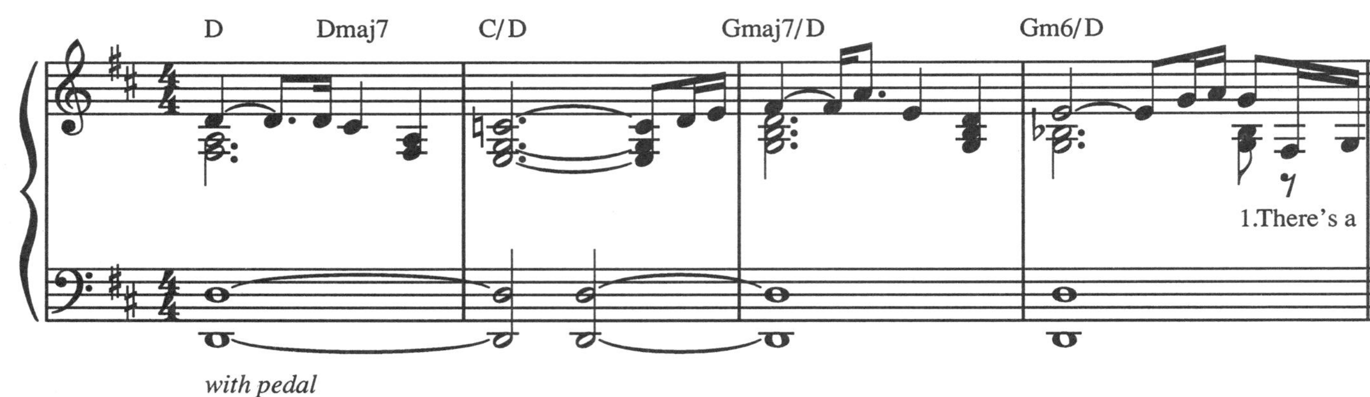

Gmaj7/D
Gm6/D
though my heart_ is break - ing_____ in___ a mil-lion bits in - side.___ I can
F#m7(♭5)/C
B7
3
Em
A
make be - lieve_ that none of this is true, ________ but I can't for - get___ you,_
mf
Chorus:
D
A/C#
Bm7
D/A
G
D/F#
_________ can't_ break free.____________ I've on - ly got___ my - self_ to blame.
Em7
A
D
A/C#
Bm7
A
Noth-ing feels the same_ with-out__ you.____________ Can't_ you see____
B7(♭9)
B+/D#
Em
D/F#
G
A
B
1.
D/A
we can find__ to - mor - row_ what we lost yes - ter - day,_ what we lost yes -
dim.

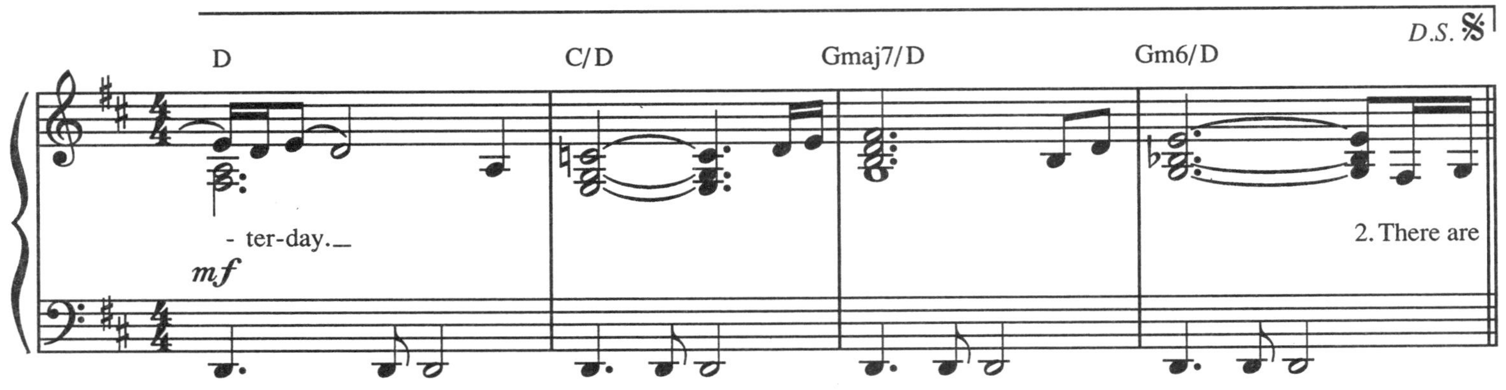
D.S. 𝄋
D
C/D
Gmaj7/D
Gm6/D
- ter-day.
mf
2. There are

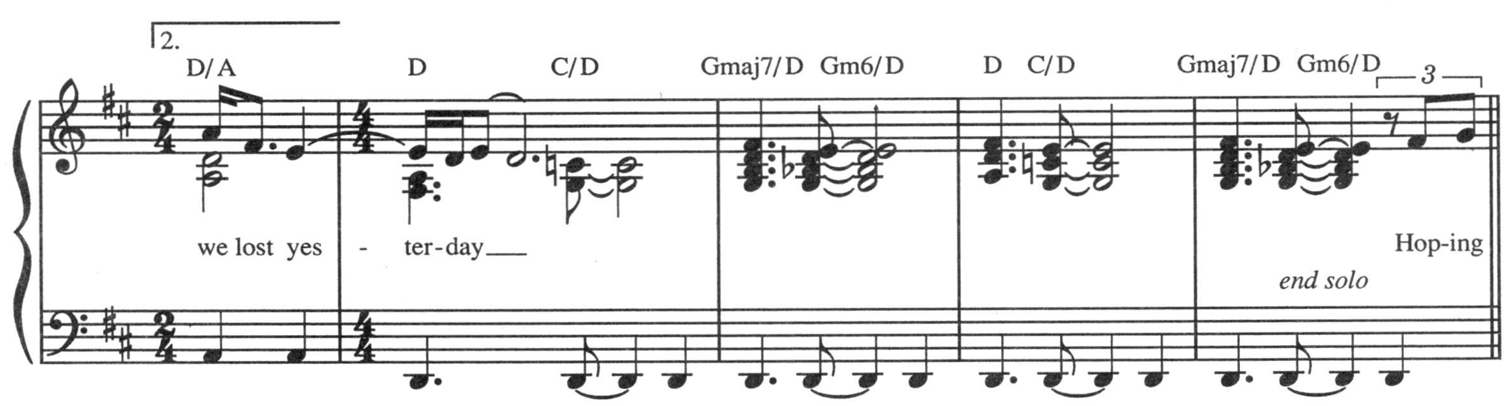
2.
D/A
D
C/D
Gmaj7/D Gm6/D
D C/D
Gmaj7/D Gm6/D
3
we lost yes - ter-day
Hop-ing
end solo

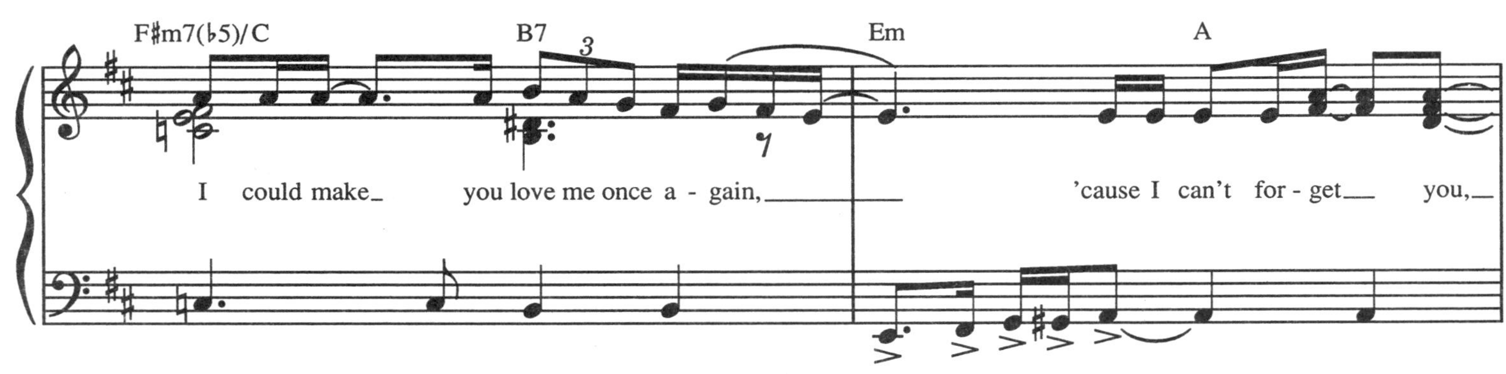
F#m7(♭5)/C
B7
3
Em
A
I could make you love me once a - gain,
'cause I can't for - get you,

D
A/C#
Bm7
D/A
G
D/F#
can't break free.
I've
on - ly got my self to blame.

Repeat ad lib. and fade

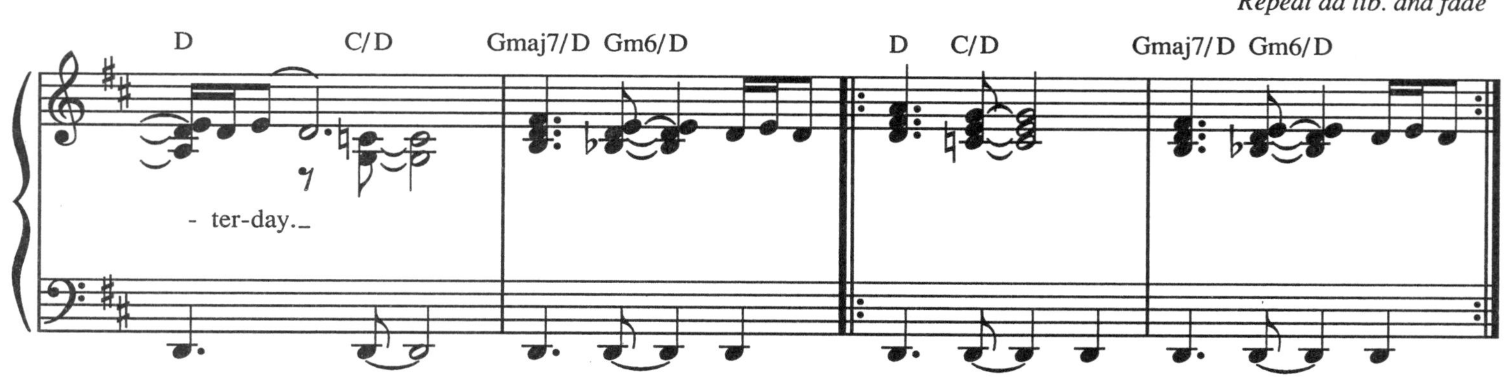

Verse 2:
There are nights when I lay wide awake
Thinking how good it could be.
Other nights I don't feel worthy
Of the love you gave to me.
I remember not too long ago,
We were both there to stay.
But it seems it happened overnight,
When I threw it all away.
I can walk away and find somebody new. . .
(To Chorus:)

CAN'T STOP THIS THING WE STARTED

Lyrics and Music by
BRYAN ADAMS and
R.J. LANGE

D/A A D/A A

oth - er guys, / I can't fly, } but if you wan - na stop me, ba - by, don't ev - en try. I'm go-in' one

D G/D D E

way, your way.

A/E E D G/D D

Now, it's such a strong way, let's make it

E F♯m7 Esus

our way, now, ba - by.

𝄋𝄋 *Chorus:*

D(2)

I can't stop this

E(2) E/F♯ F♯m7 D A

thing we start - ed. You got-ta know it's right.

To Coda
D(2)
E(2)
E/F♯
F♯m7
D
I can't stop this course we plot - ted, yeah.
A
D(2)
E(2)
This thing called love, we got it.
F♯m7
A
D(2)
No place for the brok - en heart - ed.
I can't stop this
F♯m/E
E
Esus
E
D
thing we start - ed, no way.
I'm go - ing
E
1.
D.S.
2.
A/E
E
your way.

B♭
E♭/B♭ B♭
E♭/B♭
B♭
F
Oh,
why take it slow?

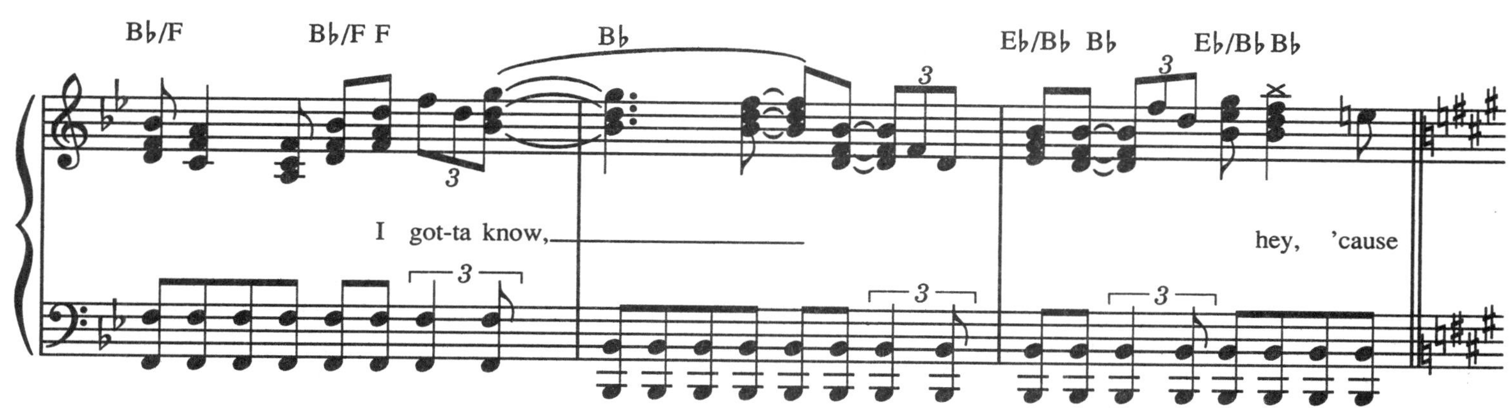
B♭/F
B♭/F F
B♭
E♭/B♭ B♭
E♭/B♭ B♭
I got-ta know,
hey, 'cause

A
D
E
noth - ing can stop this thing that we've got.
(Instrumental solo . . .

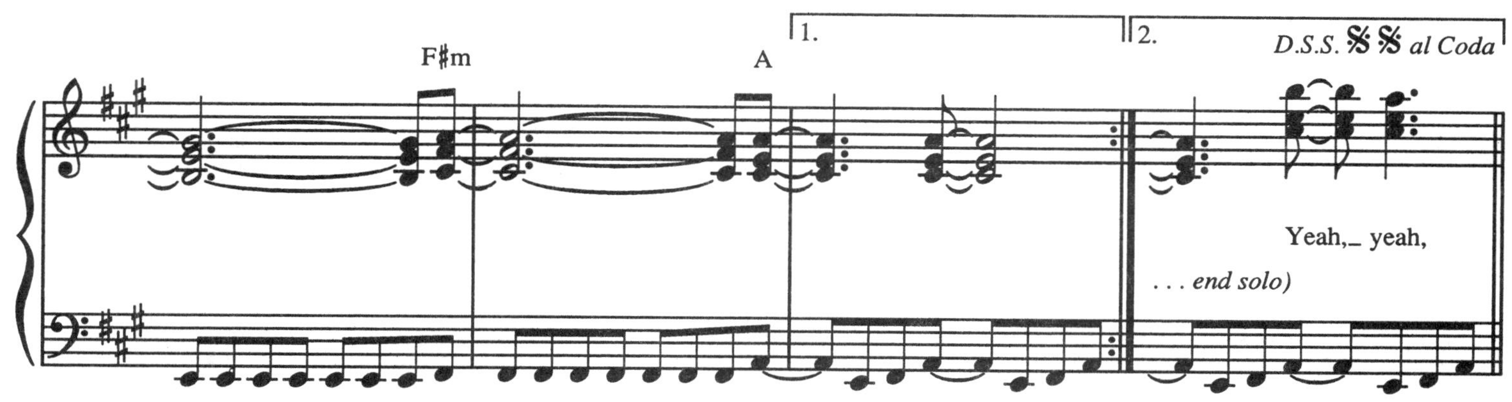
F♯m
A
1.
2.
D.S.S. 𝄋𝄋 al Coda
Yeah, yeah,
. . . end solo)

Coda
A
B♭
C
This thing called love, we got it.
F
B♭
D
Ain't no place for the brok - en heart - ed. I can't stop it.
E
D(2)
E(2)
I can't stop it. I can't stop this thing we start - ed.
E/F♯
F♯m7
D
A
D(2)
You got-ta know it's right. I can't stop this
Repeat ad lib. and fade
E(2)
E/F♯
F♯m7
D
A
course we plot - ted, yeah.

THE COMFORT ZONE

Lyrics and Music by
REGGIE STEWART &
KIPPER JONES

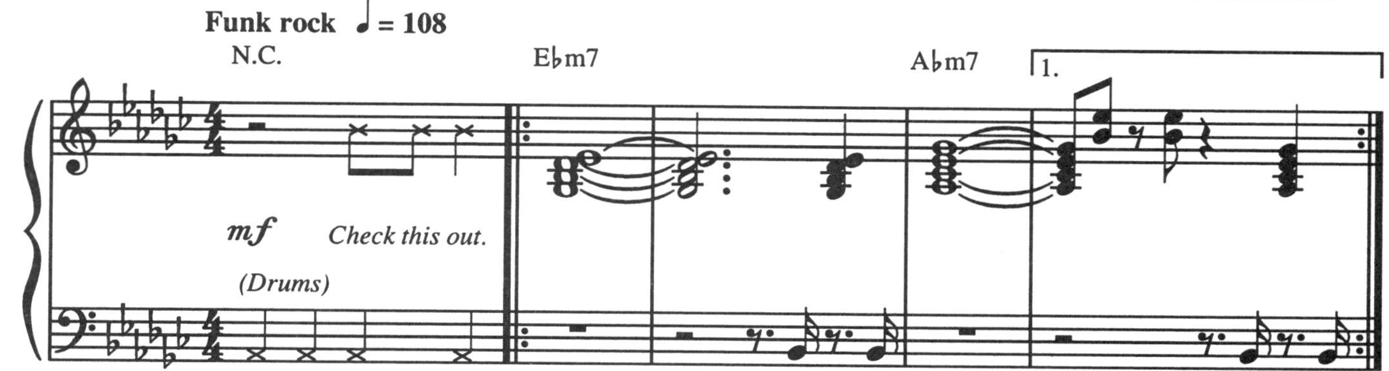

Bb7(b9)/Eb
Bb7(b9 b13)
— and where — to go.
Hey, wel - come to the

Chorus:
Ebm9
com - fort — zone. —
zone.
When you need —

Abm7/Eb
— to be loved — like you need — to be, wel - come to the

Ebm9
com - fort — zone. —
Do what - ev - er feels — right
No one ev - er has to know

Abm7/Eb
To Coda
1.3.
Bb7(b9)
Bb7(b9 b13)
To Next Strain
2.4. (After 4th ending to Coda)
Bb7/Eb
Bb7(b13)
and what } turns you on.
2. Af - ter a
3. (Ad lib. vocals . .)
Hey, wel-come to the

Verse:
Ebm9
N.C.
hard day at work, there's one
thing to be cer - tain of,

Abm7/Eb
this ol' fa - mil - iar love.
Oh,

Ebm9
N.C.
it's not un - us - u - al
to find that it's sen - su - al.

Bridge:
B♭7/E♭
B♭7(♭13)
A♭m9
It's all you need to let go.
There's no need to try,
(Instrumental solo 2nd time . . .

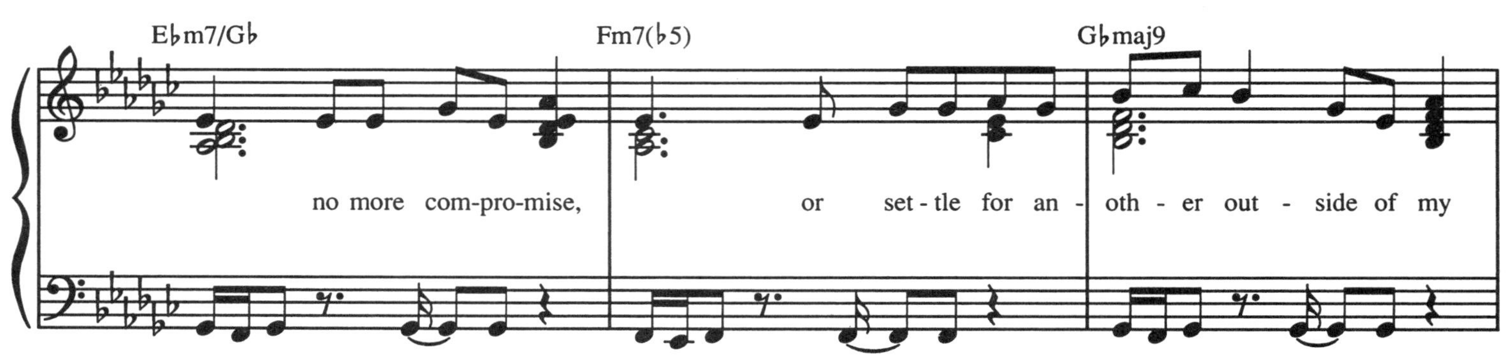
E♭m7/G♭
Fm7(♭5)
G♭maj9
no more com-pro-mise,
or set-tle for an-oth-er out-side of my

A♭m9
E♭m7/G♭
1.
Fm7(♭5)
love. The thing to do
when you get through,
heed the mes-sage,

F♭maj13
D.S.
2.
Fm7(♭5)
F♭maj7
seek the com-fort of my
Hey, wel-come to the
. . . solo ends)

Coda
B♭7/E♭
B♭7(♭13)
E♭m9
Hey, let me make you com - f'rta - ble. Let me
take con - trol and give your
A♭m7/E♭
mind a break from the
day you made. Let's turn the
E♭m9
lights down low then, oh, the
rest you know. I'll be
A♭m7/E♭
here for you, 'cause you
B♭7/E♭
B♭7(♭13)
just stepped in - to the
E♭m9
N.C.
com - fort zone.

CUTS BOTH WAYS

Slowly ♩ = 88

Words and Music by
GLORIA ESTEFAN

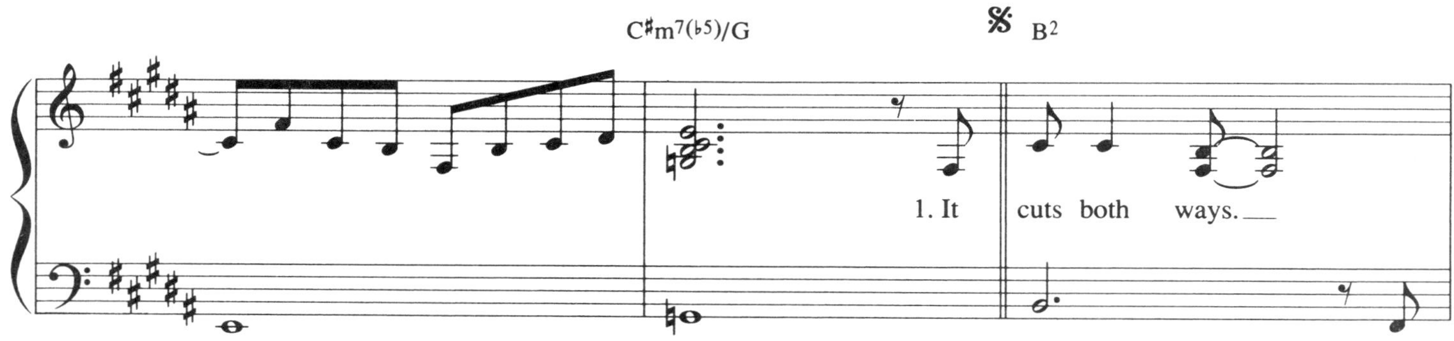

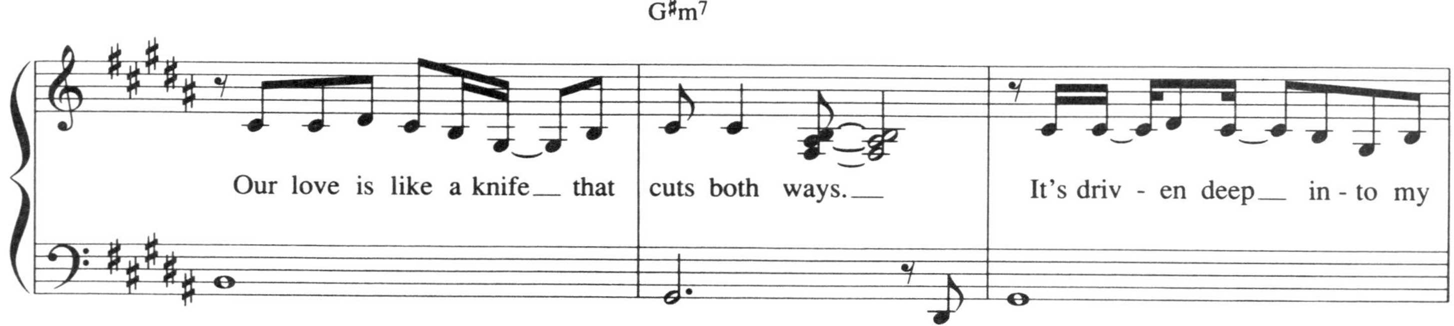

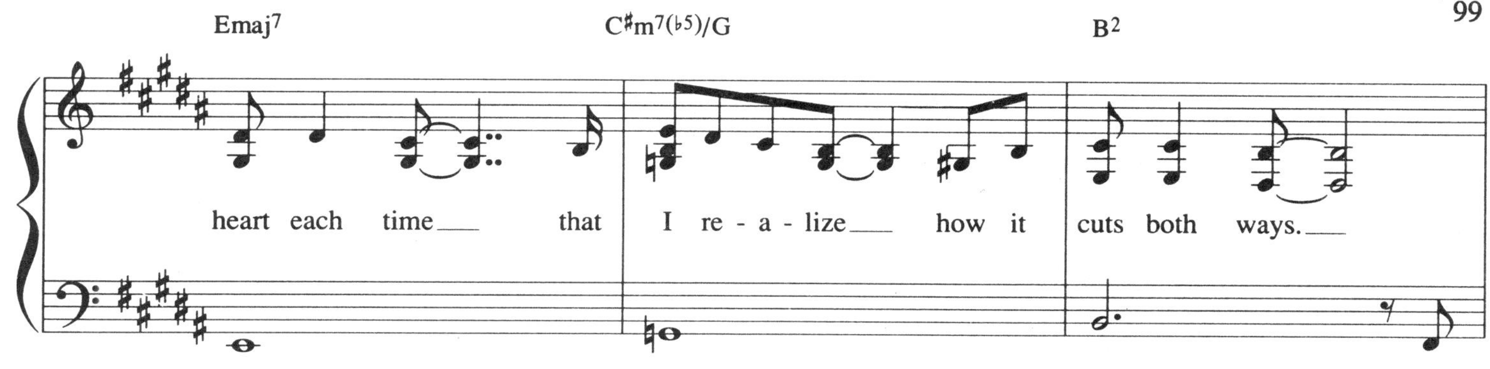
Emaj7
C#m7(b5)/G
B2
heart each time that I re - a - lize how it cuts both ways.

G#m7
Can't be to - geth - er, can - not live a - part. We're head - ing straight in - to a

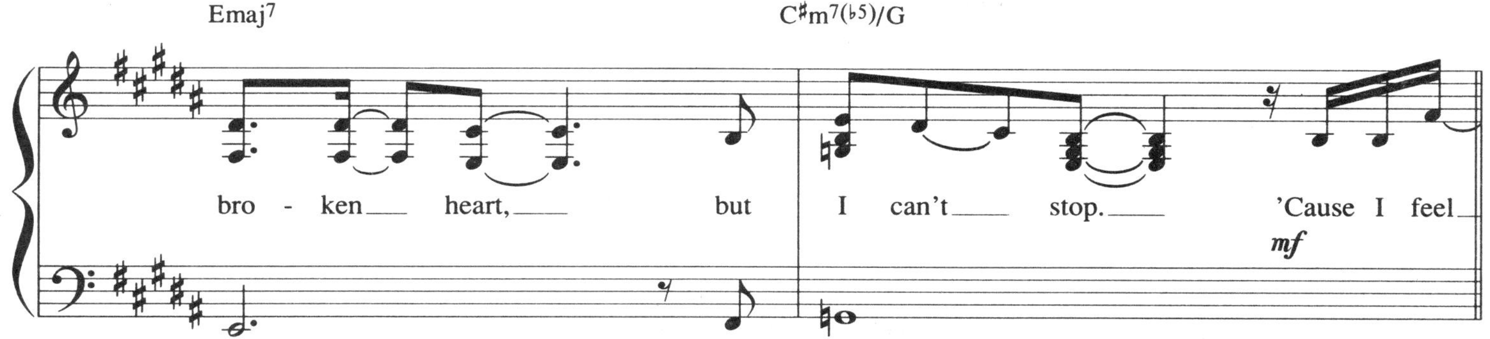
Emaj7
C#m7(b5)/G
bro - ken heart, but I can't stop. 'Cause I feel
mf

Slower and soulfully ♩ = 72
Chorus:

Emaj7
too much to let you go. I'm hurt - ing you, and it's hard I know to stay

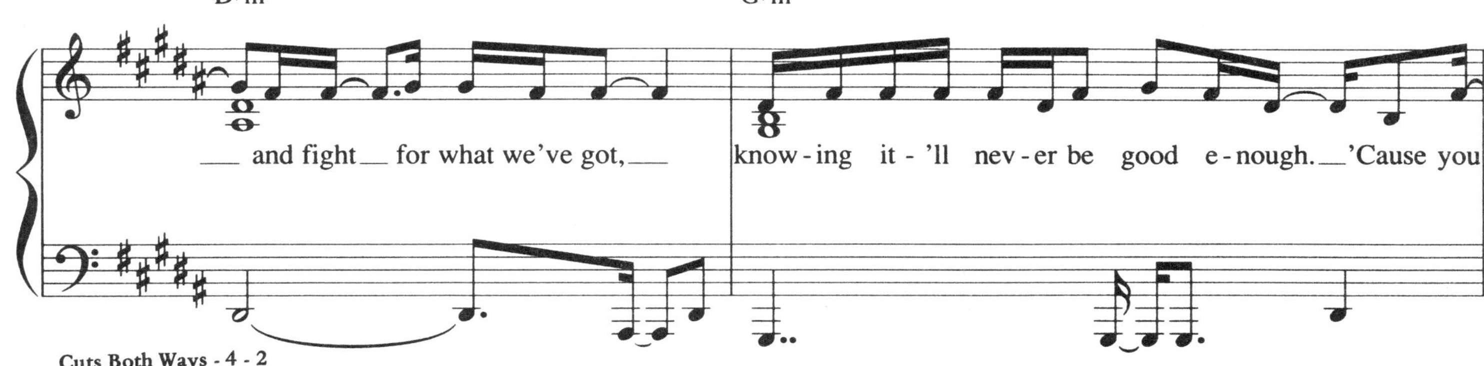
D#m7
G#m7
and fight for what we've got, know - ing it - 'll nev - er be good e - nough. 'Cause you

Emaj7
and I are dan - ger - ous. We
want too much, and life ain't that way. Don't ask

D♯m7
for more, don't be a fool.
1.
C♯m7
C♯m7(♭5)/G
Have - n't we al - read - y bro - ken ev - ery rule?

D.S. 𝄋
Slowly ♩ = 88
2. It
dim.
mp
2.
C♯m7
C♯m7(♭5)/G
Have - n't we al - read - y bro - ken ev - ery rule?

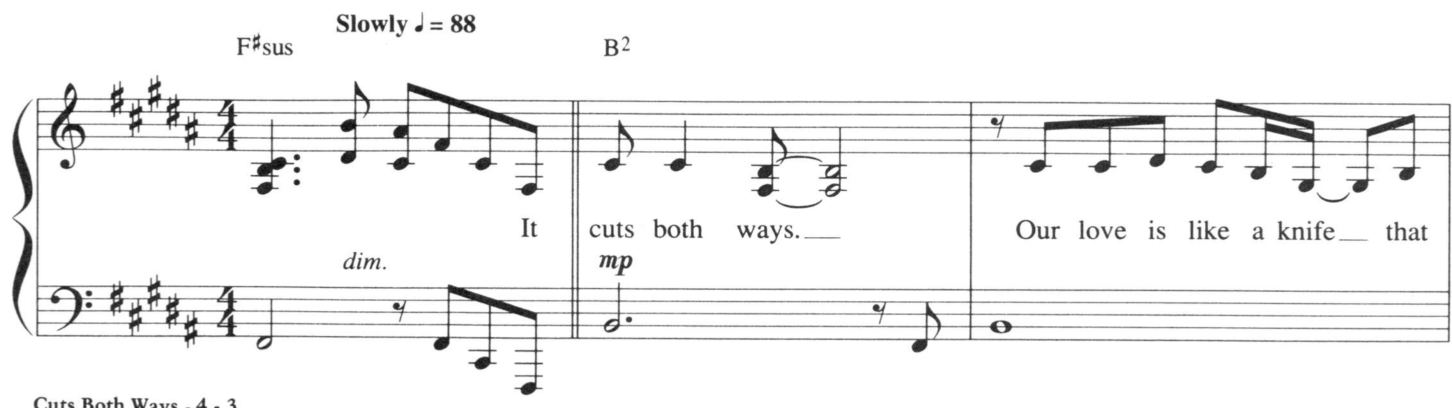
Slowly ♩ = 88
F♯sus
B2
It
dim.
cuts both ways.
mp
Our love is like a knife that

G♯m7
Emaj7
cuts both ways.
It's driv - en deep in - to my
heart each time I see we're

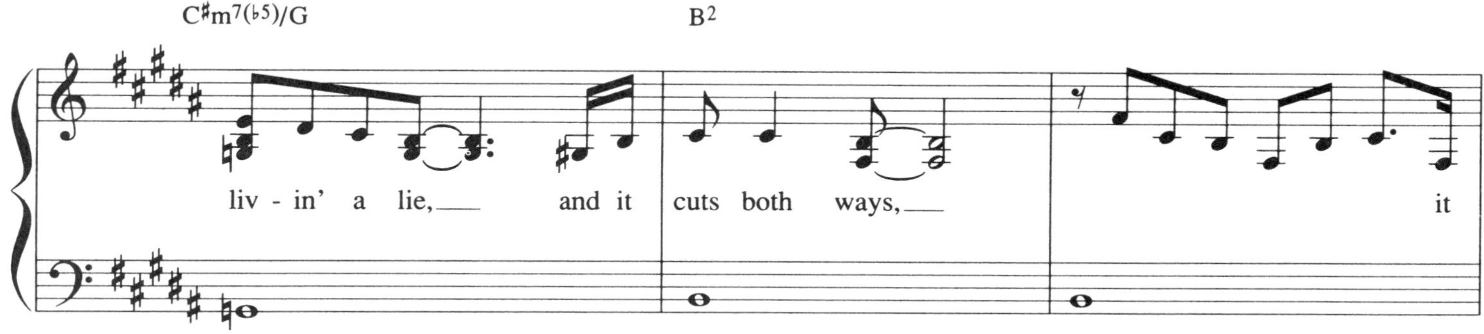
C♯m7(♭5)/G
B2
liv - in' a lie, and it
cuts both ways,
it

G♯m7
Emaj7
cuts both ways.
Mm, it
cuts both ways,

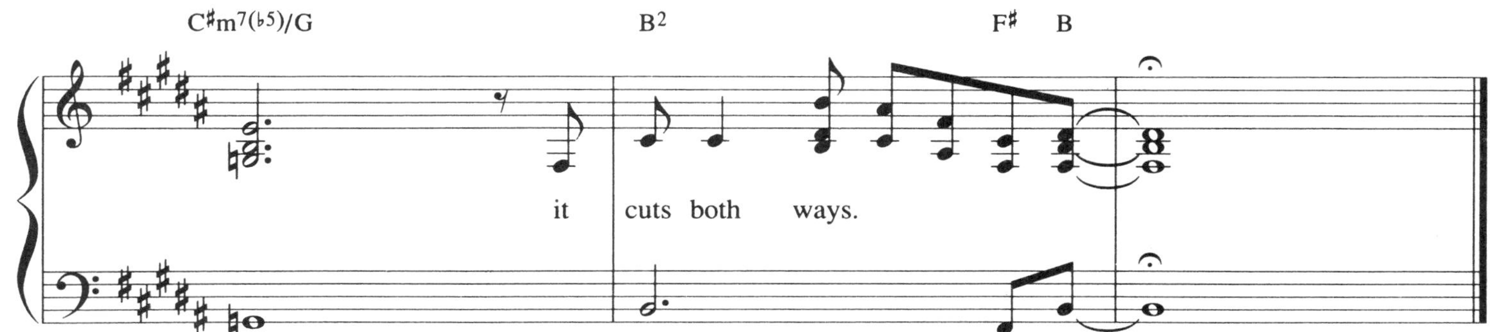
C♯m7(♭5)/G
B2
F♯ B
it
cuts both ways.

Verse 2:
It cuts both ways.
We're in too deep for sorry alibis.
Can't have regrets or even question why
We can't say goodbye,
Because it cuts both ways.
No more illusions of the love we make.
No sacrifice would ever be too great
If you would just stay.

(To Chorus:)

A FACE IN THE CROWD

Words and Music by
TOM PETTY and
JEFF LYNNE

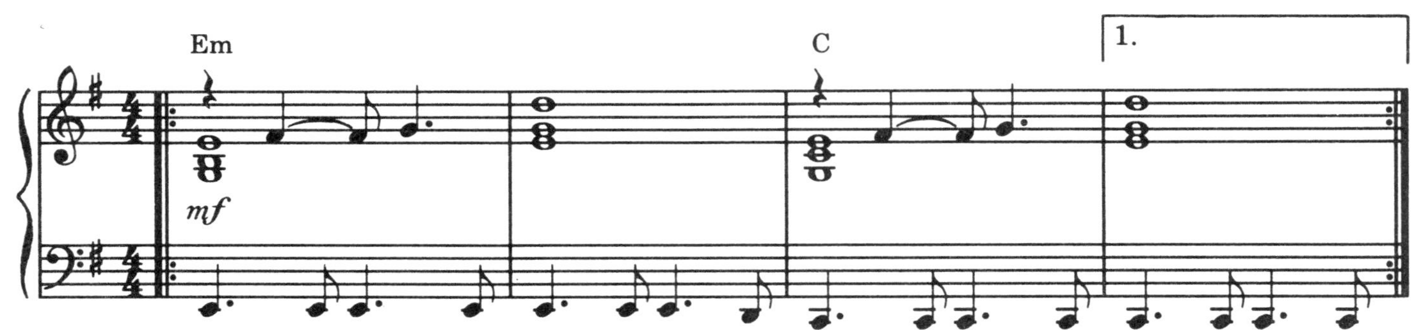

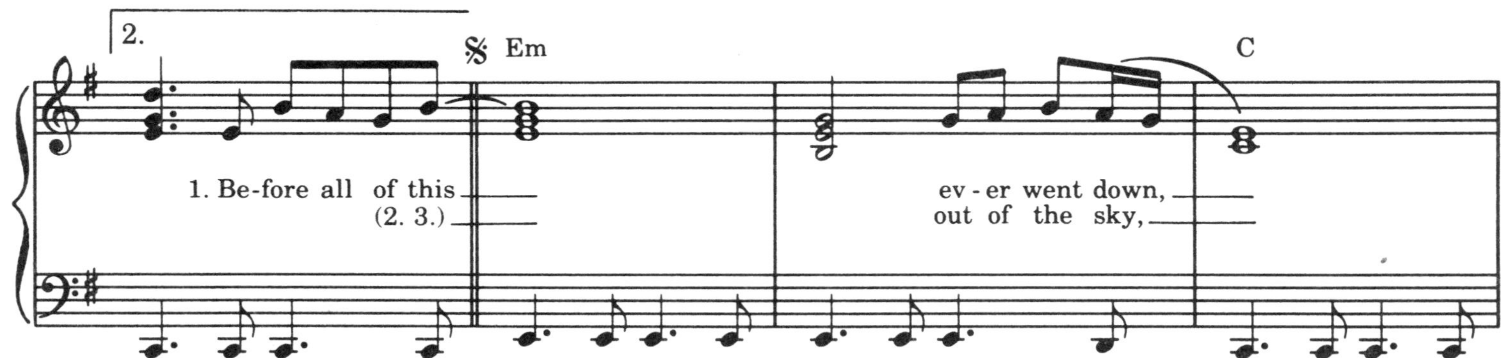

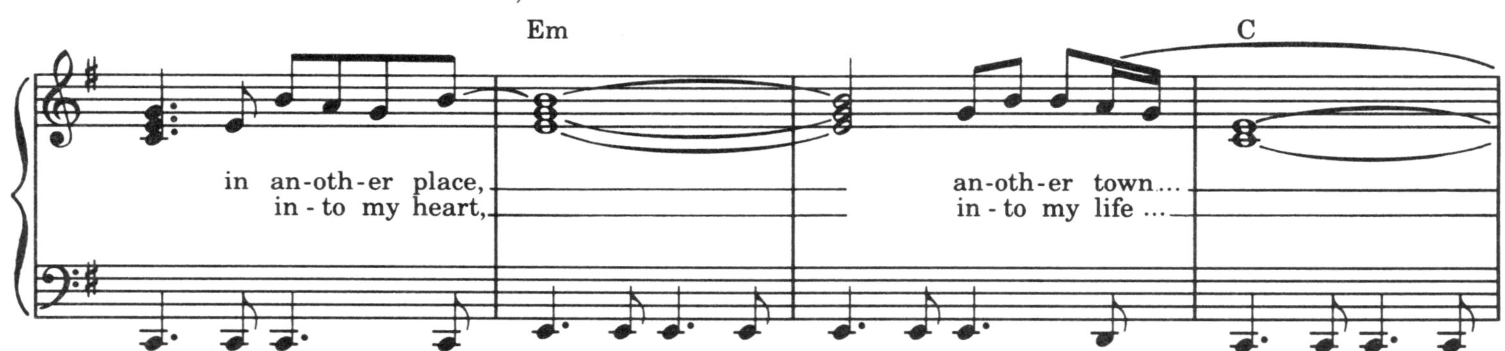

D
Am7
You were just
a face in the crowd
G/B
Am7
out in the street,
walk-ing a-round;
Em
To Coda
1.
C
a face in the crowd.
D.S.
2.
C
2. Out of a dream
D(2)
C

D.S. 𝄋 al Coda
D(2)
3. Out of a dream

Coda
C
Em
A face in the crowd,

C
Em
a face in the crowd.

Repeat ad lib. and fade
C
A face in the crowd,

GEORGIA ON MY MIND

Lyrics by
STUART GORRELL

Music by
HOAGY CARMICHAEL

E G#7(♭13) G#7 C#m Cm Bm E7
Geor-gia, I'm in Geor-gia, a song of
(Instrumental solo 2nd time . . . .
A A#dim7 E/B D13(#11) C#7 F#7 A/B
you comes as sweet and clear as moon-light through the
E A13 Emaj9 G#7 C#m A/C#
pines. Oth-er arms,
. . . . end solo)
cresc.
f
C#m6 A7 G#7(♭13) C#m A/C# C#m7 F#7
they reach out to me. Oth-er eyes smile ten-der-ly.
C#m A/C# C#m7 D#7(♭13) G#m7 (G9) C#7(♭9)
Still in peace-ful dreams I see the road leads back to

F#9 F#m7/B E D#m7(♭5) G#7
you. Geor-gia, sweet Geor - gia,
C#m E7/B A#m7(♭5) Am7 Am6 E D13(#11) C#7
no peace I find. Just an old sweet song
1.
D.S.
F#9 A/B D9(#11) C#9 F#9 A/B
keeps Geor-gia on my mind. Geor-gia on my mind.
2.
D9(#11) C#9 F#m9 E/G# A A#dim
mind. Just an old sweet, sweet, sweet
A/B E E7/G# A A#dim7 E/B F E E7(#9)
song, keeps Geor-gia for-ev-er on my mind.
mp

FAIRY TALES

Words and Music by
ANITA BAKER,
VERNON FAILS & MICHAEL POWELL

1.
2.3.4.
Eb7(#9 b13)
Ab7(#9 b13)
and kissed my face good - night.
we'd ride clean out of sight.
Db7sus4 2
Db7
She nev - er said that we would
curse, cry and scream and lie.
She nev - er said that may - be,
some - day he'd say good - bye.
cresc.
Chorus:
Gbmaj9
F7(#9 b13)
Bbm9
f {The My} sto - y ends
as sto - ries do,
re - al - i - ty
Eb9
Cm11
Cb9(#11)
steps in - to view.
No long - er liv - ing life in par - a - dise,

Db7sus4/2
Db7
Db7sus4/2
Db7
To Coda
1.
Gbm7
Fbmaj9
{ or no } fair - y tales.
Eb7(b9 #9 #11)
D13(#11)
Cbmaj7/Db
Db7
Cbmaj7/Db
Db7
D.S.
dim.
2.
Cbmaj7/Db
Db7
Dbmaj7/Db
Db7
Bridge:
Amaj9
I don't look for pie
C#m11
F#m7
up in the sky, ba - by, need
G#m7
C#7
Amaj9
re - al - i - ty now. I said I don't feel the need

Verse 2:
She spoke about happy endings, of stories not like this.
She said he'd slay all dragons, defeat the evil prince.
She said he'd come to save me, swim through the stormy seas.
I'd understand the story, it would be good for me.

You never came to save me, you let me stand alone,
Out in the wilderness, alone in the cold.
(To Chorus:)

Verse 3:
You never came to save me, you let me stand alone,
Out in this wilderness, alone in the cold.
I found no magic potion, no horse with wings to fly.
I found the poison apple, my destiny to die.

No royal kiss could save me, no magic spell to spin.
My fantasy is over, my life must now begin.
(To Chorus:)

HERE I AM

(Come and Take Me)

Words and Music by
AL GREEN and MABON HODGES

Bbm

I know it's you and me, ba - by,

Fm Bbm

that makes this world__ go 'round.__

Fm Bbm

__ I'm keep - ing you in love with me, ba -

Fm Bbm

by, lay - ing all my trou - bles down.__

Fm *Chorus:* Ab Eb Ab Eb

__ Here I am,__ ba - by, come and take me. Here I am,__

To Coda
Ab
Eb
Ab
Eb
Ab
Eb
ba - by,
come on and
take me,
take me by the hand.
Ooh,

Ab
Eb
Ab
Eb
Fm/Eb
Fm
show me,
here I am
ba - by.

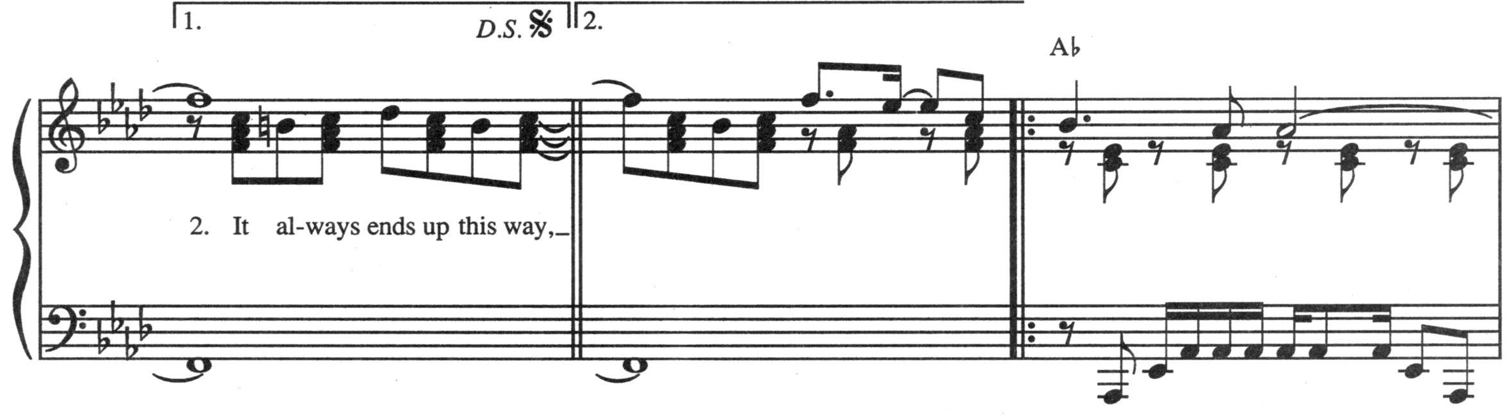
1.
D.S.
2.
Ab
2. It al-ways ends up this way,

Db

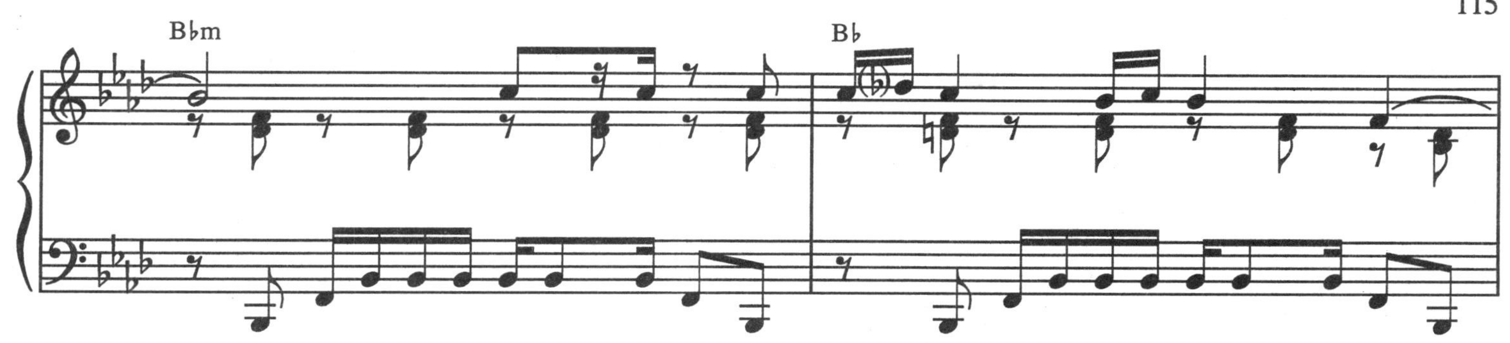

B♭m
B♭

Fm
E♭
Fm
1.
2.
D.S.S. 𝄋𝄋 al Coda
Oh, here I am

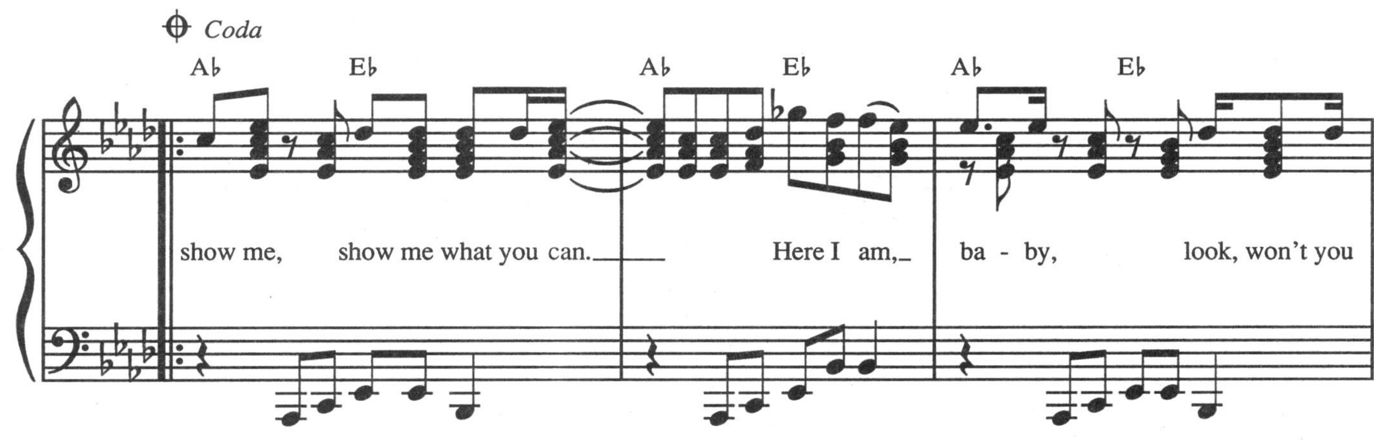

Coda
A♭
E♭
A♭
E♭
A♭
E♭
show me, show me what you can.
Here I am,
ba - by, look, won't you

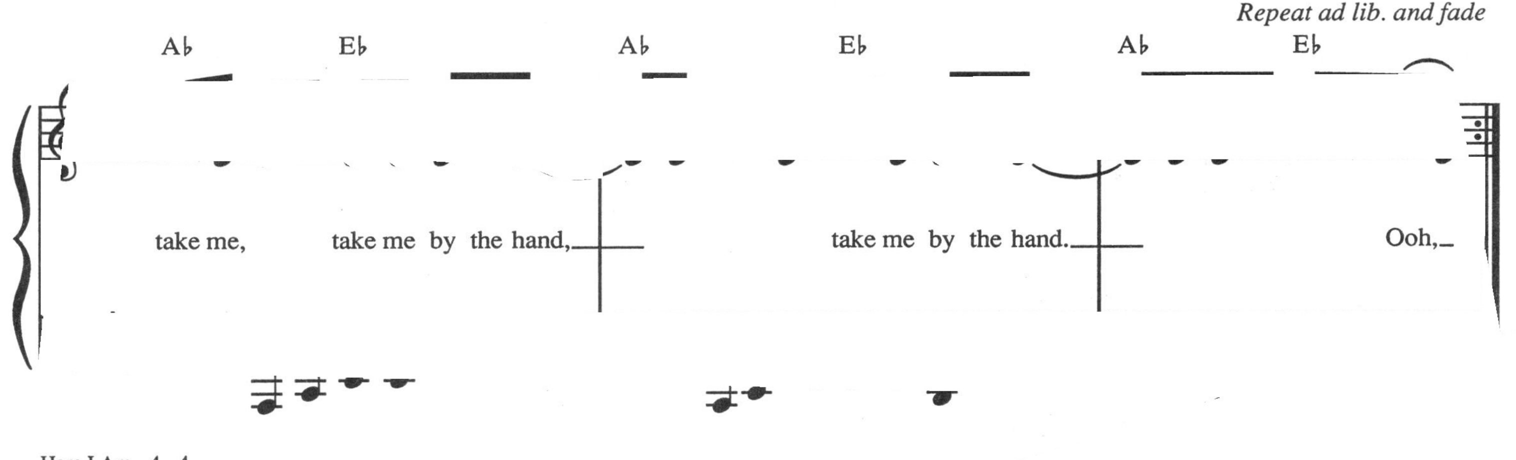

Repeat ad lib. and fade
A♭
E♭
A♭
E♭
A♭
E♭
take me, take me by the hand,
take me by the hand.
Ooh,

HOLD ON

Lyrics by
THOMAS McELROY, DENZIL FOSTER, TERRY LYNN ELLIS,
CINDY ANN HERRON, MAXINE JONES and DAWN SHERESE ROBINSON
Music by THOMAS McELROY and DENZIL FOSTER

And I won-der
(won-der)
(won-der)
who, who's

lov - in' you.
(you.)
(you.)
(you.)
Funk rock shuffle ♩= 100
B♭m

B♭m

Verse:
B♭m
Ooh, my first mis-take was

I want - ed too much
time. I had to have him
morn-ing, noon and night.
If I would have known then
the things that I know
now, I might not have lost the
Bridge:
B♭m
time I com-plain a-bout.
Don't waste your
time fight - ing
blind mind - ed
thoughts of de - spair.
Chorus:
B♭m
Hold on to your
love, you got - ta hold on.
Hold on to your
love, ooh ba - by, hold on.

Hold on to your
love, ooh, you got to hold on.
Hold on to your

1. 2.
D.S. 𝄋
3.
B♭m
love, ooh. 2. The
love, ooh.
Hold on to your
(ad lib vocals)

Repeat ad lib. and fade
love.
Hold on to your
love, ooh.

Verse 2:
The art of playing games, now, it's not the hearts you break.
It's 'bout good love you make when his heart's on fire.
Give him love every day, remember he needs space.
Be patient and he'll give his heart to you.

Verse 3:
Trust, and honesty too, must be the golden rule.
You'll feel the strength of passion in your soul, burning so deeply within.
Ooh, the magic that you share,
So, sacrifice and show how much you care.

MISSING YOU

Words and Music by
STEVE PERRY and TIM MINER

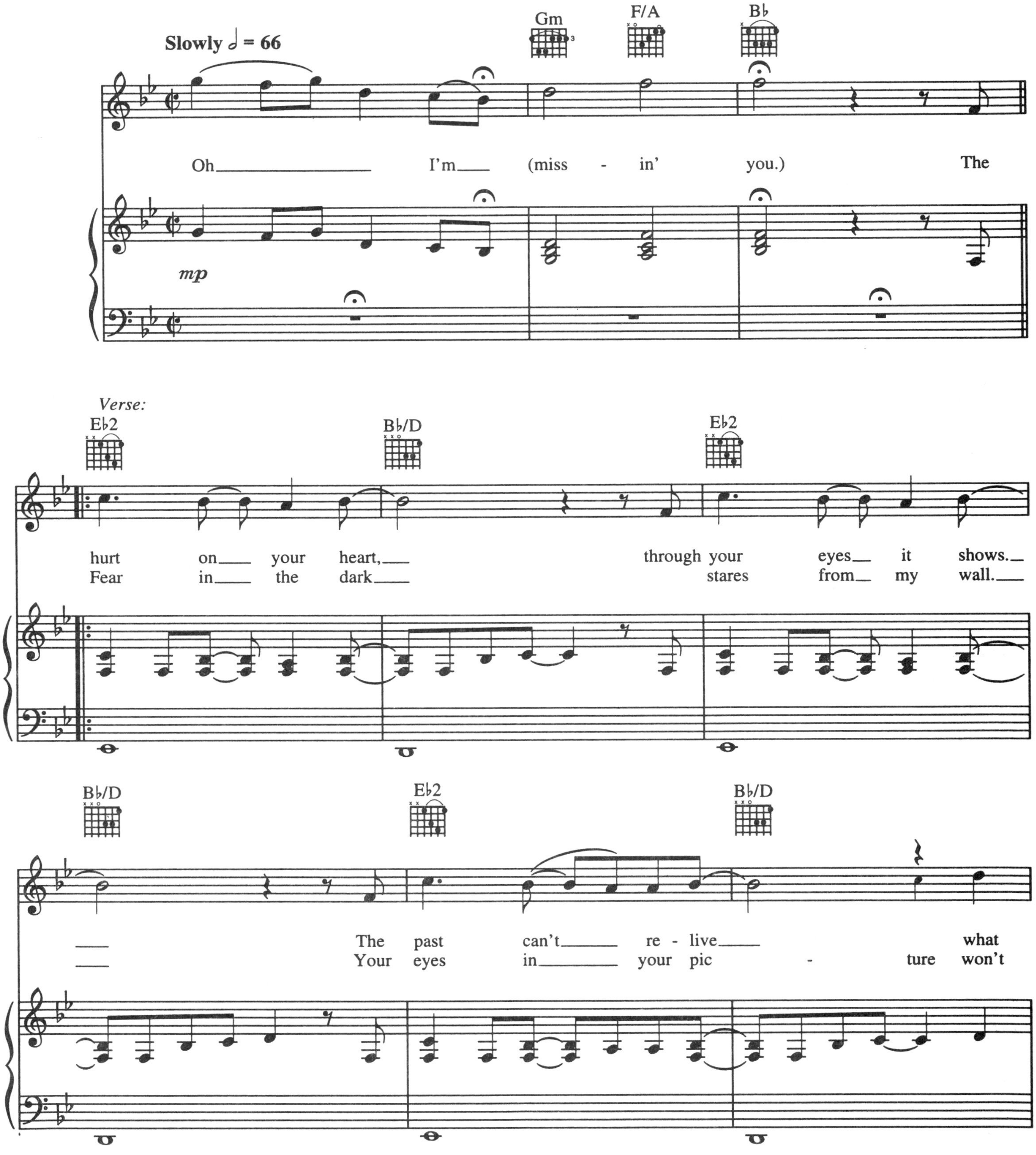

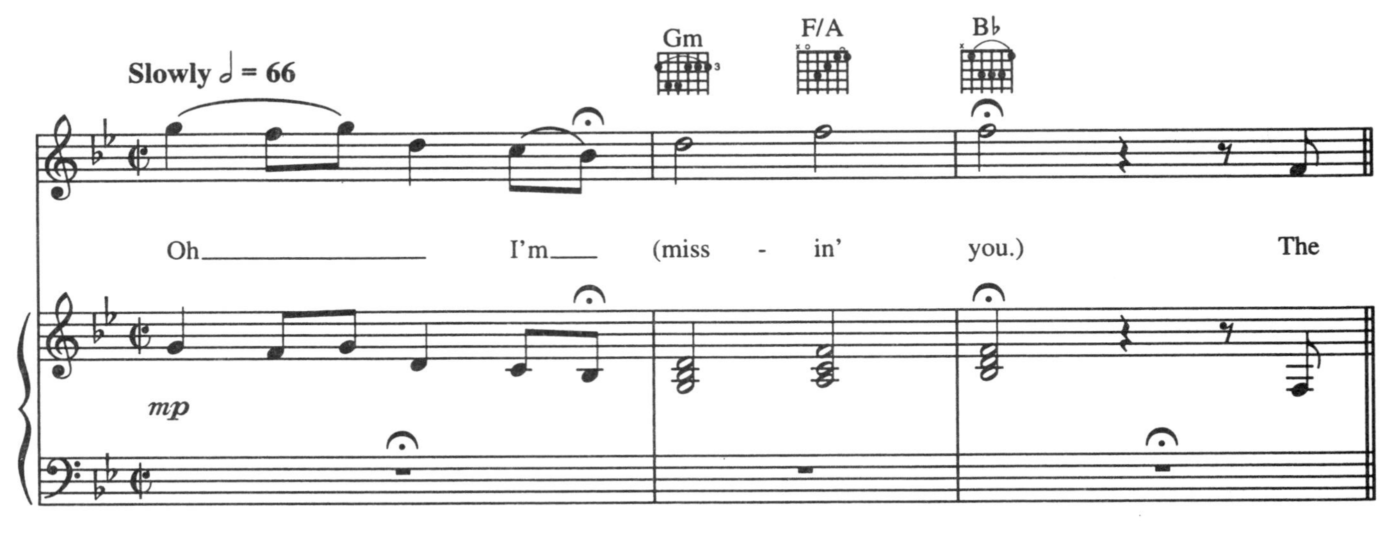

Slowly ♩ = 66
Gm
F/A
B♭
Oh I'm (miss - in' you.) The
mp
Verse:
E♭2
B♭/D
E♭2
hurt on your heart, through your eyes it shows.
Fear in the dark stares from my wall.
B♭/D
E♭2
B♭/D
The past can't re - live what
Your eyes in your pic - ture won't

Cm7 Bb/D Fsus F Eb2 Bb/D
we both know._ Still I___ re - mem - ber__
let me go.___ If I could_ re - mem - ber__
Eb2 Bb/D Eb2
things I nev - er meant.__ Mem - 'ries__ sur - round__
how you felt______ the pain.___ The king of___ pre - tend -
Bb/D Cm7 Bb/D Fsus F
___ me,__ won't let___ me for - get.
- ers__ a - lone__ in shame.
I was so
3

Chorus:
E♭maj9
Gm7
E♭maj9
wrong, the se - cret's not worth
Gm7
Cm7
Gm7
keep - ing. I had no faith that you would still be - lieve.
F/A
F
E♭maj9
Gm7
No, now my
E♭maj9
Gm7
Cm7
B♭/D
Fsus
heart's in your keep - ing. Here I am,

1.
F
E♭2
Gm7
F/A
B♭
miss - ing you.
(Miss - ing you.)
2.
F
Gm7
Cm7
B♭/D
E♭maj13
oh here I am,
(miss - ing you
)
B♭/D
Gm7
miss - ing you.
Cm7
Cm7/F
F/A
Gm7
F/A
B♭
Oh,
I'm
(miss - ing you.)
You were

E♭maj9
Dm7
Gm7
there,
now I'm
here.
You gave
Cm7
Cm7/F
F/A
Gm7
F/A
B♭
much more than I did,
I gave what I had to give.
If I
E♭maj9
Dm7
Gm7
could you know I
would,
Cm7
Cm7/F
F/A
Gm7
F/A
B♭
I'd make it up to you, in - stead I'm (miss - ing you.)
In the

E♭maj9 Dm7 Gm7

place you used to be you were

Cm7 Cm7/F F/A Gm7 F/A B♭

ly - ing next to me. Oh, I'm

E♭maj9 B♭/D Gm7

miss - ing you.

Cm7 Cm7/F F/A Gm7 F/A B♭

Oh, I'm miss - ing you.

HOW CAN I EASE THE PAIN

Words and Music by
NARADA MICHAEL WALDEN
& LISA FISCHER

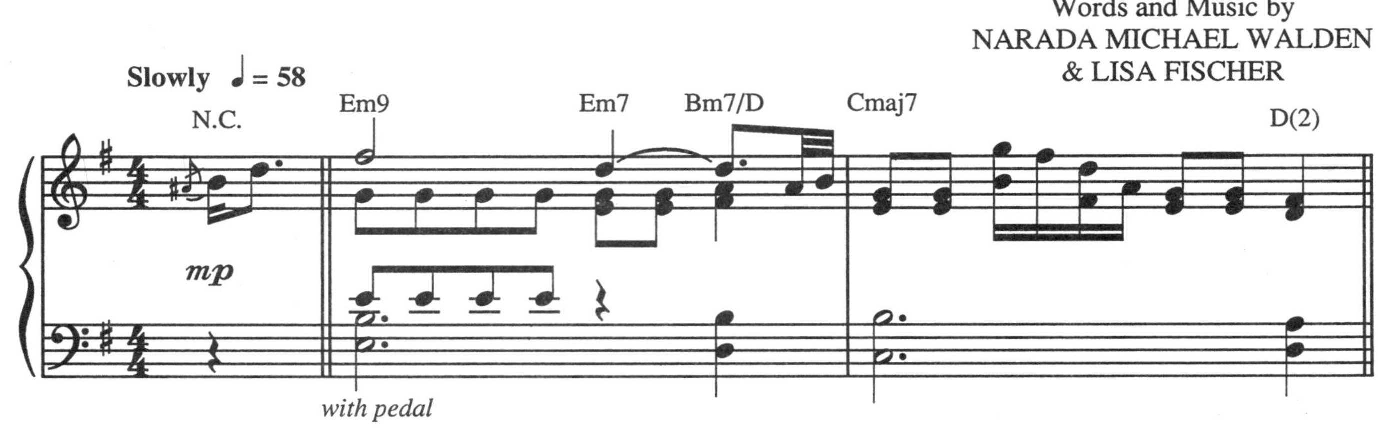

Chorus:
Am7
Bm7
D/E
Em/G
Cmaj9
Bm7(4)
ease the pain
when I know you're com-ing back a - gain? How can
Am7
Bm7
Cmaj9
I ease the pain in my heart?
1.
D
Em
Bm7/D
Cmaj7
D(2)
D.S. 𝄋
How can I ease the pain?
dim.
mp
2.
D(2)
Bridge:
Am7
G/B
How can I ease it?
cresc.
If it's not love
f
Cmaj7
D
Am7
G/B
you've come here for,
tell me, ba - by, why you're here,

Cmaj7
D(2)
Em7
Am7
G/B
knock-knock-knock-in' at my door.
I can't take it no more,

Cmaj7
D
D♯dim7
B7(♭9)/F♯
no more, no more, no more, ba - by.
Give me all or noth-ing at

B7(♭9 ♭13)/A
B7(♭9 ♭13)
Cmaj9
Bm7
Chorus:
Am7
Bm7
all.
How can I
ease the pain

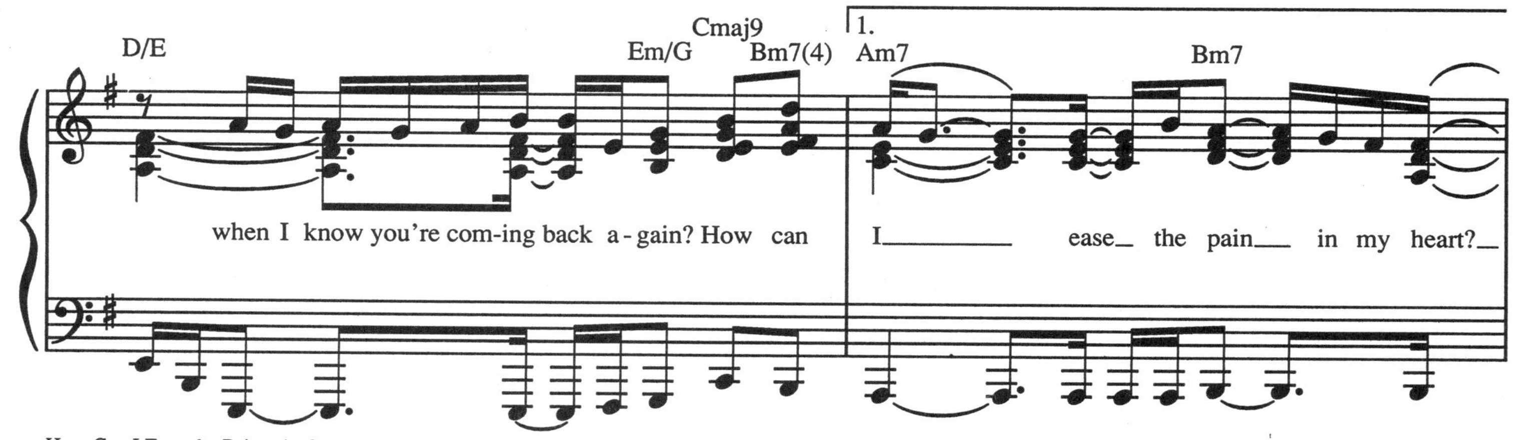
D/E
Em/G
Cmaj9
Bm7(4)
1.
Am7
Bm7
when I know you're com-ing back a-gain? How can
I ease the pain in my heart?

*Pianist should play downstemmed notes in r.h. for this section.

HOW 'BOUT US

Words and Music by
DANA WALDEN

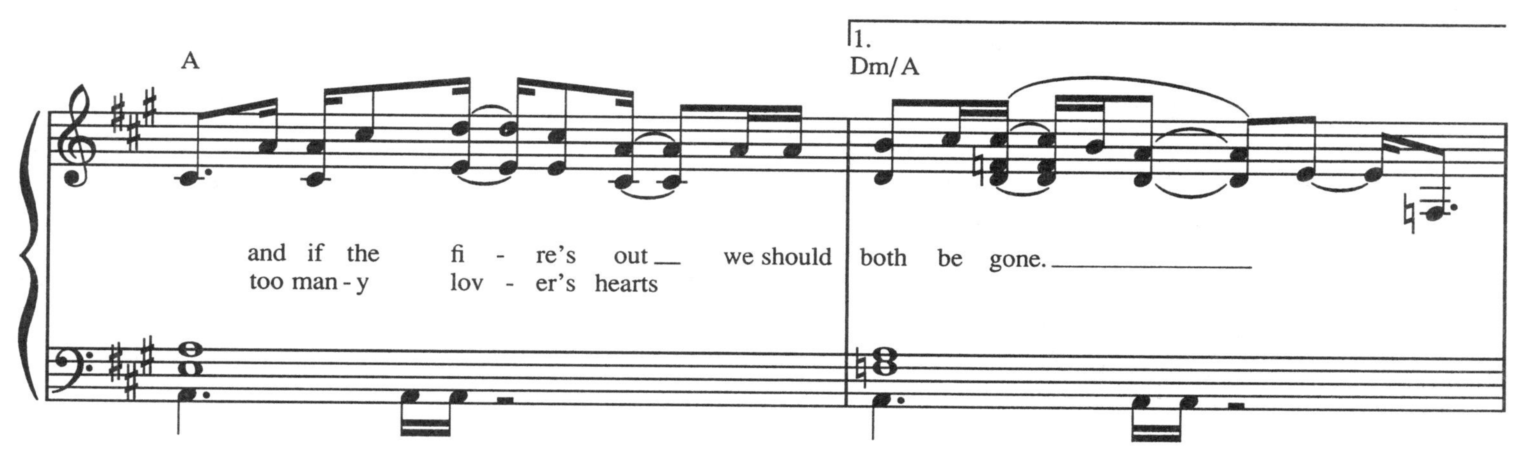
A
1.
Dm/A
and if the fi - re's out we should both be gone.
too man-y lov - er's hearts

G9
Both:
To Next Strain
2.
Dm/A
Oh.
lose their dream. (We won't lose it!)
cresc.

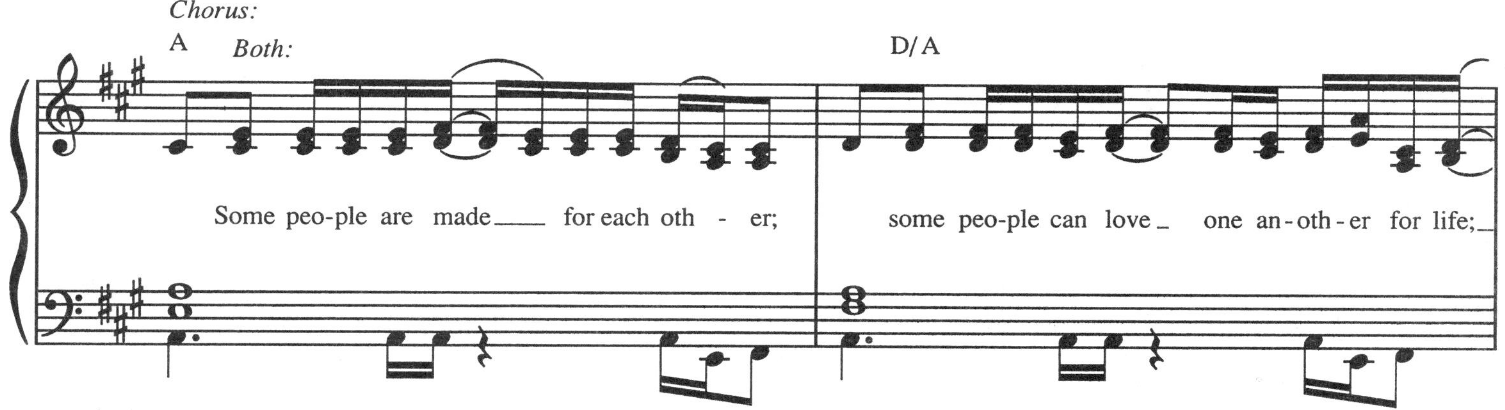
Chorus:
A
Both:
D/A
Some peo-ple are made for each oth - er;
some peo-ple can love one an-oth-er for life;

Dm/A
A
how 'bout
us?

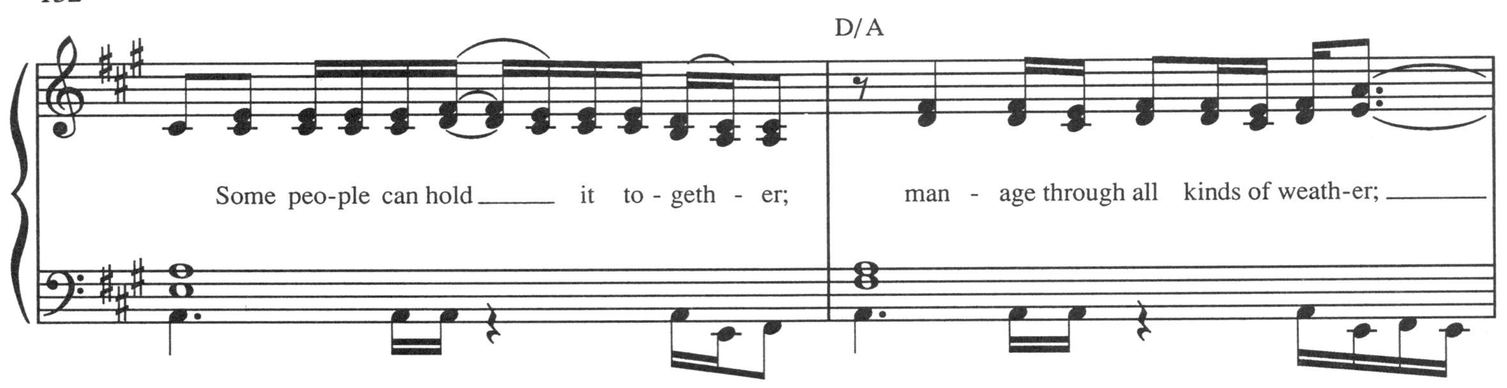
D/A
Some peo-ple can hold it to-geth - er;
man - age through all kinds of weath-er;

Dm/A
1.
A
Dm/A
Dm6/A
can
we?

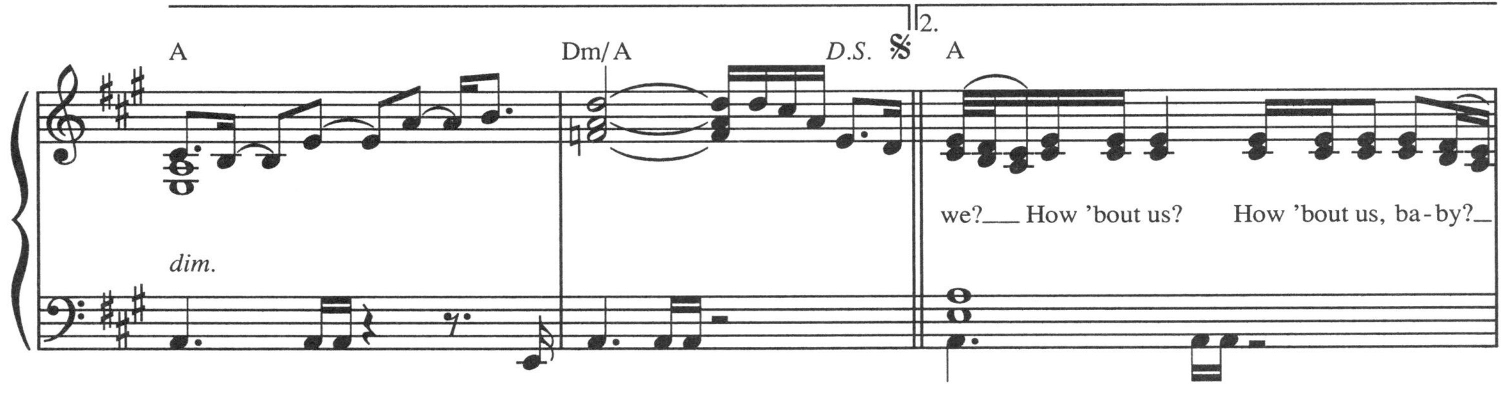
A
Dm/A
D.S.
2.
A
we? How 'bout us? How 'bout us, ba-by?
dim.

Dm6/A
A
How 'bout us? How 'bout us, ba - by?
How 'bout us? How 'bout us, ba - by?

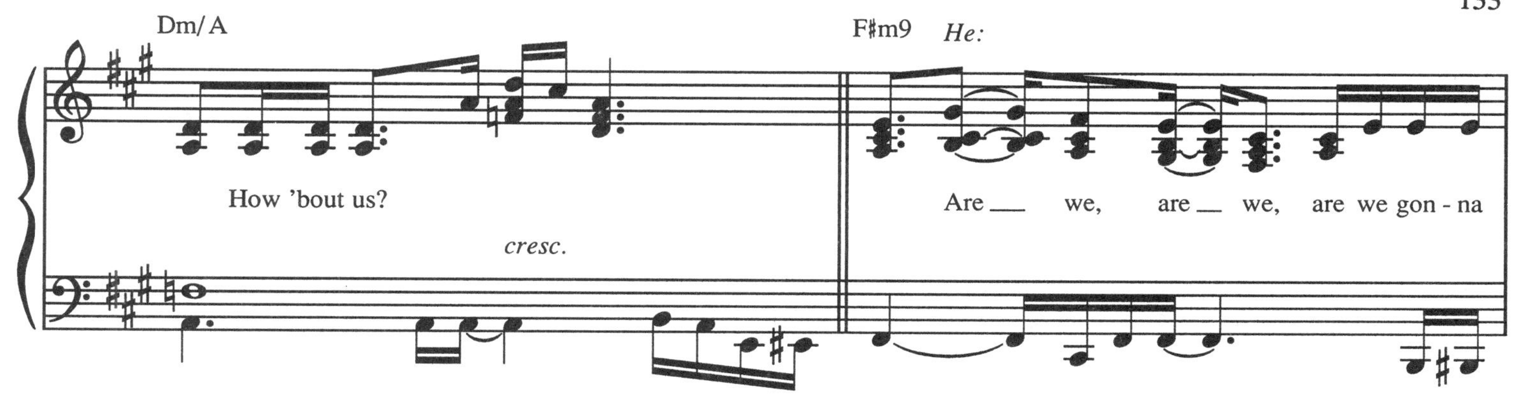
Dm/A
F♯m9
He:
How 'bout us?
cresc.
Are ___ we, are ___ we, are we gon - na

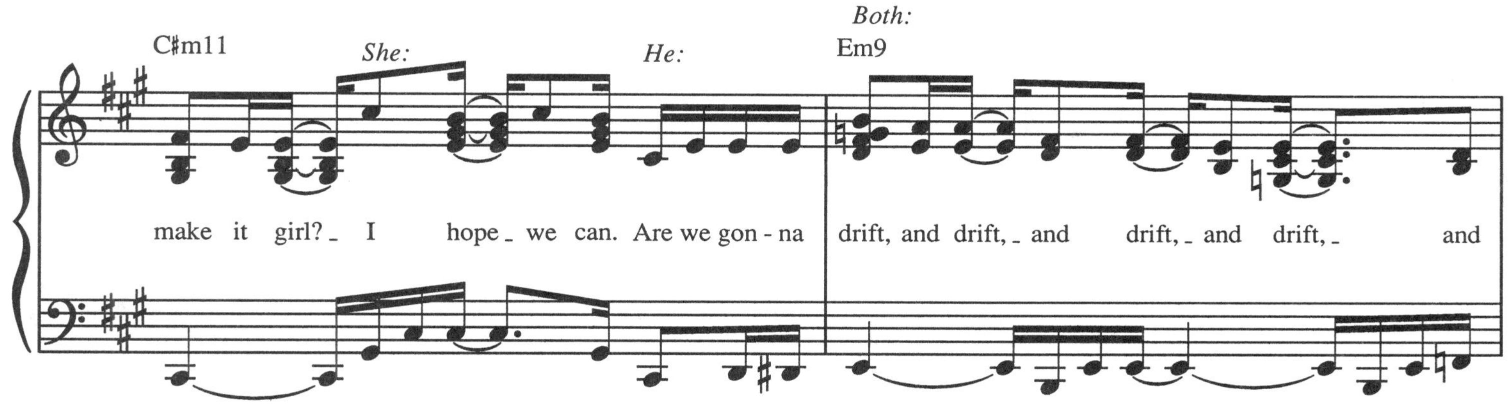
C♯m11
She:
He:
Both:
Em9
make it girl? _ I hope _ we can. Are we gon - na
drift, and drift, _ and drift, _ and drift, _ and

G9
C
drift to - geth - er? ___
Some peo - ple are made ___ for each oth - er;

F/C
Fm/C
some peo - ple can love _ one an - oth - er for life; ___ how 'bout

C
us?
Some peo-ple can hold it to-geth - er;

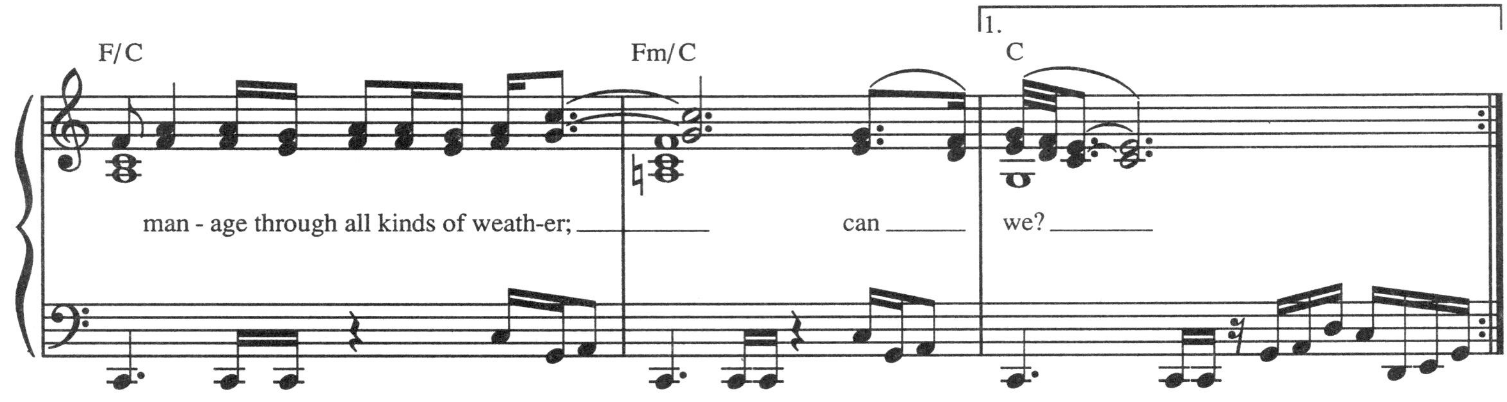
F/C
Fm/C
1.
C
man - age through all kinds of weath-er;
can
we?

2.
C
Fm/C
we?
How 'bout

C
Fm/C
Repeat ad lib. and fade
us?
How 'bout

I CAN'T WAIT ANOTHER MINUTE

B♭m7
E♭/D♭
We'll turn the lights_ down low,_
and dance so ver - y slow._
D♭maj7
B♭m7
I know that we don't
know each oth - er well,_
but I
A♭/C
3
Fm
Fm7/E♭
can't be - lieve_ I'm wast - ing your time,_
oh_ no._
D♭maj7
Dm7(♭5)
So tell me what_ to_ do
for the love_ of you_ to-night._
D♭2/E♭
Chorus:
A♭
E♭/G
'Cause I've been
hold-ing back what_ I feel, love's so

Fm7 Ab/Eb Bbm7

real, But I can't wait an - oth - er min - ute, I can't

Db/Eb Ab Eb/G

wait an - oth - er min - ute. 'Cause I've been hold - ing back all I feel, I'm for

Fm7 Ab/Eb Bbm7

real, 'cause I can't wait an - oth - er min - ute, I can't

Db/Eb *To Coda* 1. Ab Eb/G

wait an - oth - er min - ute for your love. Your love.

Fm7 Ab/Eb Bbm7 Db/Eb *D.S.*

Ooh ooh ooh ooh ooh ooh. Nuh, help now ba - by.

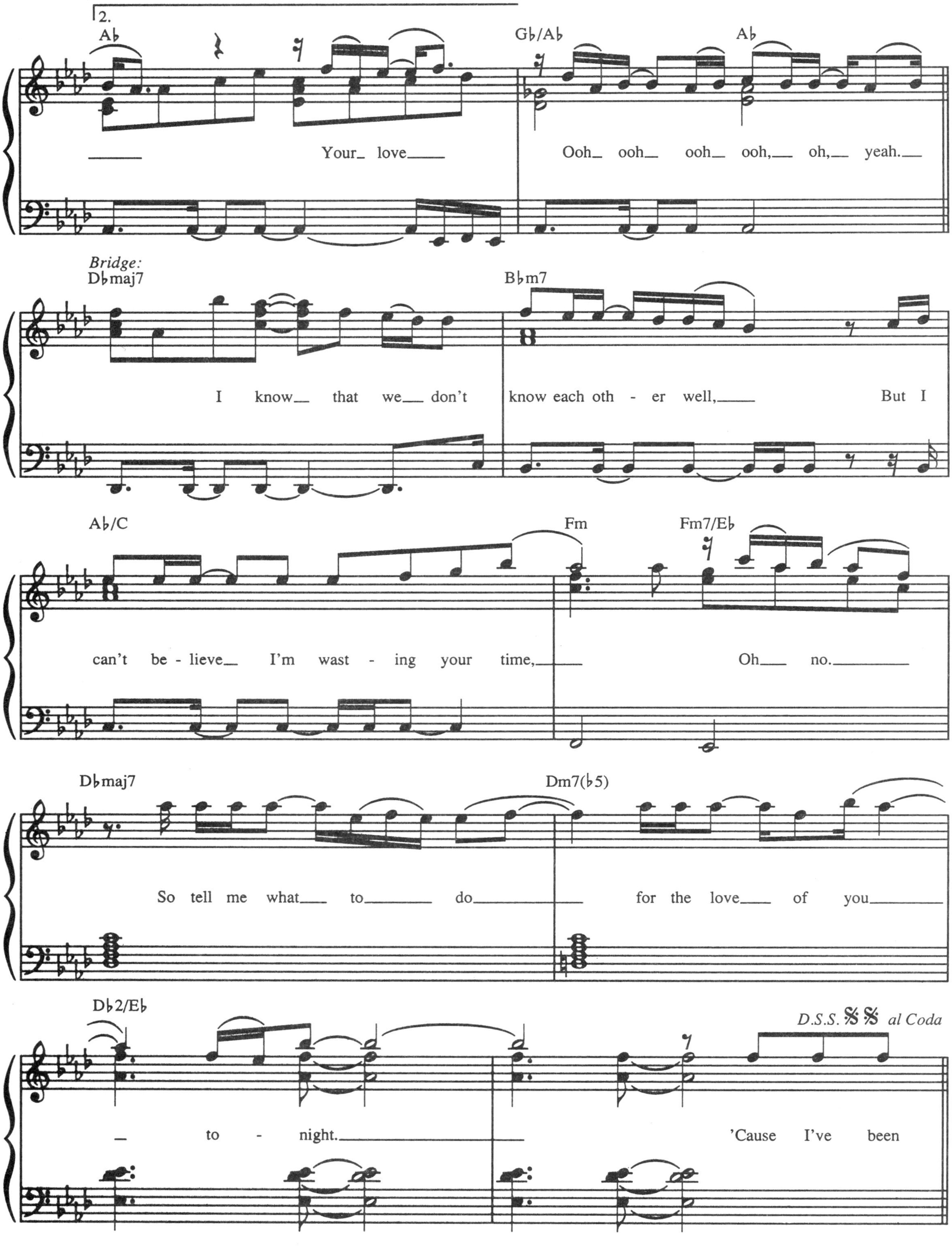

2.

Ab Gb/Ab Ab

Your love Ooh ooh ooh ooh, oh, yeah.

Bridge:

Dbmaj7 Bbm7

I know that we don't know each oth - er well, But I

Ab/C Fm Fm7/Eb

can't be - lieve I'm wast - ing your time, Oh no.

Dbmaj7 Dm7(b5)

So tell me what to do for the love of you

Verse 2:
Sweet lady, don't you look away.
I don't mean to make you shy,
But we haven't got much time.
Tonight, I know just what to say.
I'll love your cares away; you and I will find a way.
You know that there's a possibility
That we'll never get this chance once again.
So tell me what to do for the love of you tonight.
(To Chorus:)

I DON'T WANNA CRY

Words and Music by
MARIAH CAREY and
NARADA MICHAEL WALDEN

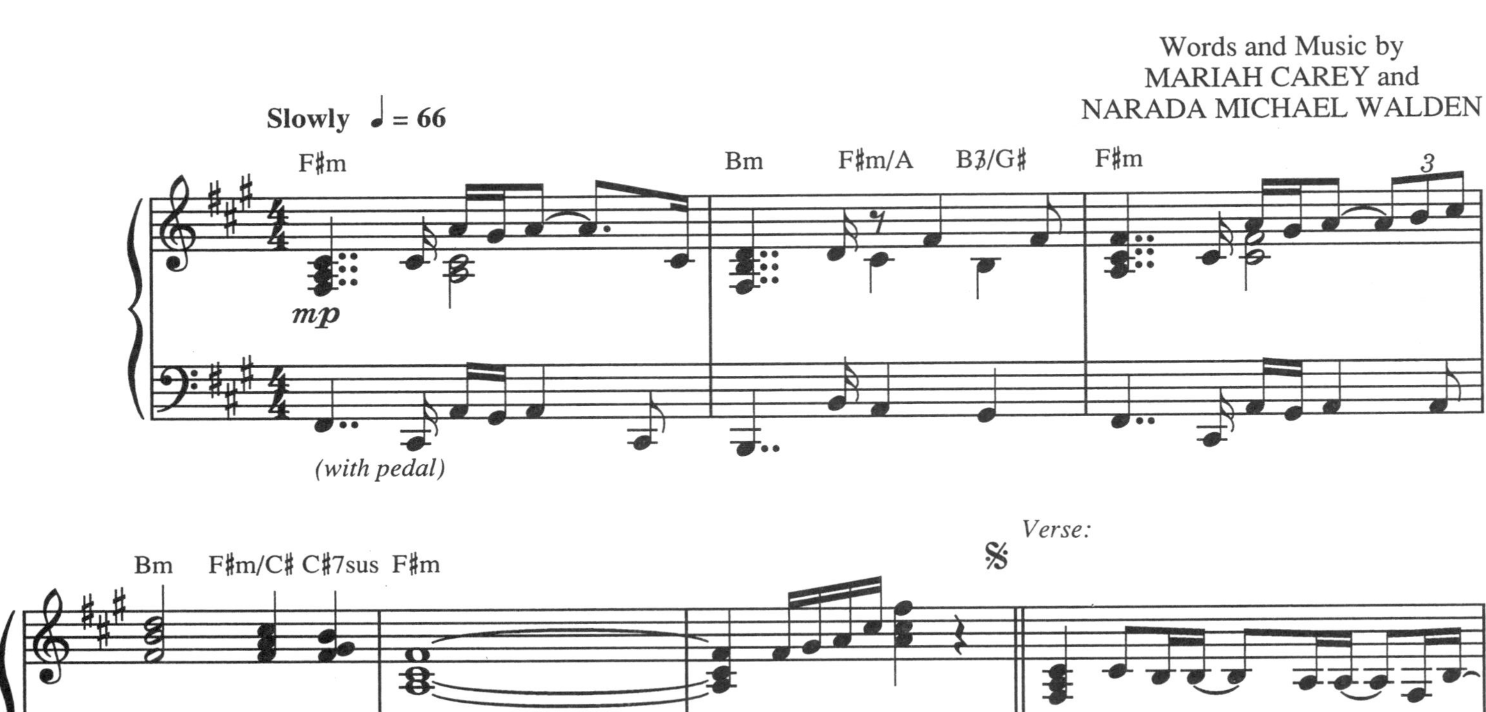

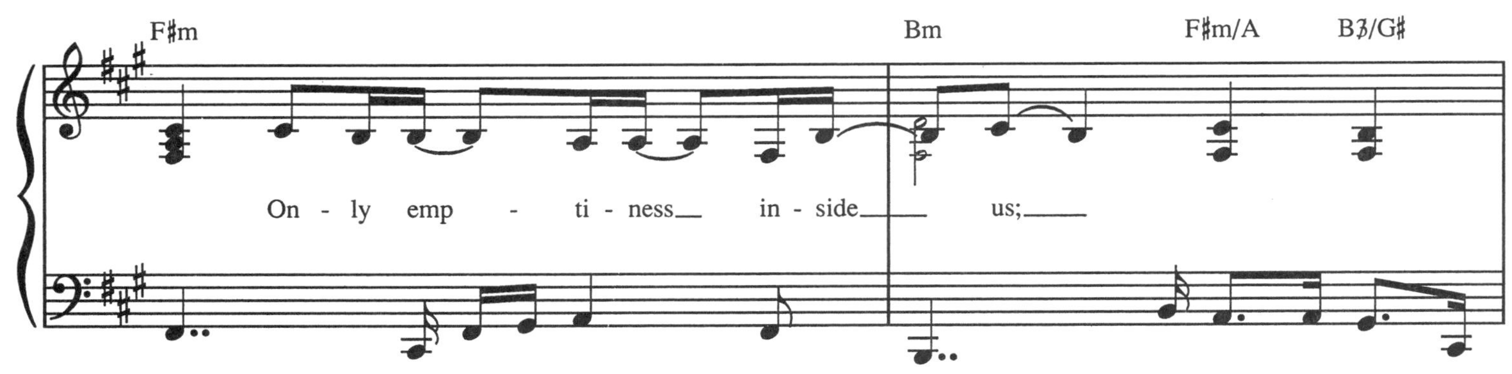

F#m
Bm
F#m/A
B7/G#
ba - by look what we've be - come.
E
Bm
A
mf
We can make a mil-lion prom - is - es, but we still won't change.
E
Bm7/E
It is - n't right to stay to - geth - er when you on - ly bring each oth - er pain.
cresc.
Chorus:
A
E/G#
f
I don't wan - na cry, don't wan - na cry.
G
Bm/F#
F#7/A#
Noth-ing in the world could take us back to where we used to be. Though I've giv-

Bm A/C♯ D E F♯m

-en you_ my heart_ and soul,_____ (giv-en you_ my heart_ and soul,) I must find_

Bm A/C♯ Dmaj9

_ a way_ of let - ting_____ go, 'cause ba - by I____ don't wan - na

dim

F♯m Bm F♯m7/A B♭/G♯ F♯m

cry.__

mp

1. Bm F♯m/C♯ C♯7sus *D.S.* 𝄋 2. Bm F♯m/C♯ C♯7sus

cresc.

Bridge:

E

All the mag - ic's gone,_ there's just a

mf

Bm A/C♯ E

sha-dow of a mem - o - ry.___ Some-thing just__ went wrong._ We can't go

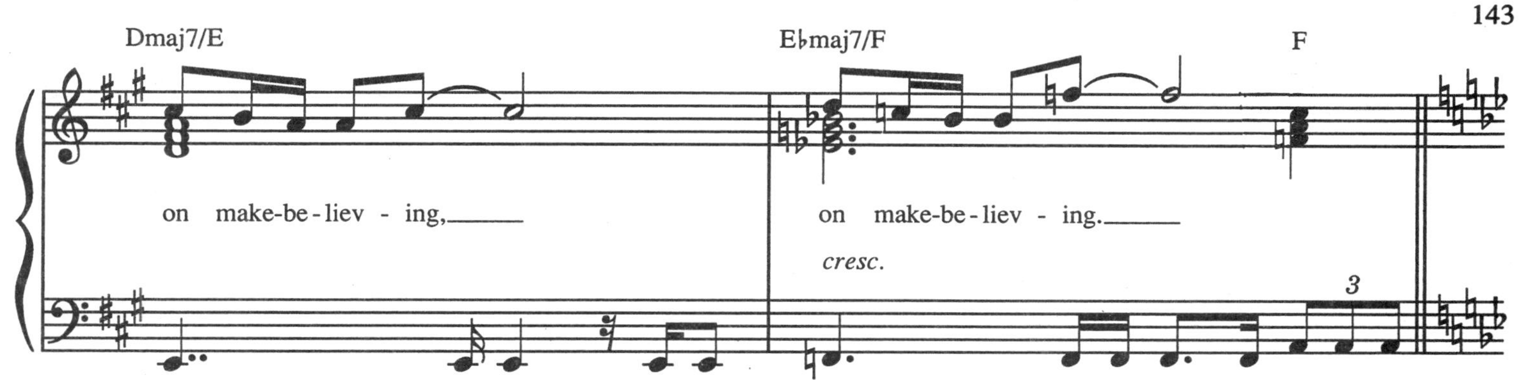
Dmaj7/E
E♭maj7/F
F
on make-be-liev - ing,
on make-be-liev - ing.
cresc.
3

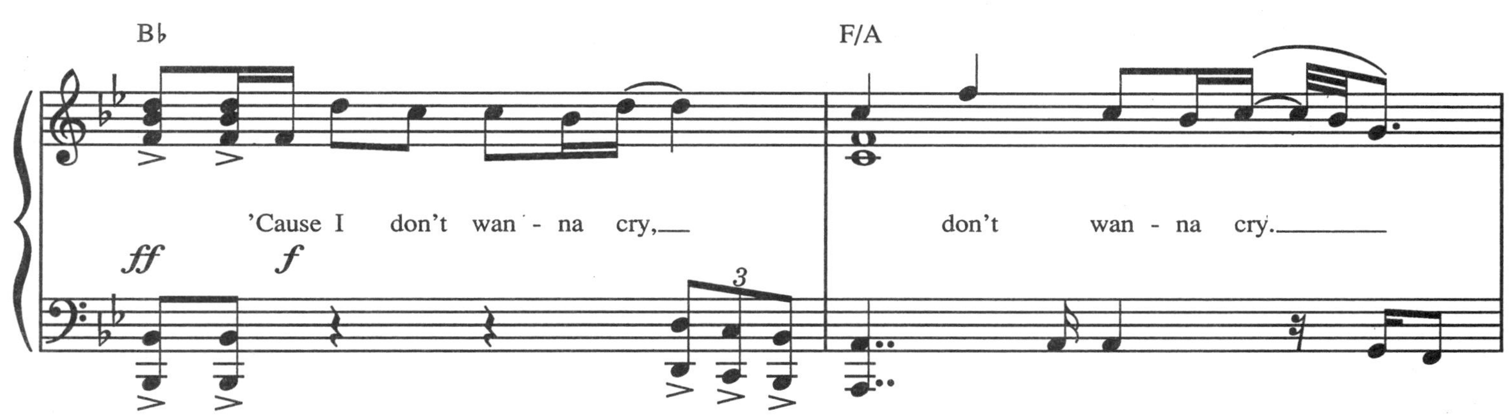
B♭
F/A
'Cause I don't wan - na cry,
don't wan - na cry.
ff
f
3

A♭
Cm/G
G7/B
Noth-ing in the world could take me back to
where we used to be. Though I've giv -

Cm
B♭/D
E♭
F
Gm
- en you my heart and soul,
(giv-en you my heart and soul,) said I've giv -

Verse 2:
Too far apart to bridge the distance,
But something keeps us hanging on and on.
Pretending not to know the difference,
Denying what we had is gone.
Every moment we're together,
It's just breaking me down.
I know we swear it was forever,
But it hurts too much to stay around.
(To Chorus:)

IF TOMORROW NEVER COMES

Words and Music by
GARTH BROOKS and
KENT BLAZY

D
Am7
D
C
would she ev - er doubt the way I feel a - bout her in my
G
3
C/G
G
Chorus:
C
heart.
If to - mor - row nev-er
comes,
will she know how much I
G
D
Am7
loved her?
Did I try in ev - ery
way to show her ev - ery-day
D
C
G
Am7
G/B
that she's my on-ly one?
And if my time on earth were
C
D
Em7
Bm7
through,
and she must face this world with - out me,

Verse 2:
'Cause I've lost loved ones in my life.
Who never knew how much I loved them.
Now I live with the regret
That my true feelings for them never were revealed.
So I made a promise to myself
To say each day how much she means to me
And avoid that circumstance
Where there's no second chance to tell her how I feel. ('Cause)
(To Chorus:)

INTO THE GREAT WIDE OPEN

Words and Music by
TOM PETTY and JEFF LYNNE

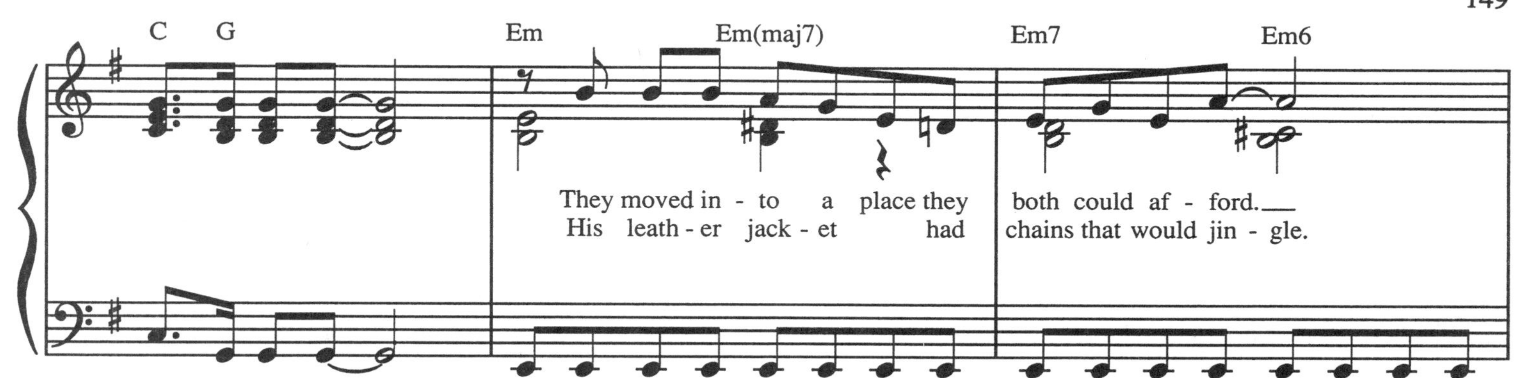
C G
Em
Em(maj7)
Em7
Em6
They moved in - to a place they both could af - ford.
His leath - er jack - et had chains that would jin - gle.

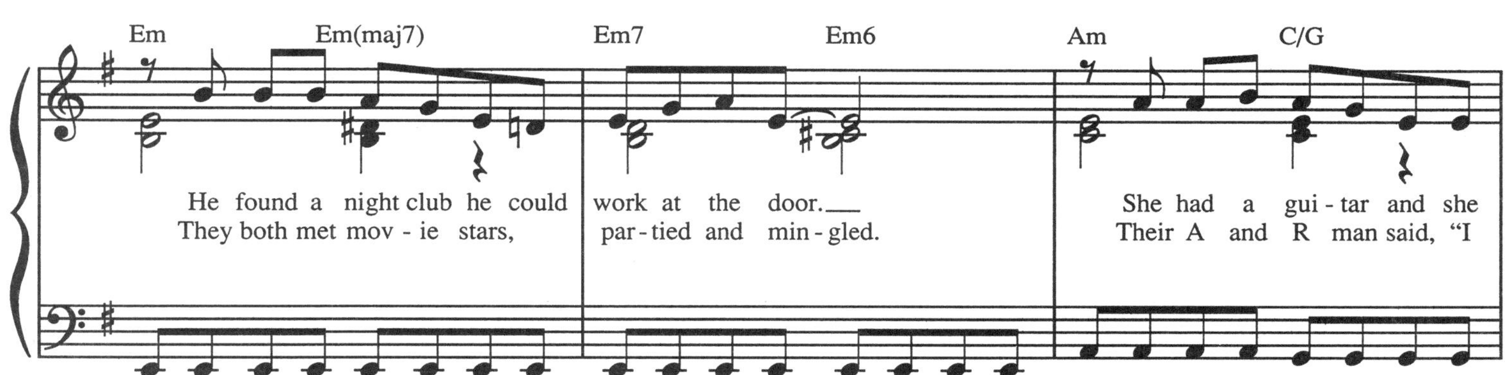
Em
Em(maj7)
Em7
Em6
Am
C/G
He found a night club he could work at the door.
They both met mov - ie stars, par - tied and min - gled.
She had a gui - tar and she
Their A and R man said, "I

F♯m7(♭5)
C/G
G
F
C
G
taught him some chords. The sky was the lim - it.
don't hear a sin - gle." The fu - ture was wide o - pen.

Chorus:
C G
C G D
G
C
In - to the great wide

D
G
Em7
D
Am
o - pen,
un - der the skies of
blue.

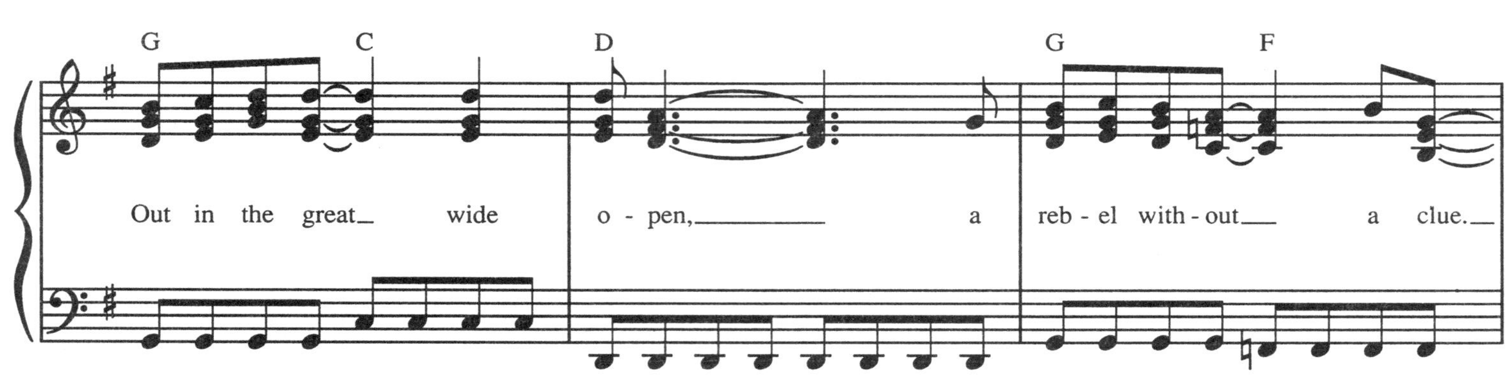
G
C
D
G
F
Out in the great wide
o - pen, a
reb - el with - out a clue.

1.
Em
A
G
C
G
C
G

Em
Em(maj7)
Em7
Em6
Em
Em(maj7)

2.
Em7
Em6
Em
A
G
C
In - to the great wide

D
G
Em7
D
Am
o - pen,
un - der the skies of
blue.

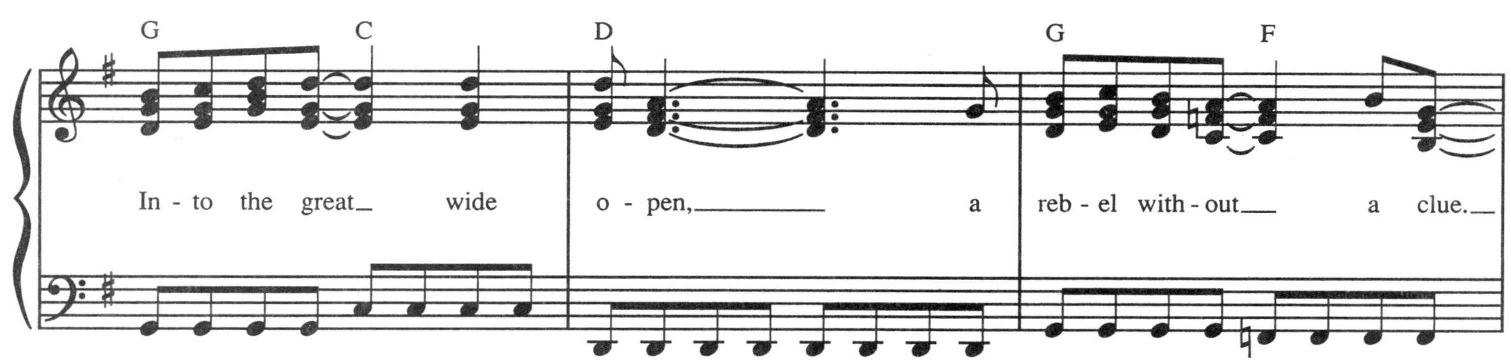
G
C
D
G
F
In - to the great wide
o - pen, a
reb - el with - out a clue.

Em
A
G
C
G
C
G

IT'S A SHAME

(My Sister)

Words and Music by
STEVIE WONDER, SYREETA WRIGHT, LEE GARRETT,
DAVID STEELE and MONIE LOVE

no, this can-not_ be ac-cept-ed. The feel-ings that be-long to you_ must be pro-tect-ed.
1.3.6.
To Next Strain
Hold up! Time out! I shout,_ "Get it to-geth-er, sis-ter." Tell him to be nice or diss the mis-ter.) I't's_ a
2.4.5
Chorus:
A♭m9/D♭
A♭m7/D♭
head at and where he's com-ing from. Get it out of your shame,_ the way you
G♭maj7/D♭
E♭m7
A♭m9/D♭
A♭m7/D♭
mess a-round with my heart._ It's_ a shame,_ the way_ you_
G♭maj7/D♭
E♭m7
A♭m9/D♭
A♭m7/D♭
_ hurt_ me._ It's_ a shame_ the way you

Verse 2:
Get back on your feet. Please, I'm begging you to check out all your own need.
Don't let nobody see you in a state of grieving over the brother.
There's another possibility, which is for you to check out where you went wrong.
I guarantee to you that it will not take long for you to make your mind up if the two of you belong.
You know where honey's head at and where he's coming from.

Verse 3:
Get it out of your system, Don't be another victim.
There stood the nerves and boy he really picked 'em.
What d'ya know, it's time for you to show your now sleeping.
A progress report on the two of you you're keeping.
Peeking through the peephole to see if honey's sneaking,
You estimated right that night the other weekend.
Collectably the facts should conclude the decision.
You caught the brother in a terrible disposition.
(To Chorus:)

Verse 4:
That's it. Pack it up. Be wise, my sister, cos the facts keep stacking up.
Tell him to kiss the you know what, make sure the door is shut behind you.
I do believe the brother's out of luck and stuck. But that's not the problem.
You got to let him go and let him know this is the end.
You been kissed, dissed, listed as a dumb one.
I hope he likes sad songs, he gonna hum one.

Verse 5:
He's been dumb and that's the way it is forever.
There comes a time when you're at the end of your tether, and you, I think, went far beyond that.
So, it was bound to back track and smack you with an irksome vengeance, as it attacks you,
Making sure you get the full entire view of who's to blame at the end of the game.
Things will never be the same, and it's a crying shame.
(To Chorus:)

MENTAL PICTURE

Words and Music by
JON SECADA and
MIGUEL A. MOREJON

G2
A
G
A
G2
can't I feel?) Say-ing my
blind side.
And if a
Chorus:
D
A/D
Dsus
D
A/B
men - tal pic - ture's all I got to go
C(9)
3
G
on, for a
while or more, girl, you
know I'll al - ways think
Asus
A
D
A/D
Dsus
of you, think of you.
And if a
men - tal pic -
D
A/B
- ture's all I've got to go on, I know your a

C(9) G(9) Asus

pic - ture to re - mem - ber.

1. D.S. 𝄋 | 2. To next strain | 3.4. etc. Repeat ad lib. and fade

A A A

dim. Re - mem - ber. And if a

G A G A G A

(Instrumental solo ad lib. . . .

G A Gmaj7 A G2 A

. . . end solo) Take me to the oth - er side. (Why can't I feel?) Out of my

Em7 A *D.S.S.* 𝄋𝄋

blind side. And I'm for

Verse 2:
Time was of the essence,
And as usual the day turns into minutes.
Sharing love and tenderness,
That's the nerve you struck in me that sent a signal.
To the other side,
(Girl, I don't know,)
Saying my blind side.
And if a . . . *(To Chorus:)*

I'LL SEE YOU IN MY DREAMS

Lyrics and Music by
ALAN PASQUA & MARK SPIRO

C♯m E B/D♯ B F♯m
yes - ter - day will al - ways be the rea - son why
Let me close my eyes and live an - oth - er day,
you keep

E/G♯ A Bsus B
com - in', you keep com-in' back, you keep com-in' back for more. I'll
cresc.
mf
cresc.
f

Dm B♭/D Dm Csus C G5
see you in my dreams. There, we'll be safe to-night from the

B♭ Csus C Dm B♭/D Dm Csus N.C.
1.
lone-ly days of mem - o - ries. I'll see you in my dreams, oh.

D.S. 𝄋 2.
G5
Csus
C
Em
C/E
Em
Dsus
D
oh.
(Instrumental solo . . .
dim.
A5
C
Dsus
D
Em
C/E
Em
Dsus
D
The
. . . end solo)
Gm
Dm/F
E♭
B♭/D
F
B♭/F
truth, oh, it's there for you to see, the echo. Sometimes it's painful to be
Cm
Dm
E♭
Fsus
F
Dm
B♭/D
Dm
on your own, on your own. I'll see you in my
mp

C/E C G5 B♭ Csus C
dreams. There, we'll be safe to-night _ from the lone-ly days _ of mem - o - ries. _ I'll
cresc.
f
Em C/E Em Dsus D A5
see _ you _ in my _ dreams, ___ back in my arms a-gain. _ And no
C Dsus D Em C Dsus
mat - ter what _ to - mor - row brings _ I'll ___ see ___ you ___ in my dreams, _
N.C. A5
1.
Em7 D/F♯ G
___ oh. ___ Oh. ___
2.
Em7 D/F♯ G A B/A Am7 Em7 D/F♯ G
Repeat ad lib. and fade

I'LL TAKE YOU THERE

Words and Music by
ALVERTIS ISBELL

C
F
F/G
Female
C
I know a place, ya'll,
F
F/G
C
F6
F/G
ain't no-bod-y
cry-in',
no,
ain't no-bod-y
C
F6
F/G
C
wor-ried.
Oh, ain't no smil-ing
fac-es
F
F/G
C
F
Male
F/G
ly-ing to the rac-es.
I said ain't no smil-ing

C
F
F/G
Bkgd.
C
faces, no smiling faces (lying to the races.) Ain't nobody
F
F/G
C
F
F/G
crying, no more crying. If you're ready now
C
Bkgd.
F
F/G
Female
come on, come on, (I'll take you there.)
Lord have mer-
C
Male
Bkgd.
F
F/G
Say if you're ready. (I'll take you there.) Oh, yeah.
cy.

C
F
F/G
Help me, help me. (I'll take you there.) Come on I said
Help me.
C
F7
come on (I'll take you there.)
Vocal ad lib.
Play 4 times.
1.
Female
If you're read - y now.
2nd time
1st time

2.
F C N.C.
Female
Oh I, oh, I I know a place ya'll
F C N.C.
Oh, there ain't no-bod-y cry-ing.
C
F F/G
Say ain't no, (ain't no-bod-y
C
cry - ing.) I said,
F F/G
I said ain't no, (ain't no-bod-y
C
wor-ried, yeah.)
F F/G
C
No smil-ing fac-es
(Ain't no smil-ing fac - es.)
F F/G
ly-ing to the rac - es,

C
F
F/G
C
help me now. (I'll take you there.)
I said if you're read - y
(I'll take you
F
F/G
C
F
F/G
there.)
I said
(I'll take you there.) Come on get read -
C
F
F/G
y.
(I'll take you there
Come, go with
C
Vocal ad lib.
F
F/G
Repeat and fade
me.)
(Come go with

SECRET

Words and Music by
MADONNA CICCONE and DALLAS AUSTIN

1.3
To Next Strain
2.
Bb7sus
Bb7
Bb7sus
Bb7
Abm7
Bb7sus
let it go.
bod-y else.
un-der-stood.
Hap - pi - ness lies in your_ own
Ebm7
Db/F
Abm7
hand.
It took me much_ too_ long_ to un-der - stand_
Bbm7
Cbmaj7
Db
Bb7(#5)/D
how it_ could be,
un - til you_ shared_ your_ se - cret_ with

Chorus:
Ebm7 Db Cm7(b5) Cb Ebm7 Db
me.
Something's coming over.
Mm,
Cm7(b5) Cb Ebm7 Db Cm7(b5) Cb
something's coming over.
Mm,
something's coming over me.
Bb7
1. D.S.
Bb7sus Bb7
My baby's got a secret.
2.
Bb7sus Bb7
baby's got a secret.
3.
Bb7sus Bb7
baby's got a secret.
Bridge:
Abm7 Bb7sus
Happiness lies in your own

Ebm7
Db/F
Abm7
hand. It took me much too long to un-der-stand
Bbm7
Cbmaj7
Db
Bb7(#5)/D
how it could be, un-til you shared your
Ebm7
Db
Cm7(b5)
Cb
Ebm7
Db
se-cret with me.
Cm7(b5)
Cb
Ebm7
Db
Cm7(b5)
Cb
Bb7

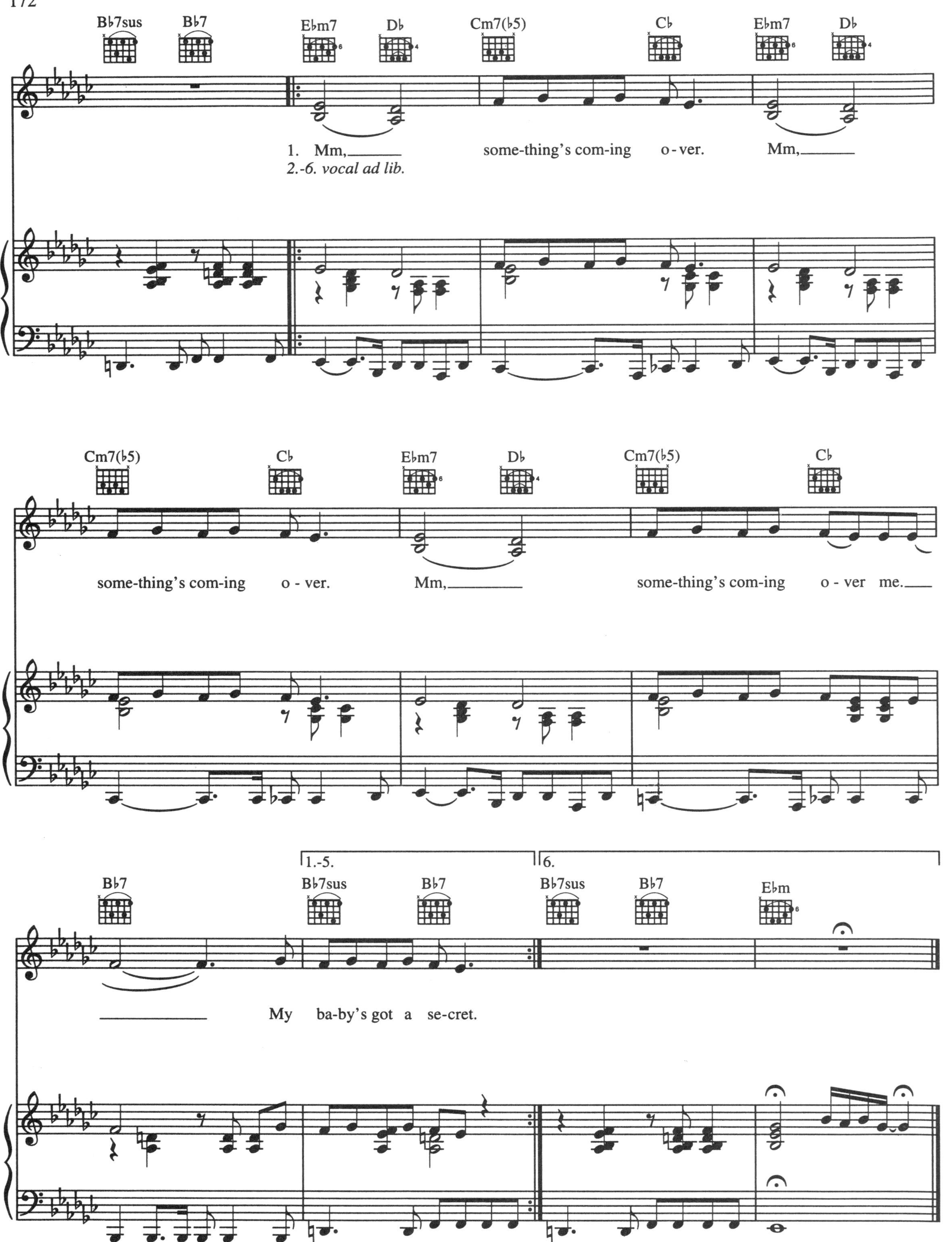
B♭7sus
B♭7
E♭m7
D♭
Cm7(♭5)
C♭
E♭m7
D♭
1. Mm,
2.-6. vocal ad lib.
some-thing's com-ing o-ver.
Mm,
Cm7(♭5)
C♭
E♭m7
D♭
Cm7(♭5)
C♭
some-thing's com-ing o-ver.
Mm,
some-thing's com-ing o-ver me.
B♭7
1.-5.
B♭7sus
B♭7
6.
B♭7sus
B♭7
E♭m
My ba-by's got a se-cret.

LEARNING TO FLY

Words and Music by
TOM PETTY and
JEFF LYNNE

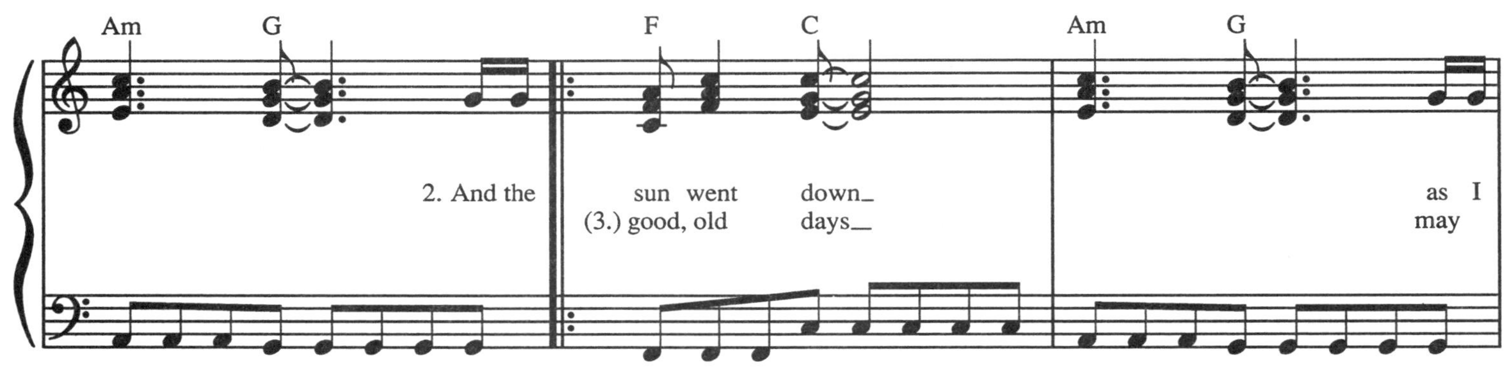
Am G F C Am G
2. And the sun went down as I
(3.) good, old days may

F C Am G F C
crossed the hill, and the town lit up,
not re - turn and the rocks might melt

Am G F C Am G
the world got still.
and the sea may burn.
1.,2. I'm

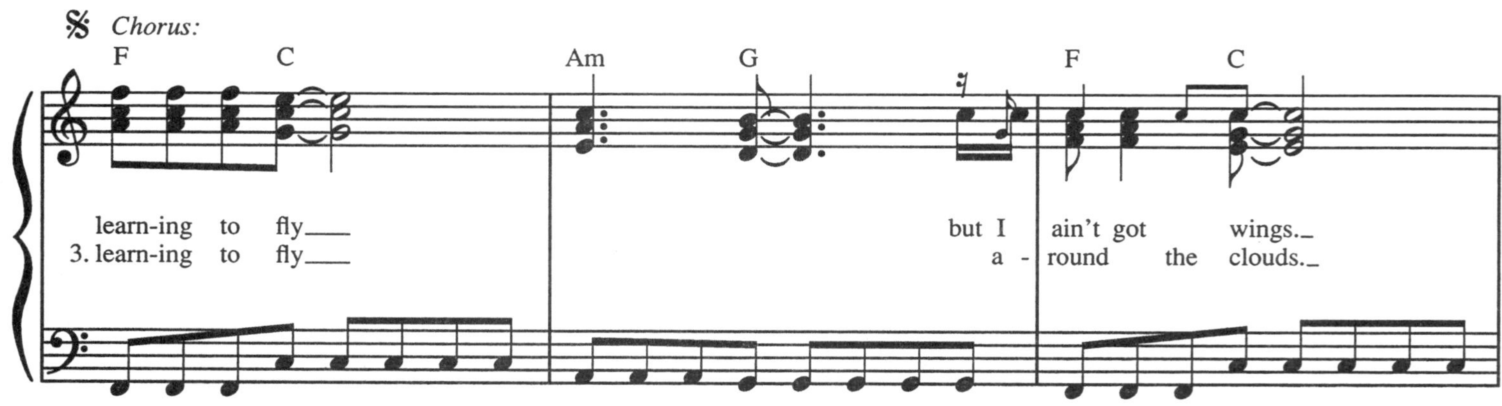
Chorus:
F C Am G F C
learn-ing to fly but I ain't got wings.
3. learn-ing to fly a - round the clouds.

Am G F C Am G

Com - ing down_ is the
What goes up___

F C | 1. Am G | 2.3. Am G

hard - est thing._ 2. Well, the
must come down._

To Coda ⊕

F C

Instrumental solo ad lib.

Am G F C | 1. Am G

| 2. Am G | *Verse:* F C Am G

4. Well, some say life___ will
(5.) start - ed out___ for

F C Am G F C
beat you down_ and break your heart,_
God knows where._ I guess I'll know_
Am G F C
when I get there._
steal your crown._
1.
Am G
5. So, I
2.
Am G
D.S. 𝄋 al Coda
I'm
Coda
F C Am G F C
Am G
I'm
F C
learn-ing to fly___
Am G
but I
F C
ain't got wings._
Am G
F C
Com-ing down_

Am G F C Am G
is the hard - est thing.
I'm
F C Am G F C
learn-ing to fly
a - round the clouds.
Am G F C Am G
What goes up
F C Am G F C
must come down.
I'm
learn-ing to fly.
Repeat ad lib. and fade
Am G F C Am G
I'm

GET OVER IT

Words and Music by
DON HENLEY and GLENN FREY

Verse:
D5
turn on the tube, what do I see? A whole lot of peo-ple cry-in',
2.3. (See additional lyrics)
"Don't blame me." They point their crook-ed lit-tle fin-gers at ev-'ry-bod-y else,
G
spend all their time feel-ing sor-ry for them-selves. Vic-tim of this,
A
vic-tim of that. Your ma-ma's too thin and your dad-dy's too fat. 1. Get ov-

Chorus:
D5
F
- er it.
Get ov - er it.
2.3. (See additional lyrics)
G
All this whin-in', and cry-in', and pitch-in' a fit. Get ov-
D5
To Coda
- er it, get ov - er it.
(Guitar solo ad. lib . . .
F

G
D5
1.
2.
Bridge:
C
. . . end solo) 2. You say you . . . end solo) It's like go-ing to con-fes-sion ev-'ry-time I hear you speak._
D5
C
You're mak-in' the most_ of your los-ing streak._
A
Some call it sick_ and I call it weak._
Yeah,_yeah, yeah,_ yeah. 3. You

Coda
- er it, get ov - er it. Get ov -
F
G
- er it. It's got - ta stop some-time, so
D5
tacet
why don't you quit? Get ov - er it. Get ov - er it.
D5
F

Verse 2:
You say you haven't been the same since you had your little crash
But you might feel better if they gave you some cash.
The more I think about it, old Billy was right.
Let's kill all the lawyers, kill 'em tonight.
You don't want to work, you want to live like a king
But the big bad world doesn't owe you a thing.
(To Chorus:)

Chorus 2:
Get over it,
Get over it.
If you don't want to play, then you might as well split.
Get over it, get over it.

Verse 3:
You drag it around like a ball and chain,
You wallow in the guilt, you wallow in the pain.
You wave it like a flag, you wear it like a crown,
Got your mind in the gutter bringin' everybody down.
You bitch about the present, you blame it on the past.
I'd like to find your inner child and kick it's little ass.
(To Chorus:)

Chorus 3:
Get over it.
Get over it.
All this bitchin', and moanin', and pitchin' a fit.
Get over it, get over it.

LIGHT MY FIRE

Words and Music by
THE DOORS

Am7
F♯m7
G
A
Girl, we could-n't get much higher;
love be-come a fune-ral pyre.
1. 2. Come on, ba - by, light my fire,
D
G
A
D
B
G
D
Come on, ba - by, light my fire,
Try to set the night on
E
fire.
1.
2. The
2
f
2. The
cresc.
Am7
F♯m7
Am7
f
time to hes - i - tate is through,
No time to wal - low in the mire,
F♯m7
Am7
F♯m7
Try now we can on - ly lose,
And our

Am7
F#m7
G
A
love be-come a fune-ral pyre.
Come on, ba - by, light my fire,
D
G
A
D
Come on, ba - by, light my fire,
F
C
D
(repeat 3 times)
F
C
Try to set the night on fire,
Try to set the night on
ff
D
G
D
fire.
F
Bb
Eb
Ab
A♮

From "Live And Let Die"

LIVE AND LET DIE

Words and Music by
PAUL and LINDA McCARTNEY

D
Bb
G7
C/G
give it a cry,
Say live and let die!
Live and let
Gdim
G7
C/G
die,
Live and let
die,
Live and let
die.
Gm
3fr
ff
To Coda
C9
8va lower ad lib. till *
What does it mat - ter to ya,
mf

G7
D7
when you got a job to do you got - ta do it well, You got - ta
Em
F
Gm
3fr
give the oth - er fel - low hell!
ff
D. C. al Coda
Coda
Eb m / Gb
T

LIVE FOR LOVING YOU

Words and Music by
GLORIA ESTEFAN, DIANE WARREN
and EMILIO ESTEFAN, JR.

C(2)
G
C(2)
_ as you are soft - ly sleep - ing._____
G
C(2)
I think_ of what_ I'd like_ to do,
while you are some - where dream - ing._____
G
C(2)
G
C(2)
_
I,_____
I feel_ so hap - py by_ your_
G
C(2)
G
side._____
Oh,_____
I,_____
1.
2.3.
C(2)
G
C(2)
I won - der, won - der, won - der why._____

Bridge:

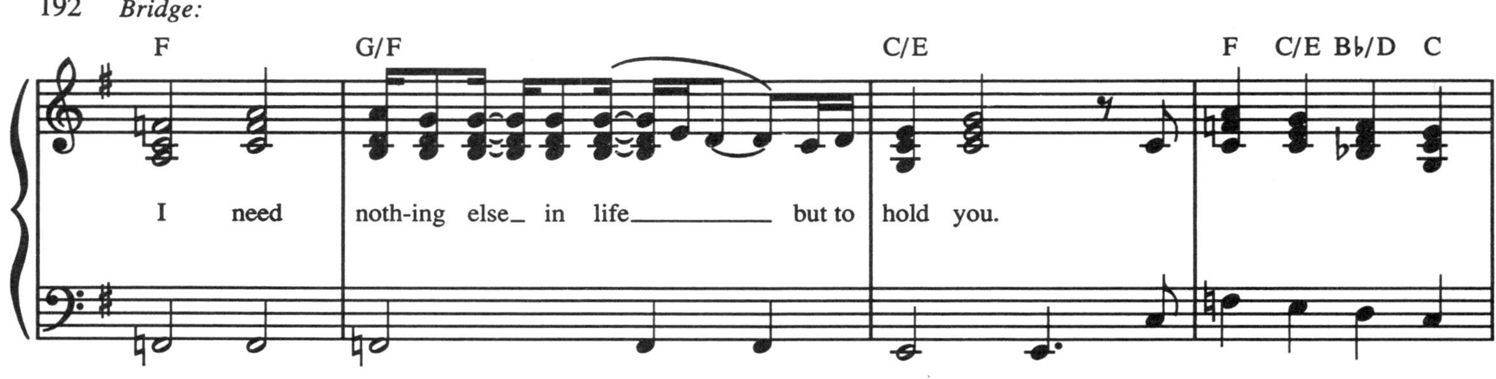

Chorus:

1.
D.S. 𝄋
G
C
G N.C.
All I want_ to do is love you, love_ you._
2.
C
G
C
G
do is live for lov - ing_ you._ Ooh.
C
G
C
la - la - la - la - la - la - la;_
I live for lov - ing_ you._
G
C
G N.C.
All I want_ to do is love you. love_ you._ Ooh,_

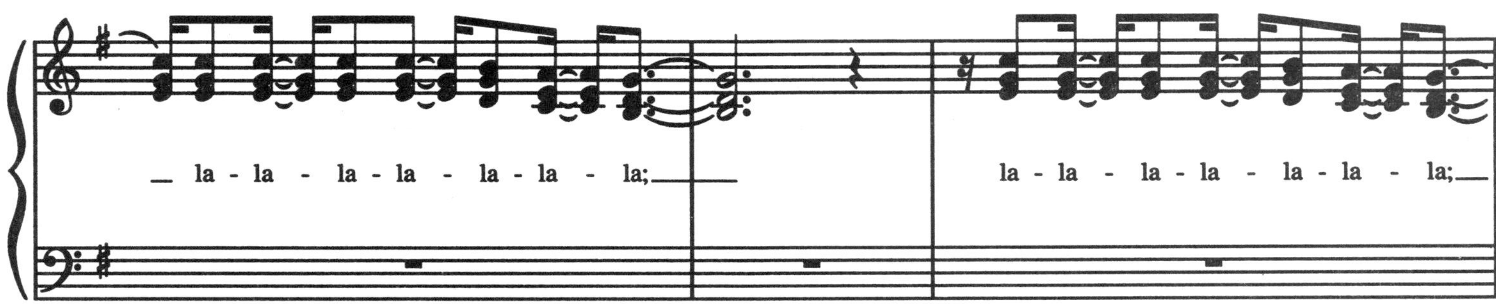

Verse 2:
I find it hard to find the words
To say what I am feeling.
I'm so in love, I'm so alive,
And I know you're the reason why,
Why I'm so happy all the time.
Oh, I, I wonder, wonder, wonder why.
(To Bridge:)

Verse 3:
It would never cross my mind,
To find another lover.
'Cause after having been with you,
There could be no other.
I, just touching you I'm satisfied.
Oh, I, I wonder, wonder, wonder why.
(To Bridge:)

LOVE AT FIRST SIGHT

Words and Music by
DENNIS DE YOUNG, JAMES YOUNG
& GLEN BURTNICK

B♭sus
B♭
B♭2
B♭
It all be - gan so eas - i - ly; a
B♭sus2 sus4/G
Gm
B♭
A♭2
look from you a glance from me. Then our eyes met
Fsus/A
E♭
like thun - der and light - ning. You and I
B♭/D
Cm
G5
F5
E♭
strang - ers lost in a mo - ment. Eye to eye,
B♭/D
B♭5/C
B♭/D
B♭5/E♭
Fsus
We were caught un - a - ware of the pass - ion in - side us.

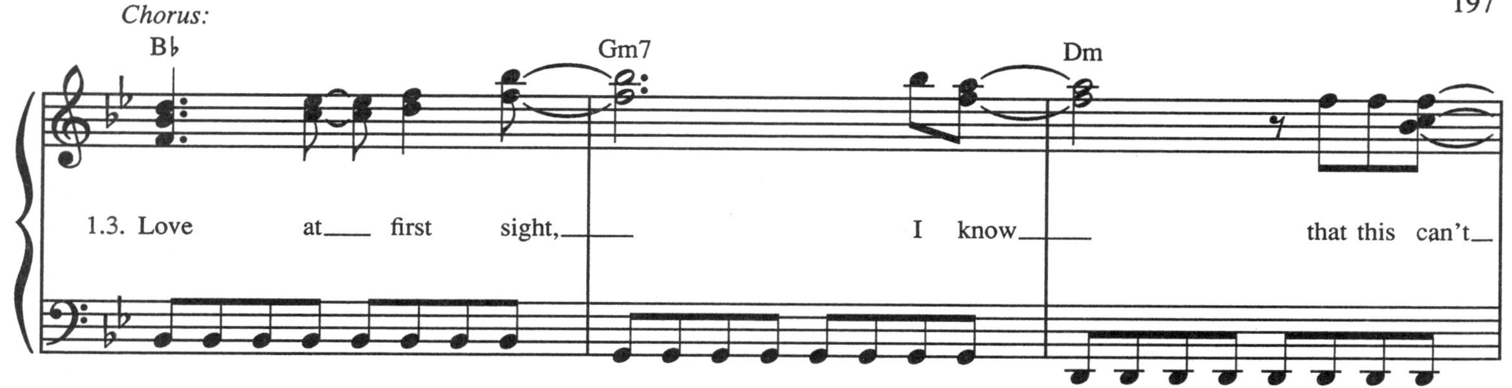
Chorus:
B♭
Gm7
Dm
1.3. Love at first sight, I know that this can't

B♭sus/E♭
B♭
B♭(9)/E♭
A♭sus2
be hap - p'ning. No, not to some - one like me.

E♭/A♭
B♭2
Gm
Love at first sight. So rare

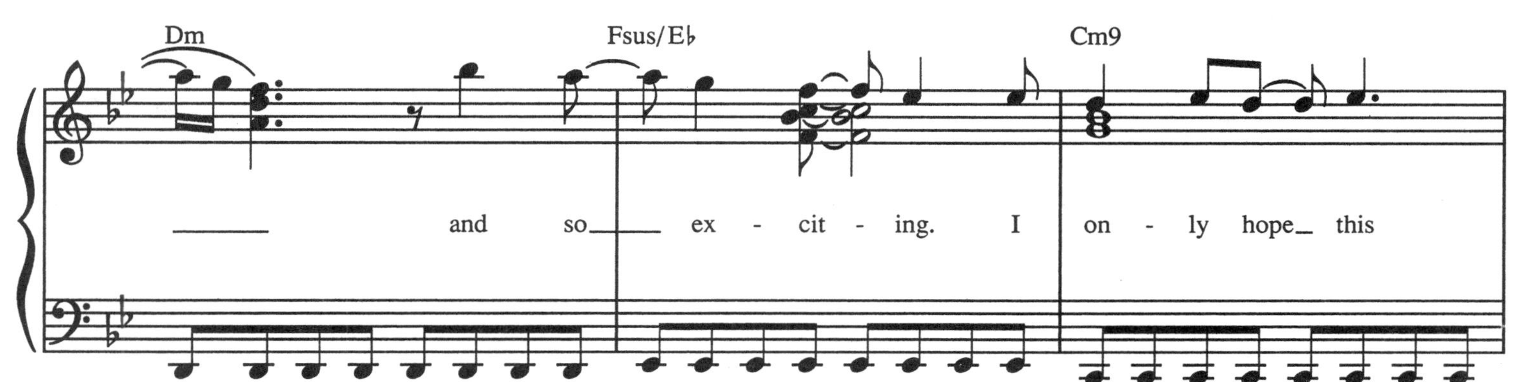
Dm
Fsus/E♭
Cm9
and so ex - cit - ing. I on - ly hope this

F7
To Coda
1.
B♭
B♭sus
B♭
F/A
love we found_ can last___
Gm
E♭/G
B♭/E♭
A♭
D.S.
2.
B♭
B♭sus
B♭
2. I'm __
F/A
Bridge:
Gm
F
If you need some time
to un-der - stand your feel -
E♭maj7
Dm7
Cm7
ings.
If you need some time a - way___
I'll be wait - ing_ for_ you with

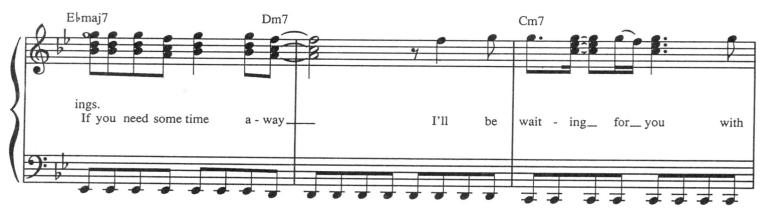

Verse 2:
I'm not a man who acts this way,
But lately I can't concentrate.
And I can't sleep, just dreaming about you.
I try to reach you on the phone,
But voices there say you're not at home.
And my heart aches, thinking I've lost you.
One more time, seeing your face in the moonlight;
One more chance to be caught unaware
Of this passion inside us.
(To Chorus 2:)

Chorus 2:
Love at first sight
I know this can't be happening
No, not to someone like me.
Love at first sight;
It's hard to keep your balance
Moving past the point of no return.

Verse 3:
All that night
We made love in the moonlight.
Eye to eye,
We were so unaware of this passion
Inside us.
(To Chorus:)

SOME PEOPLE'S LIVES

Words and Music by
JANIS IAN and
RHONDA FLEMING

C
Gm7
Am
Some lives wear out like old ten-nis shoes no one can
Gsus G Am/G G
F
Gsus G
use. Well, it's sad but it's true. Did-n't an-y-bod-y tell them?
F
G
F
Am/G G
Dm7
Did-n't an-y-bod-y see? Did-n't an-y-bod-y love them like you love

G
C
Gm7
me?
Some
peo-ple's
eyes
fade
like
their dreams,
too
Am
Gsus
G
Am/G
G
C/G
G7
C
tired
to
rise,
too
tired
to
sleep.
Some
peo-ple
Gm7
Am
Gsus
laugh
when
they
need
to
cry,
and they
nev - er
know
G
F
G
F
why.
Did-n't
an - y - bod - y
tell
them
that's not
how
it
has
to

G
F
Am/G
G
Dm7
G
Dm6/F
be?
Did-n't an - y - bod - y
love them
like you love me?
E
E7/G#
Asus4/2
Am
E/A
Am
Asus4/2
Am7
D
Em7
Some peo - ple ask
if the tears have to fall.
Then why take your chanc-
D7/F#
Gsus4/2
G
Am/G
G
C/G
G7
C
- es? Why both - er at all?
And some peo-ple's lives are as
rit.
a tempo
rit.
a tempo
Gm7
Am
Gsus4/2
cold as their lips,
they just need to be
rit.
rit.

G
F
Am/G
G
F
kissed.
Does-n't an-y-bod-y tell them?
Does-n't an-y-bod-y
a tempo
a tempo
G
F
Am/G
G
Dm/F
E
E7(♯9)
G♯dim7
see?
Does-n't an-y-bod-y love them like you love
Am
Em/G
F
C/E
Dm7
F/G
G7
C
Dm/C
C
Dm/C
F/C
me?
'Cuz that's all they need.
rit.
a tempo
rit.
a tempo
C
N.C.
rit.
8vb

MERCY, MERCY ME (THE ECOLOGY)/ I WANT YOU

"Mercy, Mercy Me" - Written by MARVIN GAYE
"I Want You" - Written by LEON WARE and ARTHUR ROSS

F♯m7
F♯maj7/B
no. Where did all the blue skies go? Poi - son is the wind that blows
1.2.
3.4.
from the north, west, south and east.
near by are dy - ing.
from the north, west, south and
Verse:
Emaj7
C♯m9
4.6. Oh, mer - cy, mer - cy me. Oh, things
east.
ain't what they used to be.
F♯m7
What a - bout this o - ver crowd-
F♯maj7/B
- ed land? How much more a - buse from man can she
C♯m9
C♯m
stand?

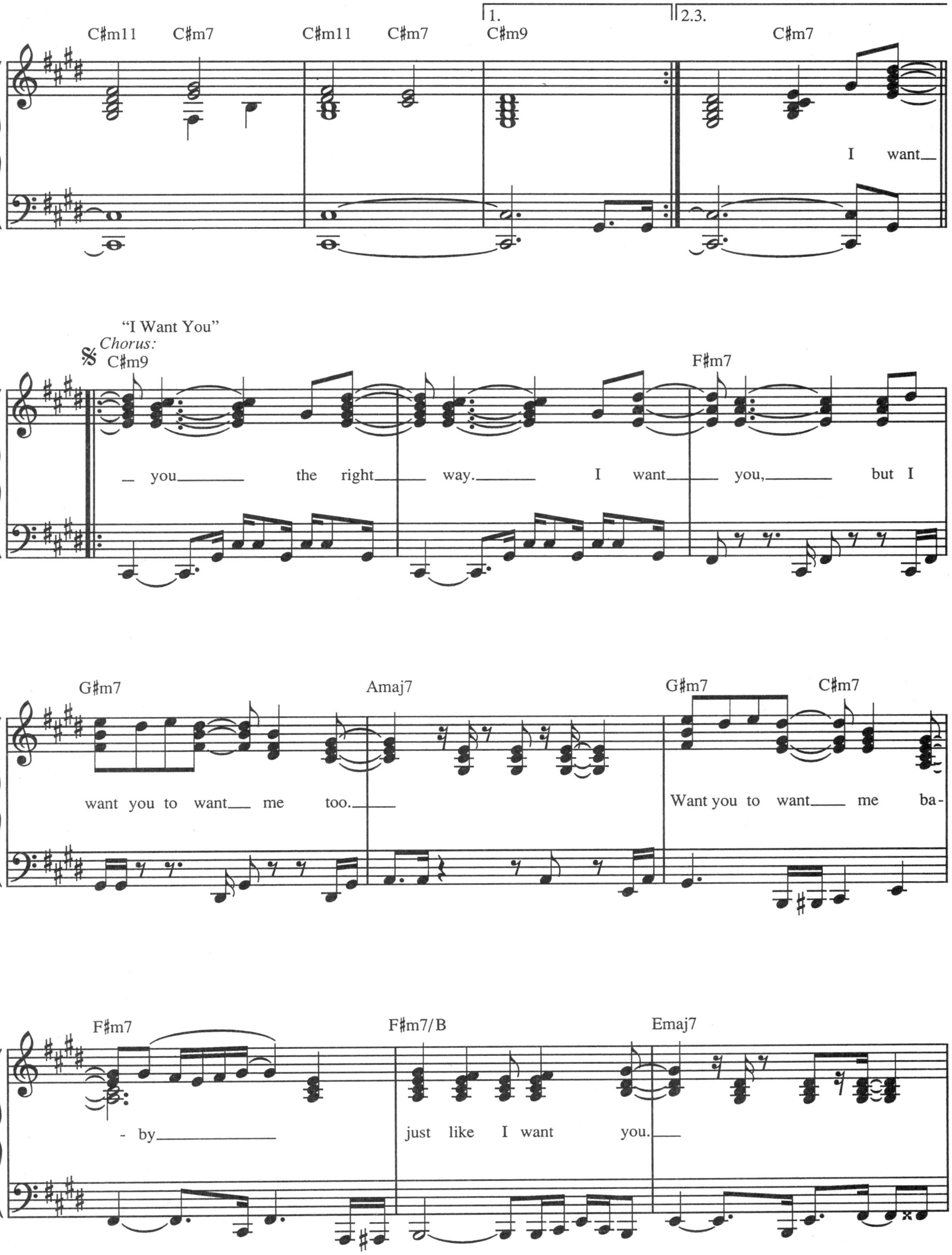

1.
2.3.
C♯m11 C♯m7 C♯m11 C♯m7 C♯m9 C♯m7
I want
"I Want You"
Chorus:
C♯m9 F♯m7
you the right way. I want you, but I
G♯m7 Amaj7 G♯m7 C♯m7
want you to want me too. Want you to want me ba-
F♯m7 F♯m7/B Emaj7
- by just like I want you.

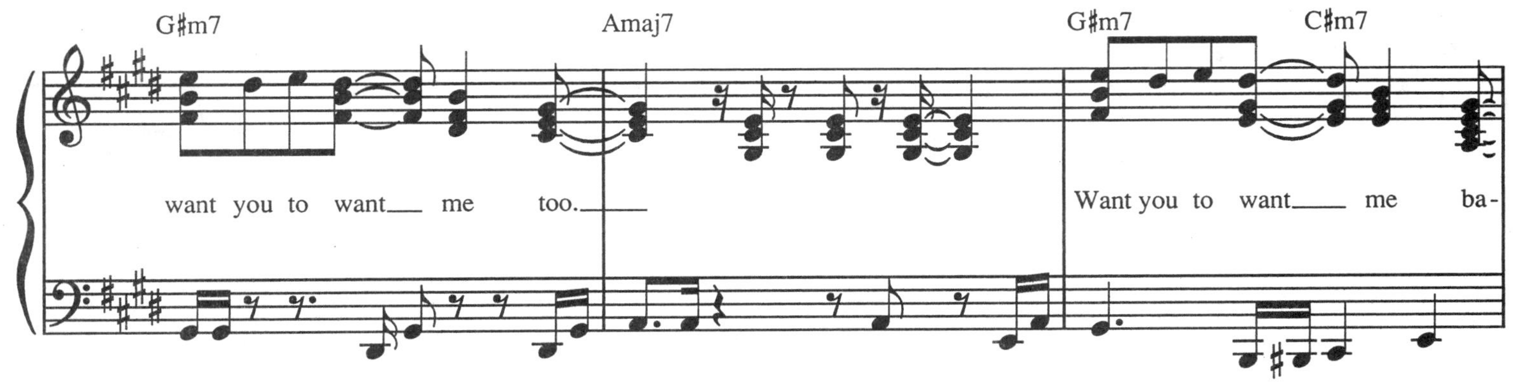

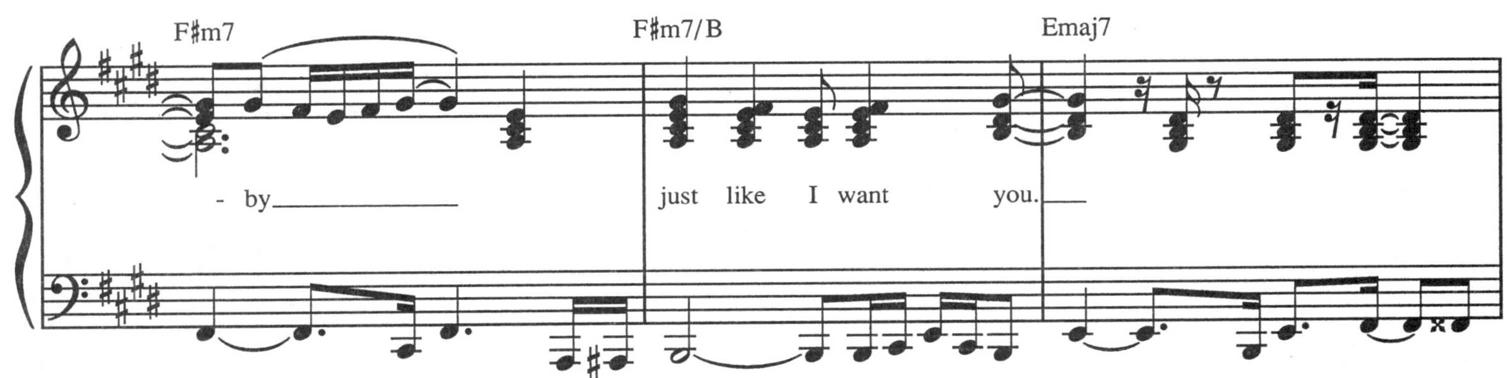

1.2.
To Next Strain
3.4.
Repeat ad lib. and fade
Verse:
G#sus
G#7(♭13)
C#m9
1. Oh,
I want
I'll give you all
the love you want in re-turn, sweet dar-lin'.
F#m7
A/B
G#7sus
Your happ-pi-ness is all I crave.
G#7(♭13)
C#m9
Ooh, it's too bad, it's just too sad you don't

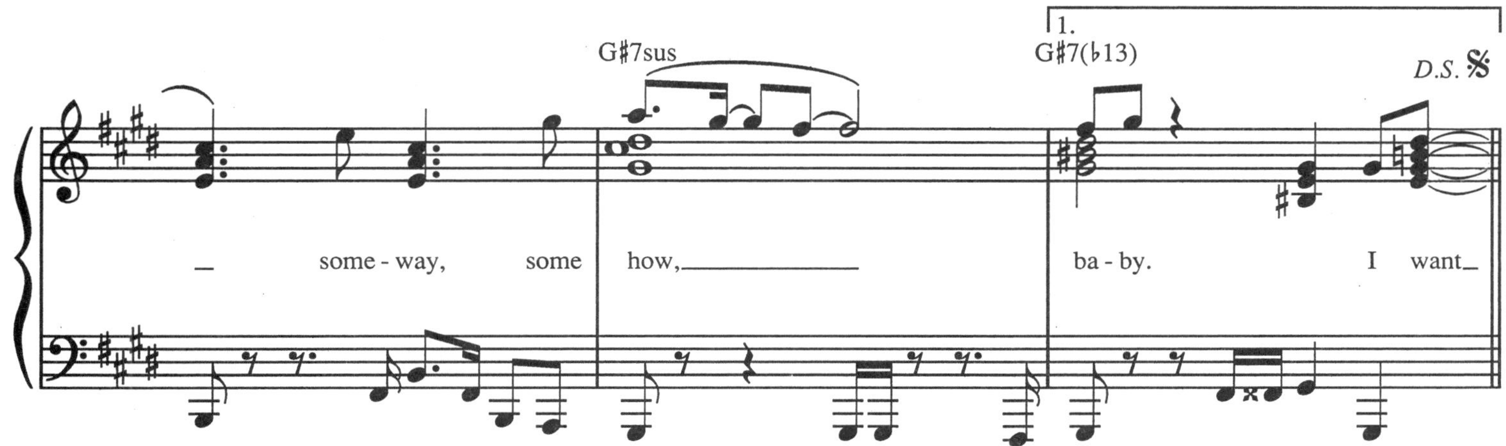

"Mercy, Mercy Me"
Verse 2:
Oh, mercy, mercy me.
Oh, things ain't what they used to be, no, no.
Oil wasted on the oceans,
And our seas are fish full of mercury.

Verse 3:
Oh, mercy, mercy me.
Oh, things ain't what they used to be, no, no.
Radiation underground and in the sky,
Animals and birds who live nearby are dying.

"I Want You"
Verse 2:
A one way love is just a fantasy.
Ah, sugar, to share is precious, pure and fair.
Don't play with something you should cherish for life, baby.
Don't you want to care?
Lonely? I'm there.

BREATHLESS

Words and Music by
JAMIE JONES and GARY ST. CLAIR

Gm7
Cm7
low,
and
turn the slow jams on the ra - di -
hot,
kiss you up and down till you say
flow,
break it down and let our pas - sion
Gm7
N.C.
o.
I
want to feel your bod - y next to
stop.
Don't stop!
Touch
all the lit - tle plac - es that you
go.
Yeah.
To -
night, I wan - na make sweet love to
To Coda
mine,
so
let's slow down and ba - by, take our
like,
girl, you know I wan - na take you
you.
Girl, that's all I wan - na do,
time.
'Cause when I
look in - to your eyes al - ways
high - er.
I
wan - na fill you up till you've

Gm7
Cm7
make my temp - 'ture rise.
said you've had e - nough.
Oh ba - by, ooh ba -
- by.
When I get you in the mood, 'cause to -
I wan - na hear you moan, call my
night we're gon - na groove.
name out all night long.
Oh, ba - by.
Oh, Jam - ie.
We're
We're
1.
D.C.
2.
mak - in' love un - til we're breath - less.
mak - in' love un - til we're breath - less.

Gm7
Cm7
Gm7
Cm7
Gm7
Cm7
1.
Gm7
Cm7
Mak - in' love un - til we're breath - less.
2.
Gm7
Cm7
N.C.
Ooh.
Ooh.
1.

2.
Gm
Eb/G
You know there's not a soul__ a - round.__ So,
come on, can we break__ it down?__
Ba - by, don't say stop.
Girl, you know we're hot.
La - dy, won't you leave me breath - less?__
D.S. % al Coda
3. To -
Coda
Gm7
Cm7
mak - in'__ love un - til we're breath - less.

N.C.
Gm7
Cm7
Mak - in' love un - til we're breath - less.
(Ad lib. vocals)
Gm7
Cm7
Gm7
Cm7
1. 3. etc.
Repeat ad lib. and fade
2. 4. etc.
Repeat ad lib. and fade
Gm7
Cm7
Gm7
Cm7
Mak - in' love un - til we're breath - less.

MAKE IT LIKE IT WAS

Words and Music by
CARVIN WINANS

Chorus:
D♭/A♭ E♭m7/A♭ G♭6 Fm7 B♭m7
hol - low call.
hap - pen - ing.
Make it like it was, the way it used to be,
cresc.
mf
C♭maj9 C♭/D♭ D♭/F G♭maj9 E♭m7
when I hun - gered for your love con - stant - ly.
G♭/A♭ A♭ E♭m7/A♭ G♭6 Fm7 B♭m7
Make it like it was, it was eas - i - er for
E♭9 D♭/A♭ E♭m7/A♭
me. I know you're a - ble to make it like it was.
mp
1.
D♭ D♭/F G♭maj9 A♭7sus
D. S. 𝄋
2. At a

2.
Bridge:
D♭
G♭/D♭
D♭
D♭/F
A♭/G♭
G♭
E♭m7
Now when I com-pare there's real-ly no com-
cresc.
mf
Fm7
A♭/B♭
B♭m7
A♭/G♭
G♭
E♭m7
G♭/A♭
par-ing. I just want it the way it used to be.
D♭
A♭/D♭
D♭
A♭/G♭
G♭
E♭m7
Just the thought of liv-ing with-out your
Fm7
A♭/B♭
B♭m7
E♭m7
love makes me ask that you make it like it was.
cresc.
Chorus:
E♭m7/A
Amaj7/B
B/A
A
G♯m7
C♯m7
Make it like it was, the way it used to be,
f

Dmaj9 D/E E/G♯ Amaj9 F♯m7
when I hun-gered for your love con - stant-ly.
A/B B F♯m7/B A6 G♯m7 C♯m7
Make it like it was, it was eas - i - er for
F♯9 1. 2. E/B A/B E/B F♯m7/B A6
me. I know you're a - ble to make it like it was
dim. mf cresc. f
3. E/B F♯m7/B E E/G♯ E/A A F♯m/B
- ble to make it like it was. Make it like it was.
dim. mp
E E/G♯ E/A A F♯m7 E(2)
Make it like it was.
molto rit.

MUSTANG SALLY

Words and Music by
BONNY RICE

Moderate rock ♩ = 120

C7
You been

G7
F
N.C.
run - nin' all o - ver town,
ooh, I guess you got - ta
put your flat feet

C7
on the ground.

Chorus:
All you wan-na do is ride a-round, Sal-ly.
(Ride, Sal-ly, ride.)

All you wan-na do is ride a-round, Sal-ly.
(Ride, Sal-ly ride.)

F7
All you wan-na do is ride a-round, Sal-ly.
(Ride, Sal-ly ride.

)
C7
All you wan-na do is ride a-round, Sal-ly.

(Ride, Sal-ly, ride.)
G7
One of these ear-ly morn-

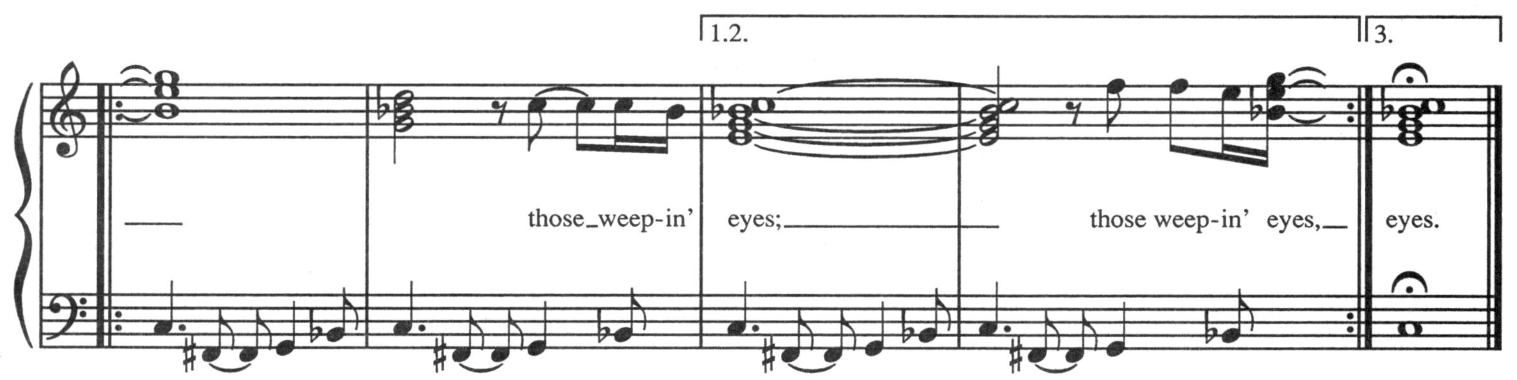

Verse 2:
I bought you a brand new Mustang,
It was a nineteen sixty five.
Now you come around, signifying a woman.
Girl, you won't, you won't let me ride.
Mustang Sally, now baby,
Guess you better slow that Mustang down.
You been runnin' all over town.
Oh, guess you gotta put your flat feet on the ground.
(To Chorus:)

THINK TWICE

Words and Music by
ANDY HILL and PETE SINFIELD

Gm | C | Gm7

This is get - ting ser - i - ous. Are you think-ing 'bout

cresc.

C

you or us? 1.-3.,5. Don't say

mf

𝄋𝄋 *Chorus:*

F Bb C

what you're a - bout to say. Look back

F Am Bb C F Bb

be - fore you leave my life. Be sure be - fore you close that door,

C Gm7 1. Bb

be - fore you roll those dice, ba - by, think

F Gm

twice. 2. Ba - by, think

D.S. 𝄋

2. *To next strain*

Bb

ba - by, think

3.4. etc. *Repeat ad lib. and fade*

Bb

4. Don't do
5. Don't say

Verse 2:
Baby, think twice for the sake of our love, for the memory,
For the fire and the faith that was you and me.
Baby, I know it ain't easy when your soul cries out for higher ground,
'Cos when you're halfway up, you're always halfway down.
But baby, this is serious.
Are you thinking 'bout you or us?
(To Chorus:)

Chorus 4:
Don't do what you're about to do.
My everything depends on you,
And whatever it takes, I'll sacrifice.
Before you roll those dice,
Baby, think twice.

HERE I AM

Words and Music by
TONY ARATA

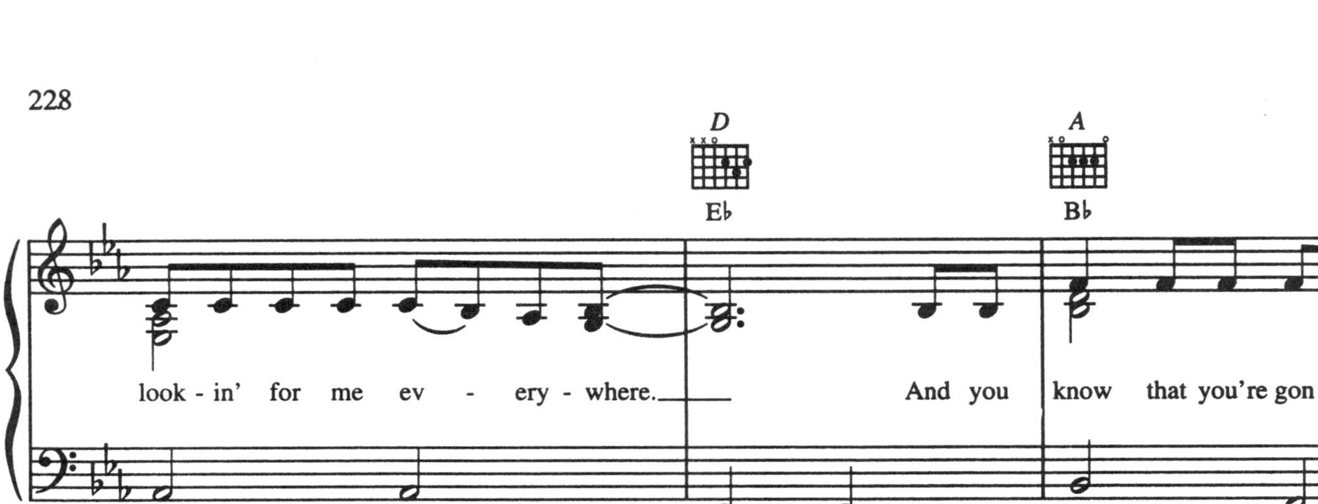
D
A
E♭
B♭
look - in' for me ev - ery - where.
And you
know that you're gon - na find

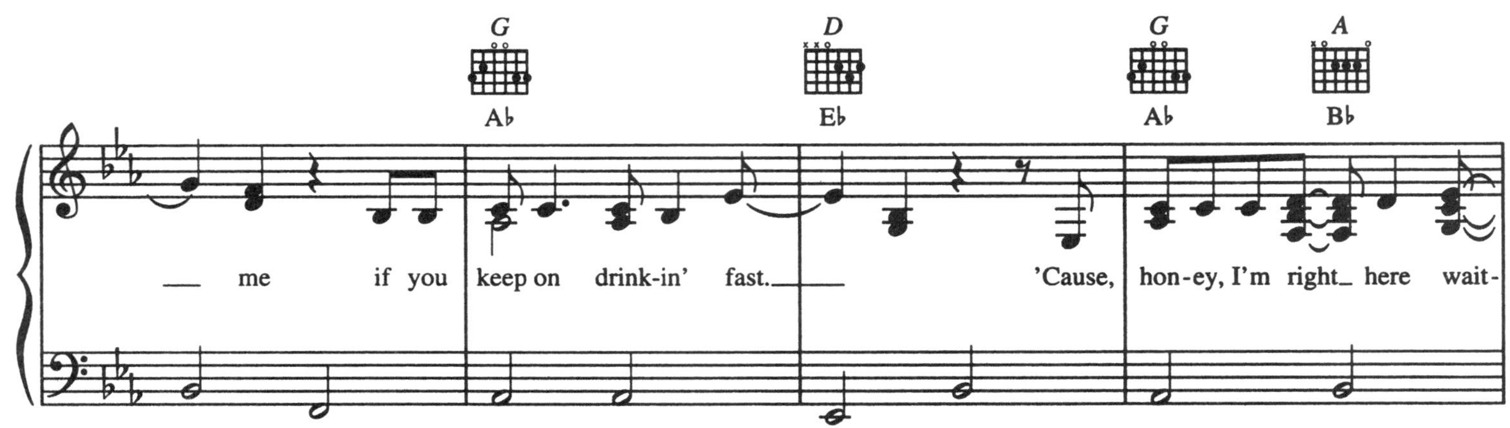
G
D
G
A
A♭
E♭
A♭
B♭
me if you
keep on drink-in' fast.
'Cause,
hon-ey, I'm right here wait-

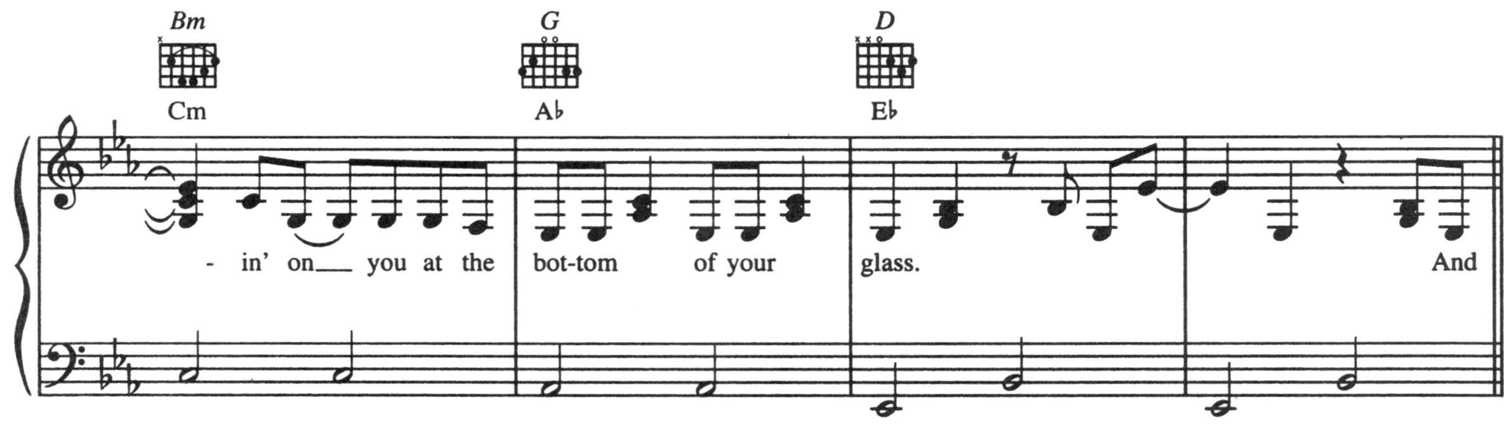
Bm
G
D
Cm
A♭
E♭
- in' on you at the
bot-tom of your
glass.
And

Chorus:
G
A♭
here I am,
here I am,

D
E♭
G
A♭
D
E♭
in the bour - bon and the wat - er that
To Coda
A
B♭
G
A♭
A
B♭
burn you just like a brand, here I am.
1.
2.
D
E♭
D
E♭
And hon - ey,
Bridge:
Em7
Fm7
D/F♯
E♭/G
G
A♭
A
B♭
I got o - ver you pass - in' me o - ver a long

Bm7
D/F♯
G
Cm7
E♭/G
A♭
time a - go.
And my pride
Em7
D/F♯
G
A
F♯7/A♯
Fm7
E♭/G
A♭
B♭
G7/B
was strong - er when I was young - er now I'd
D.S. 𝄋 al Coda
Bm
Bm/A
G
G(9)
Cm
Cm/B♭
A♭
A♭(9)
rath - er have you to know, that
⊕ Coda
D
G
E♭
A♭
Mm, mm.

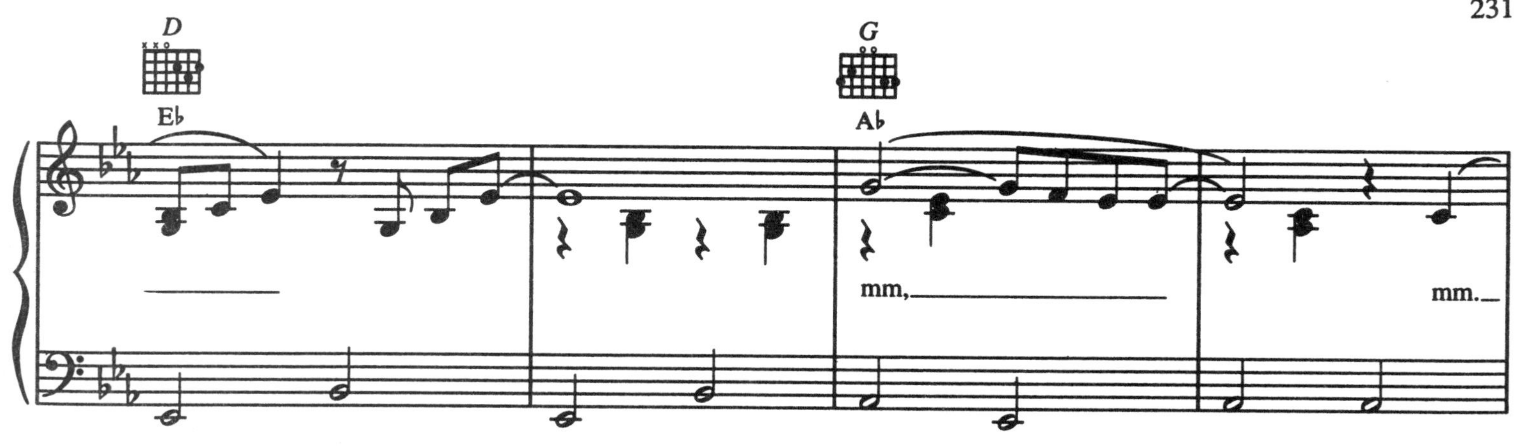

Verse 2:
It ain't workin' darlin', hard as you may try.
You keep hearin' the words you told me in everyone's goodbyes.
And you know that you're just one step from another one being gone.
I know I've seen 'em all unravel,
I've been watchin' it all along.

Chorus 2:
Here I am, here I am,
In every lie you're hearin'
That burn you just like a brand,
Here I am.
(To Bridge:)

Chorus 3:
Here I am, here I am,
I still carry a flame for you
Burnin' me like a brand,
Here I am.

COME TO MY WINDOW

Lyrics and Music by
MELISSA ETHERIDGE

D
C(9)
G
the hand of death.
You don't know how far I'd go to
use this precious ache.
And
you don't know how much I'd give or
how much I can take.
Just to reach
Em
you.
Just to reach
you.
Oh, to reach you,
oh.
Chorus:
Am
Come to my win - dow.
Crawl in - side, wait

Am D G C(9) Am Dsus
by the light of the moon. Come to my win - dow, I'll be home
1.
G C(9) Am7 D Dsus D
D.S. 𝄋
2.
G C(9)
soon.
soon.
Am7 D Dsus D
To Next Strain
3.4. etc.
G C(9) Am7 D
Repeat ad lib. and fade
soon. I'll be home, I'll be home. I'm com-in' home.
Bridge:
Em D/E C
I don't care what they think. I don't care what
C/B Am Am7
they say. What do they know a-bout this love,

Verse 2:
Keeping my eyes open, I cannot afford to sleep.
Giving away promises I know that I can't keep.
Nothing fills the blackness that has seeped into my chest.
I need you in my blood, I am forsaking all the rest.
Just to reach you,
Just to reach you.
Oh, to reach you.
(To Chorus:)

OYE, MI CANTO

(Hear My Voice)
(English/Spanish Version)

Lyrics by
GLORIA ESTEFAN

Music by
GLORIA ESTEFAN, JORGE CASAS
and CLAY OSTWALD

Latin rock ♩ = 120

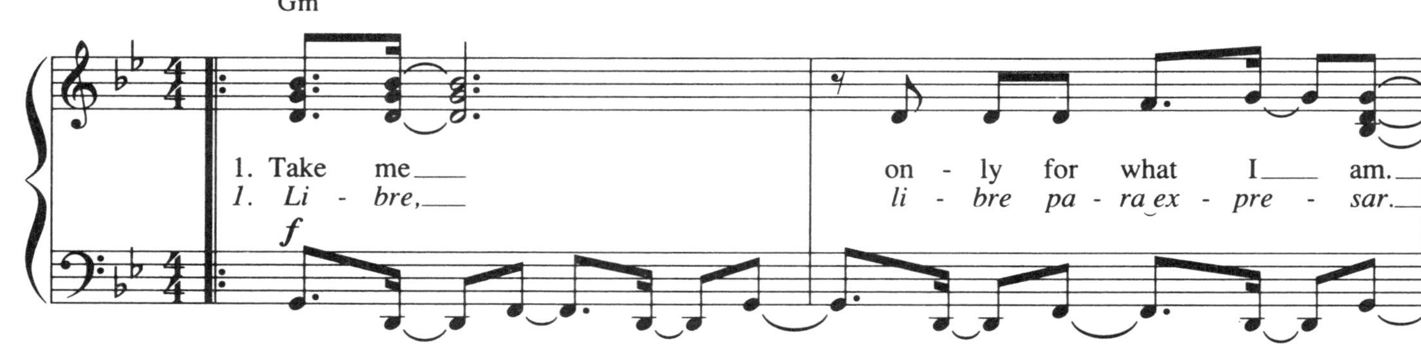

F/G
E♭/G
this is right or this is wrong. It is-n't just one way.
que es di - fí - cil de com - par - tir y tú lo sa - bes bién.
Gm
Cm7
3
Find com - mon
Hay que bus -
Dm7
E♭maj7
Cm7
Dm7
E♭maj7
ground, go in be - tween. Things aren't al - ways what they seem.
car la so - lu - ción en vez de de - cir a - diós.
Gm/F
F
Some - day it - 'll
Al - guien tie - ne
Gm
Gm/F
F
be al - right. Chang - es
que es - cu - char. O - ye es - te can - to

1.
F Gm
hap - pen o - ver - night.
que ya va a em - pe - zar.
2.
F/G Gm
o - ver - night.
va a em - pe - zar.
F
Some - day
it - 'll
Gm
be al - right.
Gm/F F
Chang - es
F Gm
hap - pen o - ver - night.
N.C.

Gm
D7
Gm
O - ye mi can - to.
D7
Gm
O - ye mi can - to. I be -
Cre - o en
D7
Gm
lieve in love but with no con - di - tions. And giv - ing
el a - mor pe - ro sin con - di - cio - nes. Y en a - yu -
(O - ye mi can - to.)
D7
Gm
in some - times does - n't make it sub - mis - sion.
dar - nos sin te - ner o - tras ra - zo - nes. Los
(O - ye mi can - to.)

D7
Gm
Hate is so com-mon it's al-most tra-di-tion.
ce-los y el o-dio son ya tra-di-cio-nes.
(O - ye mi can - to.)
Come on let's
Hay que de-
D7
Gm
leave it be-hind and make that tran - si - tion.
jar-las a-trás, no bus-car ex - pli-ca-cio - nes.
(O - ye mi can - to.)
D7
Gm
D7
O - ye mi can-to.
O-
Gm
D7
- ye mi can - to.
O -
Gm
D7
- ye mi can - to.
O -

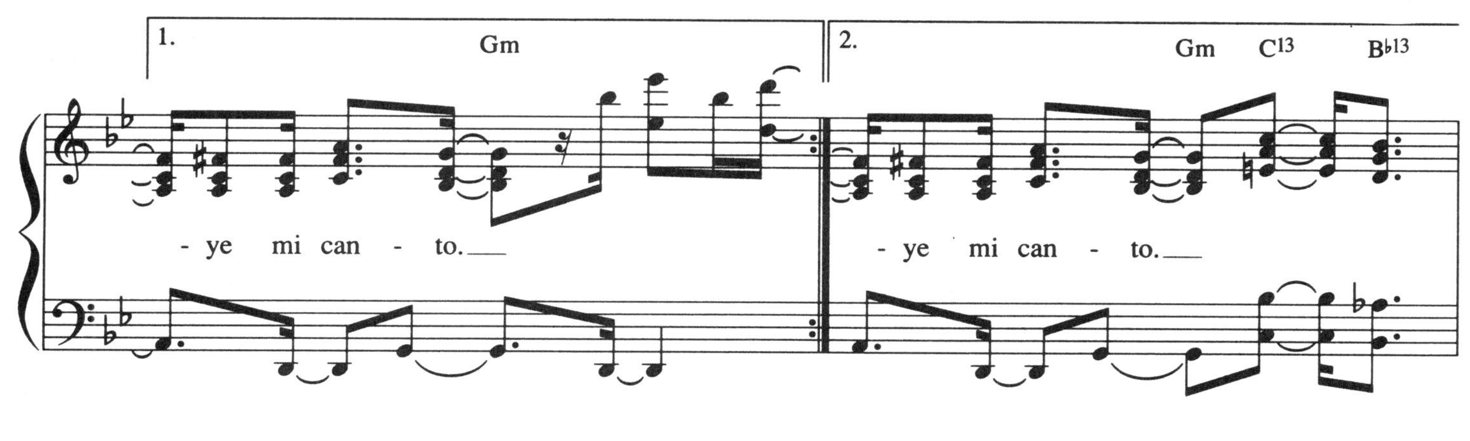

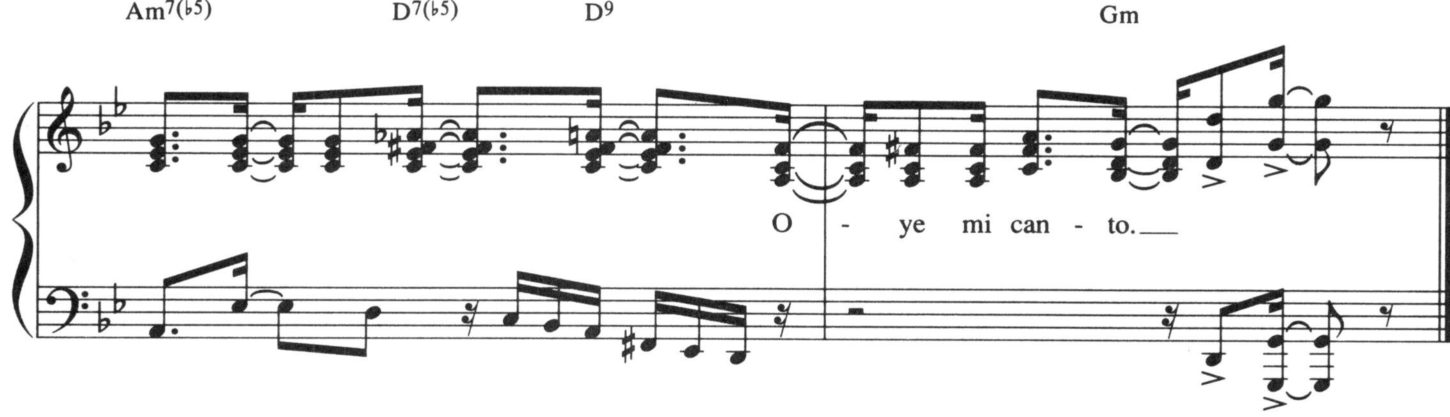

Verse 2:

People, let's give each other room.
If we're gonna work it out
We better make it soon.
Love is, love is such a common word.
When it's pride we mistake for love,
Isn't that absurd.
Why always take the upper hand?
It's better to understand.
Someday it'll be alright.
Changes happen overnight.

Verso 2:

Pronto los años pasarán
Y no quiero un dia despertar
Y ver que es tarde ya.
Algo…algo tiene que pasar.
Si miramos alrededor
Está por comenzar.
Hablamos de amor…palabra común,
Y no lo ofrecemos nunca.
Alguien tiene que escuchar,
Oye este canto que ya va a empezar.

ROAM

Lyrics by
ROBERT WALDROP

Music by
CATHERINE PIERSON, FRED SCHNEIDER,
KEITH STRICKLAND and CINDY WILSON

"Chant-like" free tempo

Moderate Rock (♩= 120)

B7sus
B♮*
E7
A
Oh, girl, danc-in' down those dirt - y and dust -

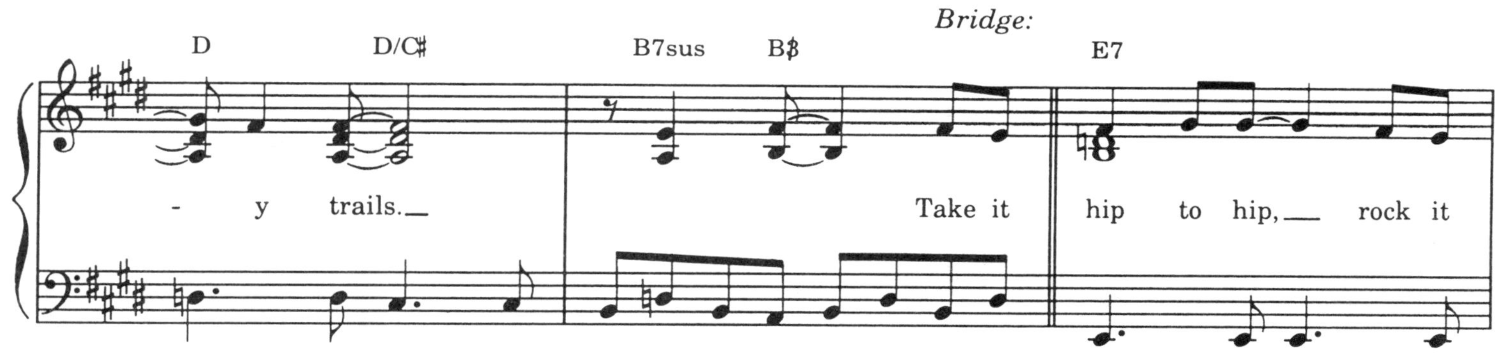
D
D/C♯
B7sus
B♮
Bridge:
E7
- y trails.
Take it
hip to hip, rock it

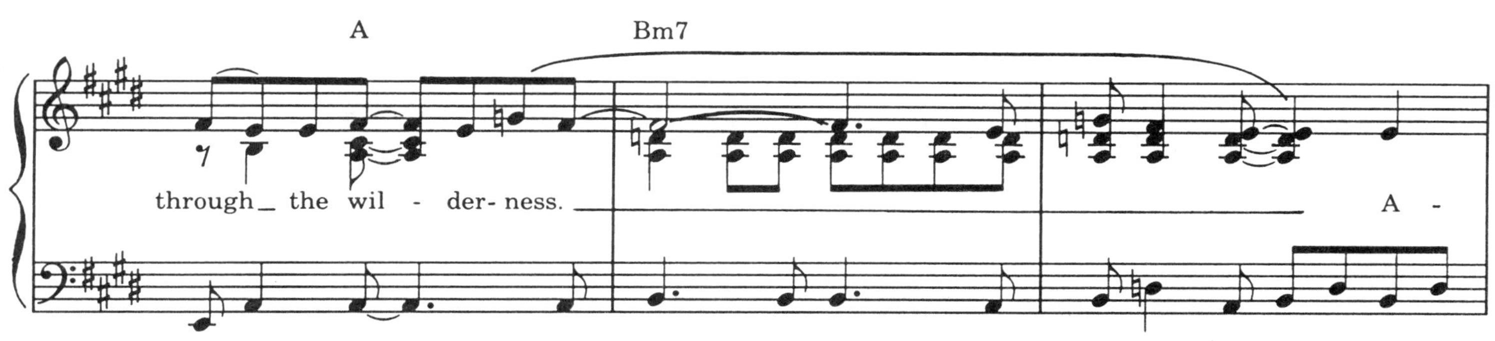
A
Bm7
through the wil - der- ness.
A -

E7
A
D
D/C♯
B7sus
round the world, the trip be - gins with a kiss.

*omit third

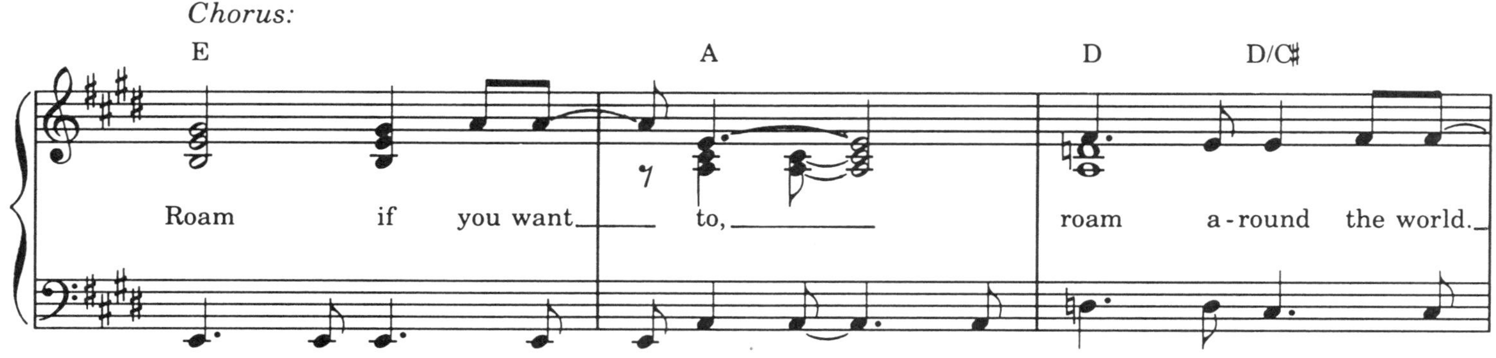
Chorus:
E
A
D
D/C♯
Roam if you want to,
roam a-round the world.

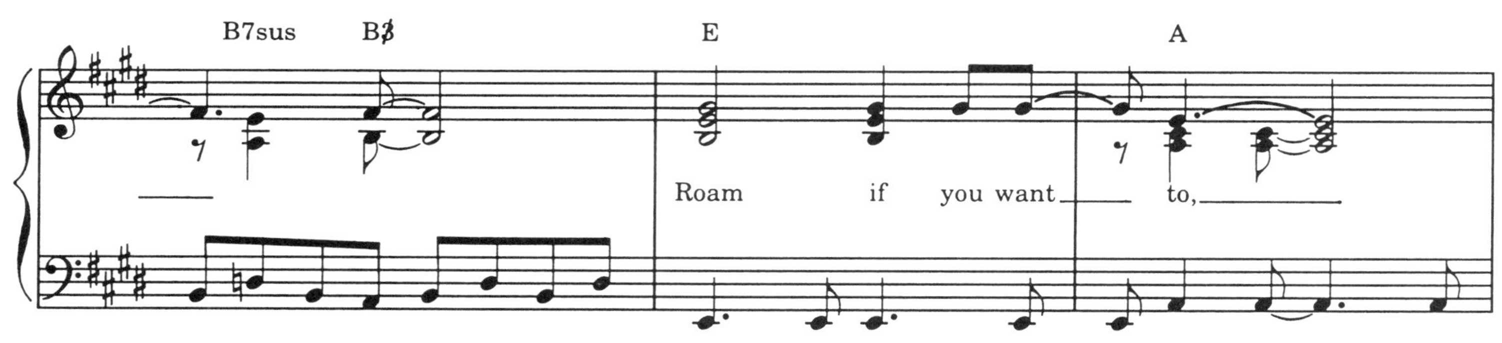
B7sus
B♭
E
A
Roam if you want to,

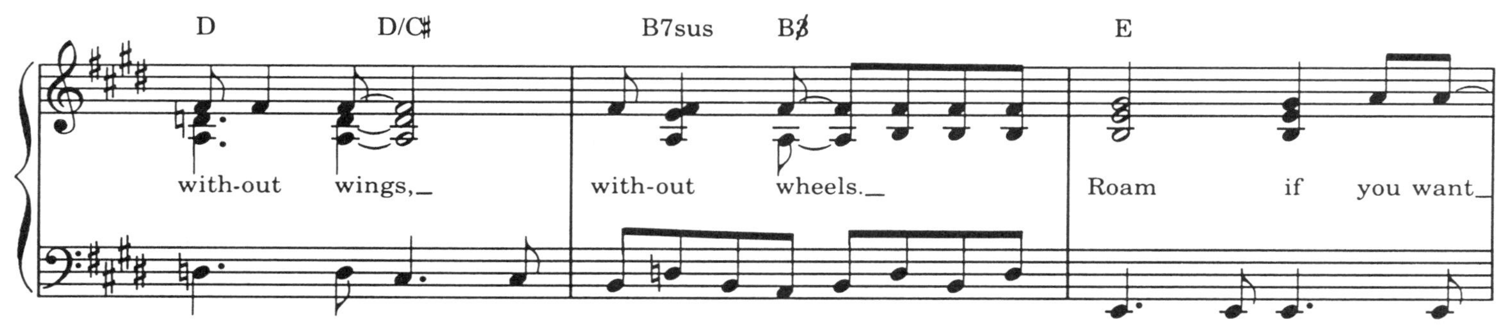
D
D/C♯
B7sus
B♭
E
with-out wings,
with-out wheels.
Roam if you want

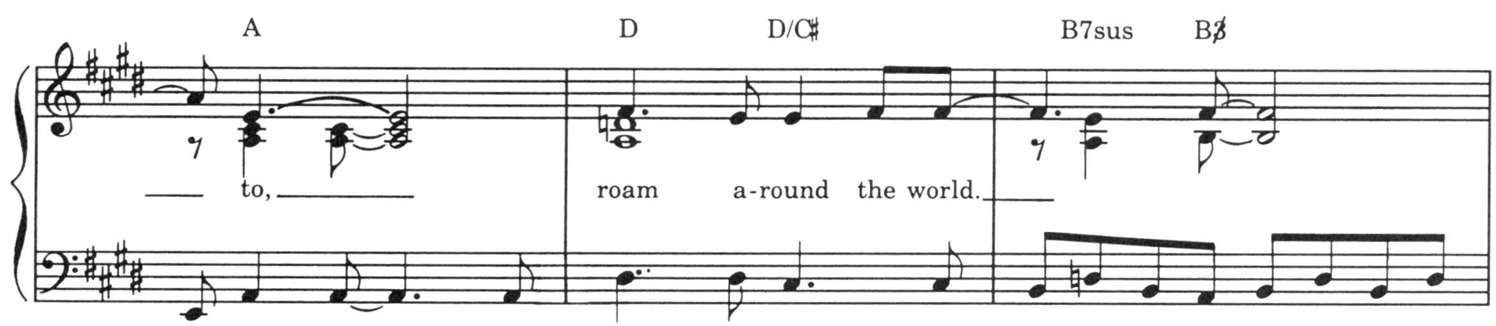
A
D
D/C♯
B7sus
B♭
to,
roam a-round the world.

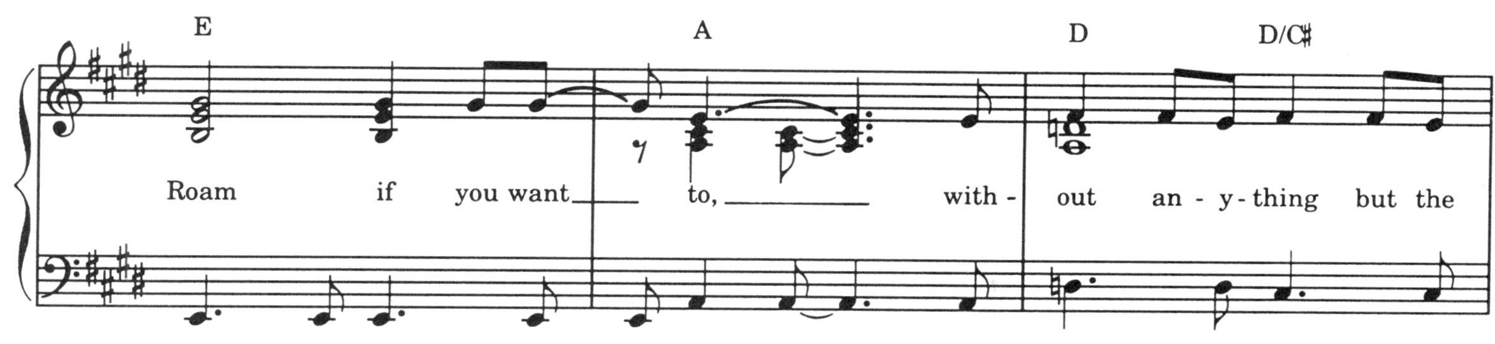

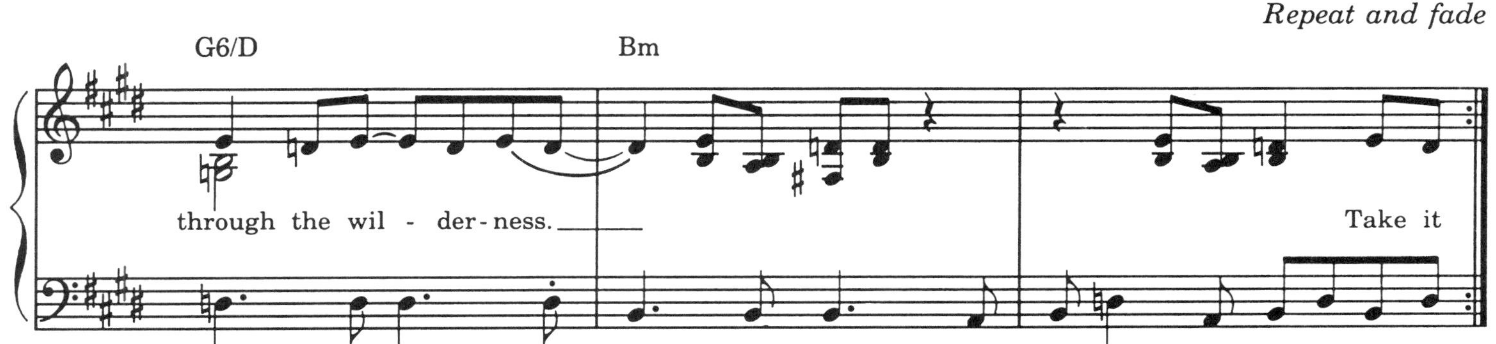

Verse 2:
Skip the air, strip for the sunset,
Ride the arrow to the target was.
(To Bridge:)

Verse 3:
Fly the great big sky, see the great big sea,
Kick through the continents, bustin' boundaries.
(To Bridge:)

ROCKIN' YEARS

Words and Music by
FLOYD PARTON

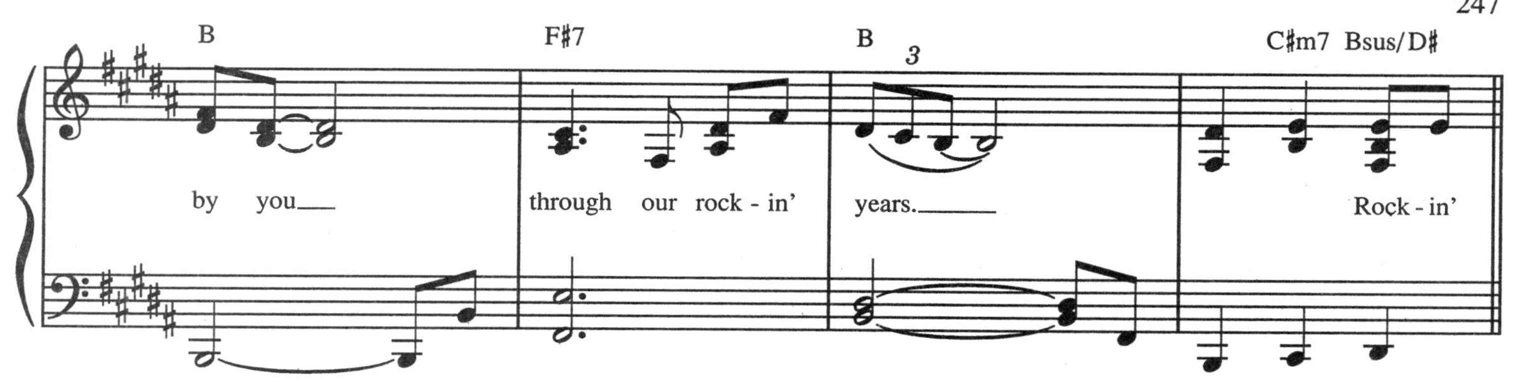
B
F♯7
B
C♯m7 Bsus/D♯
by you___ through our rock - in' years.___ Rock - in'

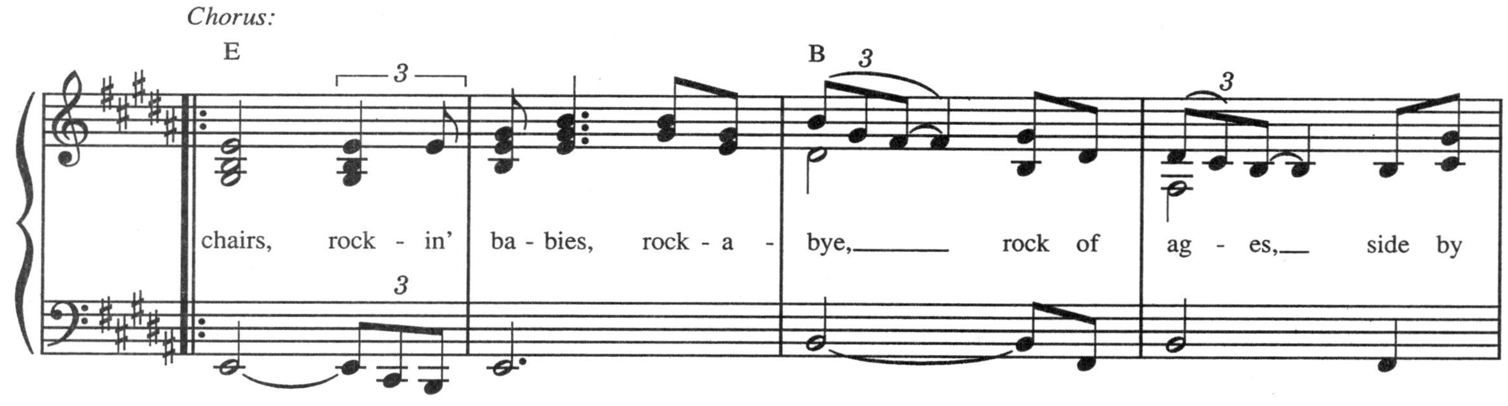
Chorus:
E
B
chairs, rock - in' ba - bies, rock - a - bye,___ rock of ag - es,___ side by

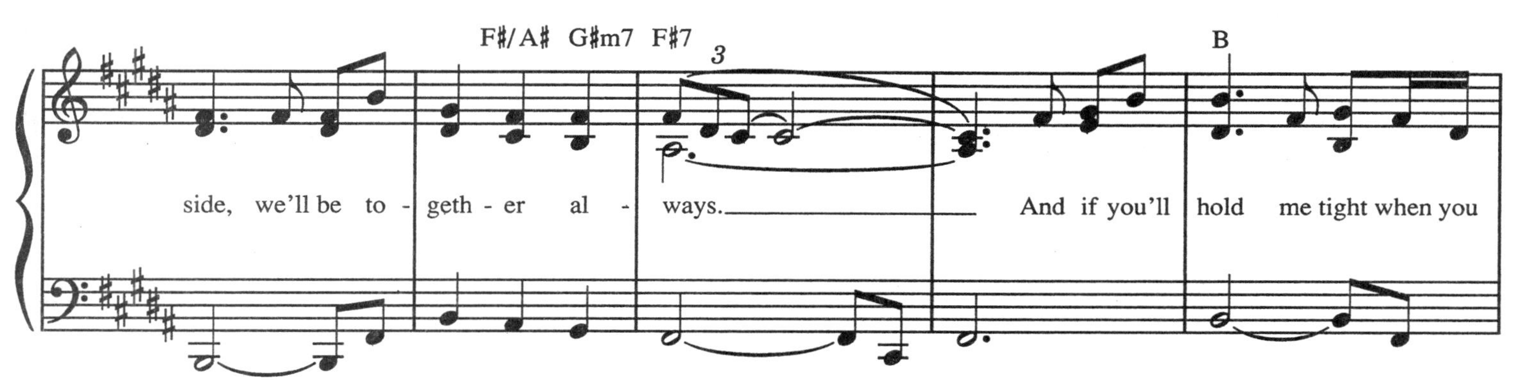
F♯/A♯ G♯m7 F♯7
B
side, we'll be to - geth - er al - ways.___ And if you'll hold me tight when you

B7
E
B
love me, that's all I'll___ ask of you. And I'll stand by you___

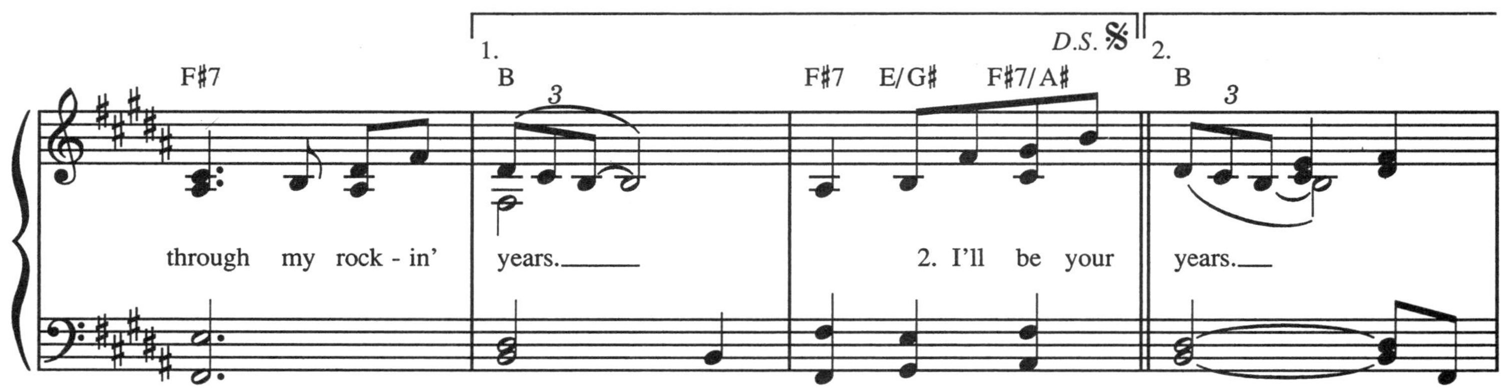

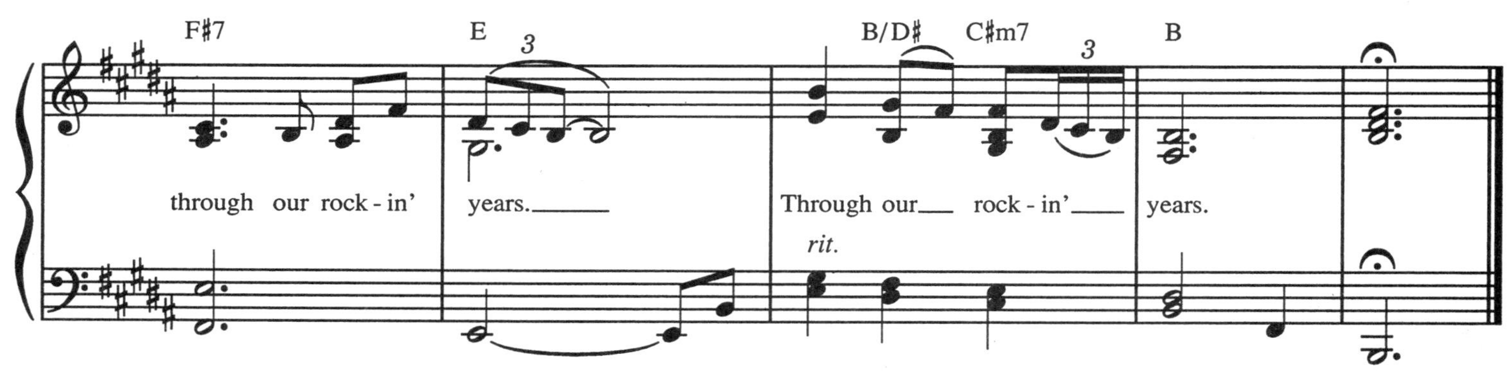

Verse 2:
I'll be your friend, I'll be your lover,
Until the end, there'll be no other,
And my heart has only room for one.
Yes, I'll always love you, and I'll always be here for you.
And I'll stand by you through our rockin' years.
(To Chorus:)

SHE'S MY BABY

By
THE TRAVELING WILBURYS

N.C. A5 E7

— She got the best pud - din' in the neigh-bor - hood.__

F♯m G C5 *To Coda* ⊕ A5 G5/A A5 G5

She's my________________

A5 G5/A A5 C5 A5 G5/A A5 G5 1. A5 G5/A A5 C5

— ba - by. 2. She can

2.3. A5 G5/A A5 *Bridge:* D7

She's com-in' down the side - walk,_ she's com-in' through the door. She's

A7 D7

com-in' home from plac - es__ she's nev - er been been before. She sits down on the so - fa, she

Verse 2:
She can drive a truck, she can drive a train.
She can even drive an aeroplane.
She's so good to look at in the rain.
She's my baby.
(to Bridge:)

Verse 3:
(Instrumental solo)
She's my baby.
(to Bridge:)

Bridge 2:
She's got a body for business, got a head for sin.
She knocks me over like a bowling pin.
She came home last night and said,
"Honey, honey, honey, it's hard to get ahead."
My baby. My baby.

Verse 4:
She can build a boat, she can make it float.
She can play my guitar, note by note.
She loves to stick her tongue right down my throat.
She's my baby.

SEAL OUR FATE

Words and Music by
GLORIA ESTEFAN

Bridge:

G♯m E

gone. Where will you be a few years ____ down the line? _ Will it be

2.3. *See additional lyrics.*

G♯m E

ev - ery - thing you dreamed _ of? __________ Al - ways hard - er to

C♯m7 D♯

do what is right __ some - times one bad de - ci - sion can mess up your life. We

Chorus:

C♯9 G♯m

seal our fate with the choic - es we made, _ but don't give ____ a sec - ond thought to all the

C♯9

chanc - es we take. _ It could come up an - y - time, _ bet - ter be wide a - wake _ 'cause we seal _

G♯m C♯9

our fate with the choic-es we make. Seal our fate;

G♯m

we seal our fate; seal

C♯9 G♯m *To Coda* ⊕ 1.

our fate; seal our fate with the choic-es we make.

2.

choic-es we make. Hey! Hey!

Hey! Hey! Hey! Hey!

Verse 2:
Surely, you say it's not as
Bad as I make it sound.
If we make a mistake we can
Always turn it back around.
Get back on the straight and narrow
When I'm through havin' all my fun.
After all, it's my decision,
I'm not really hurtin' anyone.
(To Bridge:)

Bridges 2 & 3:
Before you know it's gotten way out of hand
In ways that you have never dreamed of.
It's never worth the price you pay in the end,
Instead of being ahead, you're starting over again.
(To Chorus:)

THE SECRET GARDEN

Lyrics and Music by
ROD TEMPERTON & SIEDAH GARRETT &
QUINCY JONES & EL DeBARGE

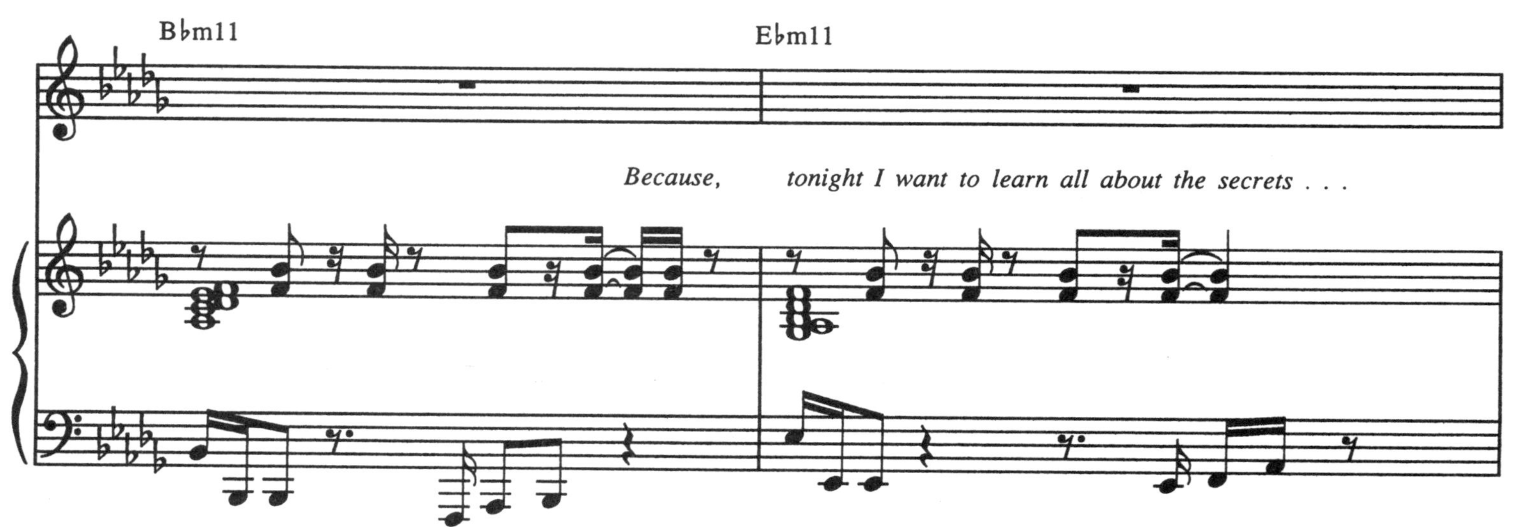

B♭m11
E♭m11
Fm7(11)
G♭maj9
in your garden.
I wan-na
cresc.
B♭m11
E♭m11
read your mind, know your deep - est feel - ings. I wan - na
be with you. Let me lay be - side you, do what you
mp
B♭m11
E♭m11
make it right for you. Ba - by,
want me to all night. Gon - na
B♭m11
E♭m11
3
show me, let me share the mys - t'ry. Oh,
hold you. Ooh, ba - by, can I touch you there?

B♭m11
E♭m11
(Come on, come on, come on, come on.)
Lis - ten to your heart to - night.
I can keep you sat - is - fied,
B♭m11
E♭m11
ba-by,
(Come on, come on, come on,)
Make it al -
whoo-ie, whoo - ie
B♭m11
E♭m11
Fm7(11) G♭maj9
right, yeah, yeah, yeah. Come on, come on, come on.
I know a
ba - by, please ba - by, all night.
Spoken: Yeah, baby.
I'll take good
cresc.
B♭m11
E♭m11
mel - o - dy that we could sing to - geth - er.
I've got the
care of you, that's what a man is sup-posed to do.
mf

Bbm11
Ebm11
se - cret key to you, ba - by. Let's make
And I'll be there for you all the time. Let your
mu - sic, har-mo - niz - ing ec - sta-sy.
hair down, let me get you in the mood.
Come on and sing it to me. Here in the
(Come on, come on, come on, come on.)
Spoken 2nd time: Come on, take me, take me with you in-to the
cresc.

Chorus:
Gbmaj7
Ab/Gb
Fm7
Bbm7
gar - den where temp - ta - tion feels so right, pas - sion can
f
Ebm9
Ebm7/Ab
Dbmaj9
Bbsus
Bb9
make you fall for what you feel.
make you fall for what you feel.
In the
Gbmaj7
Ab/Gb
Fm7
Bbm7
Ab Fm Ebm7 Fm7
gar - den, we can make it come a - live ev - ery night.
1.
Gbm7 Ebm7/Ab N.C.
Bbm11
Gbmaj7/Bb
Oh, wom-an! Your se-cret gar - den.
Whoo.
mp

Bbm11
Gbmaj7/Bb
Fm11
Gbmaj9
D.S.
2.
Gbm7
Ebm7/Ab N.C.
Spoken: Oh, baby.
I need to
Oh, wom-an! Ah, here in the
gar-den.
Gbmaj7/Bb
woo
Spoken: You know, I've never wanted anyone . . .
mp
I've never wanted anyone as much as I . . .
Ebm11
. . . as much as I want you.
I want you to
show me. I want you to tell me. I want to feel . . .
. . . all the secrets.
If you
cresc.

Bbm11
Ebm11
think I, I'm gon-na take care of you, if you think I, I got what-cha need,
think I, I'm gon-na be good to you, if you think I, I like what-cha do,
sho ya right.
Spoken:
mf
Bbm11
1.
Ebm11
I want us to take our time because . . .
. . . we have all night.
If you
2.
Ebm11
Fm11 Gbmaj9
Bbm11
If you
think I, I'm gon-na take care of you, if you
think I, I'm gon-na be good to you, if you

Ebm11
Bbm11
think I, I got what-cha need,
think I, I like what-cha do,
sho ya right.
Spoken: Let me find the secrets.
sho ya right.
1.
2.
If you
Baby, you know you're right.
If you
think I, I'm gon-na take care of you, if you think I, I got what-cha need,
think I, I'm gon-na be good to you, if you think I, I like what-cha do,
sho ya right.
1. 3. (fade)
Fm11
Gbmaj9
If you
If you

THE WAY SHE LOVES ME

Music and Lyrics by
RICHARD MARX

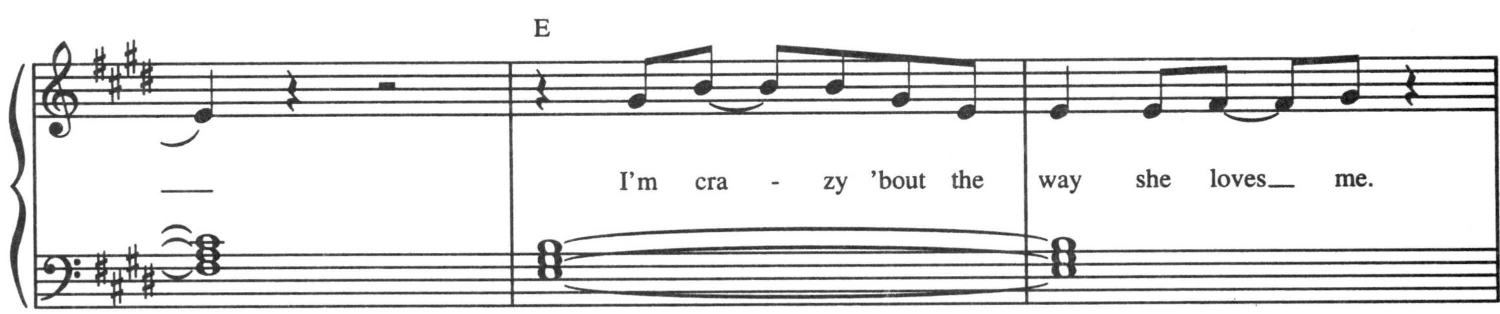

Db
Verse:
1. I'll have this feel - ing 'till the day that I die,
2. Came close to let - ting this train pass me by,
3. (Instrumental solo ad lib....
Cb
when I hear my ba - by call - in'.
just like a fool sec - ond guess - in'.
Db
A sim - ple mo - tion, a look in her eyes
I could have spent my life won - der - ing why
Cb
and I'm help - less - ly fall - in'.
I did - n't cher - ish the bless - ing.
...end solo)
Ebm7
I'd give all of
If I'd have known she'd
No - bod - y else could
Ab
some - bod - y else
come my way
do me so right,

D♭
G♭
for an - y piece of her heart___ that's left.___
the lone - ly nights would - 've been___ o - kay.___
a breath of heav - en in my dark - est night.___
E♭m7
A♭sus
A♭
She knows me bet - ter than I know my - self.___
I have her prom - ise that she's gon - na stay.___
I'm gon - na hold on with all of my might.___
Chorus:
E
F♯m7
Let me tell you 'bout the way she loves_ me. Ooh,___ I want the world to know._
E
I'm cra - zy 'bout the way she loves_ me. Ooh,__
F♯m7
1. 2.
D.S. 𝄋
3.
Repeat ad lib. and fade
__ I'm proud to let it show.___

SIGNS

Signs - 3 - 1

Chorus:
D C G D G G
sign, sign, ev - ery-where a sign, block - ing out the scen-er - y, break - ing my mind.
D A 1. C(2) C D.C.
Do this, don't_ do___ that._ Can't you read_ the sign?
2. C(2) C To Next Strain D N.C.
3. C(2) C 4. C(2) C Fine D
Bridge:
A G D
Hey now,___ mis - ter, can't_ you read?___ You got to have a shirt and tie___ to get a seat.___

A G D

You can't watch, no, you can't eat. You ain't sup-posed to be here.

N.C.

And the sign says, "You got to have a mem-ber-ship card to get in - side." *Huh!*

D C G D G

(Instrumental solo . . .

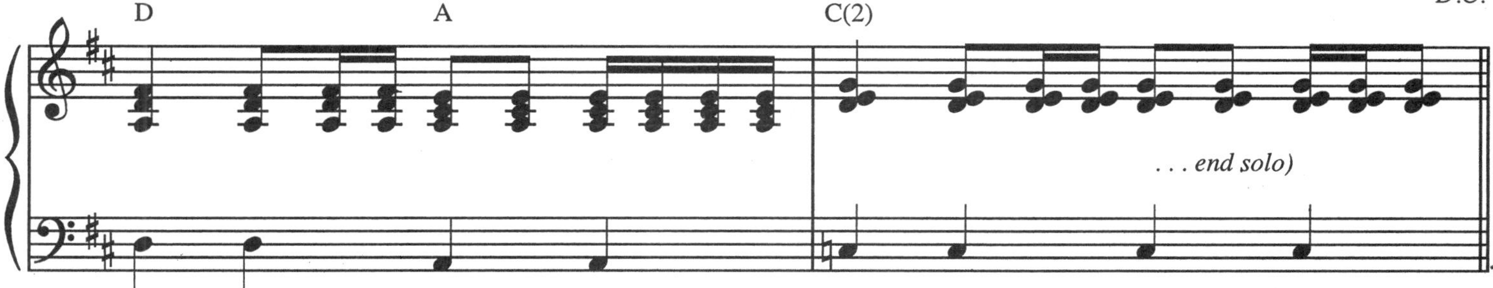

Verse 2:
And the sign says, "Anybody caught trespassing will be shot on sight."
So, I jumped the fence and I yelled at a house, "Hey! What gives you the right
To put up a fence and keep me out, or to keep Mother Nature in?
If God was here, He'd tell you to your face, "Man, you're some kind of sinner."
(To Chorus:)

Verse 3:
And the sign says, "Everybody welcome! Come in and kneel down and pray."
But when they passed around the plate at the end of it all, I didn't have a penny to pay.
So, I got me a pen and a paper, and I made up my own little sign.
I said, "Thank you, Lord, for thinkin' 'bout me. I'm alive and doin' fine."
(To Chorus:)

SOUL INSPIRATION

Words and Music by
TERRY BRITTEN &
GRAHAM LYLE

1.
N.C. Fmaj7/G
2.
C6
Ddim/C
Bridge:
Am7
Lately
Now, if
I for - got to
Fm9
Bbmaj9
Fmaj7/G
tell you I love you,
I've real - ly got no ex - cuse,
no ex - cuse.
cresc.
Chorus:
Cmaj9
Ebmaj7/F
Be - cause you're
beau - ti - ful, my
one de - sire.
f
Bbmaj9
Dm7/G
Cmaj9
You're my soul's in - spi - ra - tion.
And if I
did - n't say it, then
Ebmaj7/F
Bbmaj9
Dm7/G
I do now.
You're my soul's in - spi - ra - tion.

Cmaj9
dim.
Fm9
Bb9
mf
Am9
Verse:
Bb9
Dbmaj7
Db7
Db6
Ebdim/Db
If I'm
feel - in' low
res - cue me,
I've on - ly got my -
ba - by, you bring out the
Dbmaj7
Db7
Db6
Ebdim/Db
self to blame,
best in me.
'cause I can
I'm the
Cbmaj7
Cb7
Ebm7/Ab
Dbmaj7
Db7
al - ways share the load
girl I want to be
when I'm near
when I'm near
you, uh huh.
you, uh huh.
1.
N.C. Gbmaj7/Ab
You can
2.
Db6
Ebdim/Db
Bridge:
Bbm7
I may
need re - mind - ing to

Gbm9
Cbmaj9
Gbmaj7/Ab
say I love you,
but heav - en knows that I do,
yes, I do.
cresc.

Chorus:
Dbmaj9
Fbmaj7/Gb
Be - cause you're
beau - ti - ful, my
one de - sire,
f

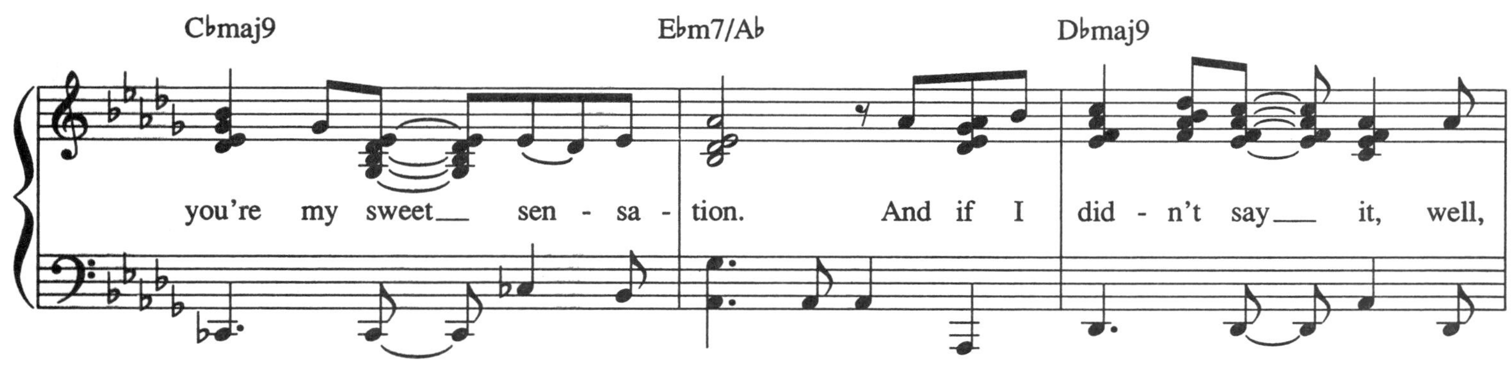
Cbmaj9
Ebm7/Ab
Dbmaj9
you're my sweet sen - sa -
tion. And if I
did - n't say it, well,

1.3.4.5. etc. Repeat ad lib. & fade
Fbmaj7/Gb
Cbmaj9
Ebma7/Ab
I do now.
You're my soul's in - spi - ra -
tion. Be - cause you're

2.
Bridge:
E♭m7/A♭
Amaj9
tion. From the day I met you, ba - by, yes, I

D13(♯11)
C♯m7
knew in - stinc - tive - ly what -

Dmaj9
Bmaj7
- ev - er our fu - ture, to -

E♭m7/A♭
D.S. 𝄋
geth - er we were gon - na be. Be - cause you're

TALK TO ME

Words and Music by
ANITA BAKER, MICHAEL POWELL
and VERNON FAILS

Chorus:
G6 Gmaj7 F#7(♭9) F#7(♭13) A/B Bm7
What's wrong, wrong with you? Why don't you tell me what you're

Am7 C/D D7 C/D G6 Gmaj7 F#7(♭9) F#7(♭13)
go - in' through, dar - lin'? What's wrong, wrong with you?

A/B Bm7 1. Am Am7/D
Why don't you tell me what you're I can help you if you
(go - in' through?)

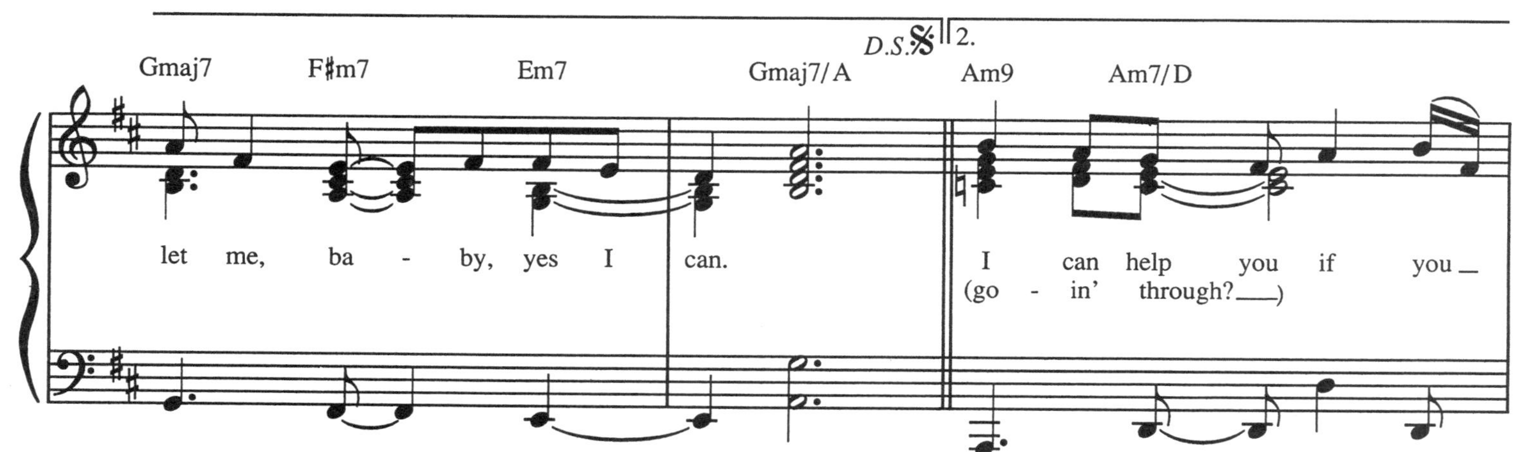
Gmaj7 F#m7 Em7 Gmaj7/A D.S. 2. Am9 Am7/D
let me, ba - by, yes I can. I can help you if you
(go - in' through?)

Verse 2:
Stare into space, I see shadows of pain cross your face.
You avoid my advice, you avoid my embrace, baby.
(To Chorus:)

HOW MANY WAYS

Words and Music by
V. HERBERT, T. BRAXTON, N. GORLING,
K. MILLER and P. FIELD

Am7(4)
E7sus
You know you make me feel so good
C/D
E7sus
E7
inside and boy, it's a feel-ing I just can't hide. And ba-by, words
Am7(4)
E7sus
can't ex-press my grat-i-tude for
C/D
D/E
E7
each and ev-er-y lit-tle thing you do. I want you to un-

Am7(4)
E7sus
- der - stand___ you're all___ the man___ that I love___

1.
To Next Strain
C/D
D/E
E7
___ and I know_ that I need_ and I want_ and more.___ Ba - by, let___ me count_ the__ ways.
cresc.

2.
D/E
E7
N.C.
cresc.
Dar - ling, let___ me count_ the__ ways.

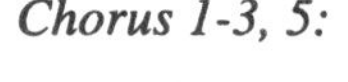
Chorus 1-3, 5:

Am7(4)
G/B
Cmaj9
Am7(4)
G/B
Cmaj9
How man - y ways I love you.___ Let me count the ways.___
mf

Verse 2:
You know you're so very special to me, my baby,
I'll never let you go.
When I'm with you,
I feel so free I could count from
1 up to 99 and still believe.
Although sometimes now, baby, we disagree,
There ain't never or will ever be another love for me.
And I want you to know I appreciate
All the things that you do when you do what you do for me.
Darling, let me count the ways.
(To Chorus:)

Chorus 4:
1, 2 I love you.
3, 4 So much more,
5, 6 I can't get enough of this.
7 Let me show you my love and take you to heaven.
8, 9, 10 Let me start love over and over . . . again.
(To Chorus 5:)

TELL ME WHAT YOU WANT ME TO DO

Words and Music by
NARADA MICHAEL WALDEN, SALLY JO DAKOTA
and TEVIN CAMPBELL

E♭m7
E♭m7/A♭
D♭
A♭/C
night.
you.
I'm so sorry.
It hurts me deep in - side when I
Now, don't keep say - in' it's too
B♭m
B♭m/A♭
G♭maj7
Fm7
see you cry - in'.
late to think it o - ver, ba - by,
What-ev - er's wrong, I'll
af - ter all that
Bridges 1 & 2:
E♭m7
Fm7(4)
make it right.
we've been through.
If you un - der - stand how
Girl, I'm beg - gin' you, I'm down
B♭m7
E♭m7(4)
I feel,
on my knees.
ooh, you should know that my
Don't walk a - way, ba - by,

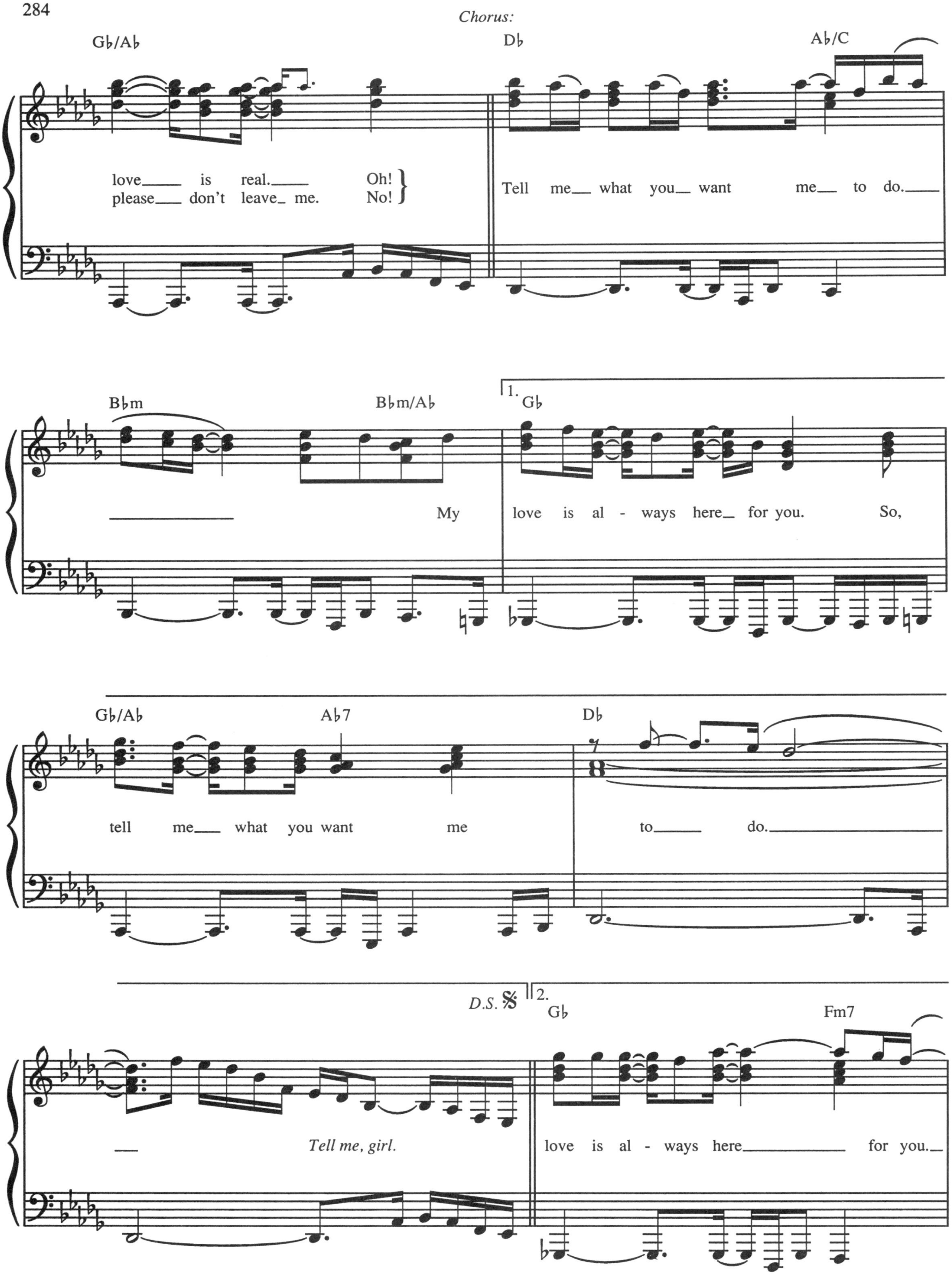

Chorus:

Gb/Ab Db Ab/C

love___ is real.___ Oh!
please___ don't leave_ me. No!

Tell me_ what you_ want me_ to do.___

Bbm Bbm/Ab 1. Gb

___ My love is al - ways here_ for you. So,

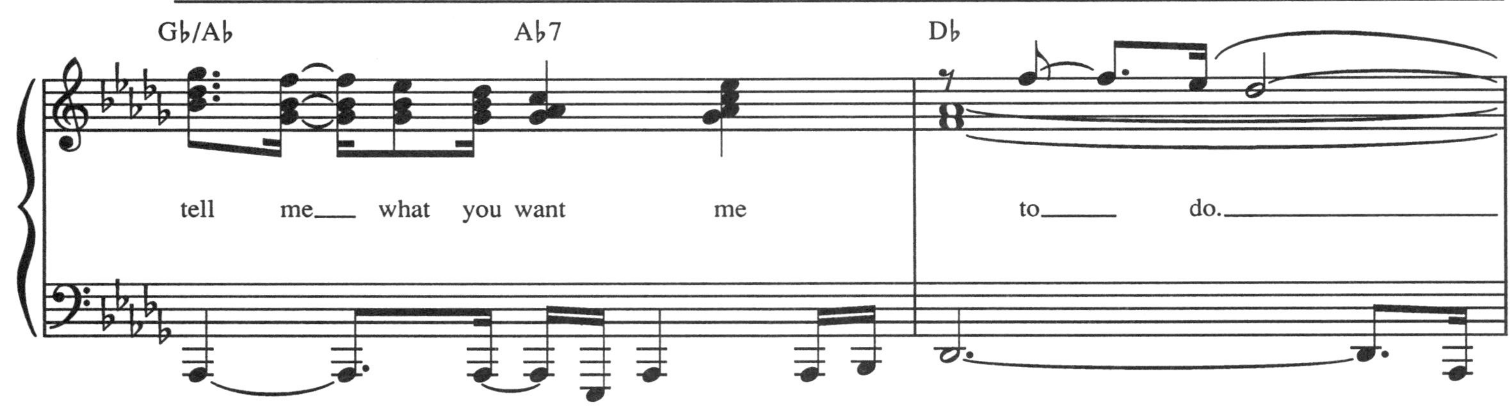

Ebm7
Ebm7/Ab
Ab
Db
Ab/C
Oh,
tell me what you want me to do.
Bbm
Bbm/Ab
Gb
My
love is al - ways here for you. So,
Gb/Ab
Ab7
Db
tell me what you want me
to do.
Bridge 3:
Cb/Db
Db7/F
Gbmaj7
Oh, ba - by, yeah.
Girl, I know that we

Fm7
B♭m
G♭maj7
could work it out some-how.
Is-n't that what love's
Fm7
B♭m7
G9(♭5)
G♭maj7
all a-bout?
I'm gon-na be by your side, we're
Fm7
B♭m
A♭/B♭
B♭m
G♭/A♭
A♭
gon-na see it through this time. I won't
let you slip a-way.
Say you'll
G♭/A♭
A♭
G/A
A
stay with me.
Stay with me, girl.
'Cause you're the fin-est girl that I've

*vocal sung 8va this measure only

THESE THREE WORDS

Music and Lyrics by
STEVIE WONDER

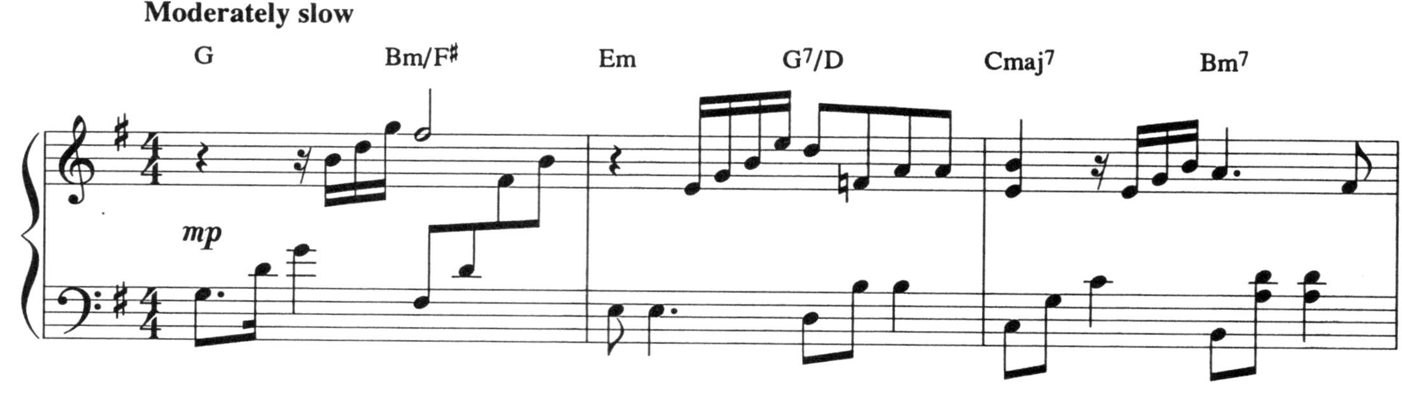
Moderately slow
G
Bm/F♯
Em
G7/D
Cmaj7
Bm7
mp

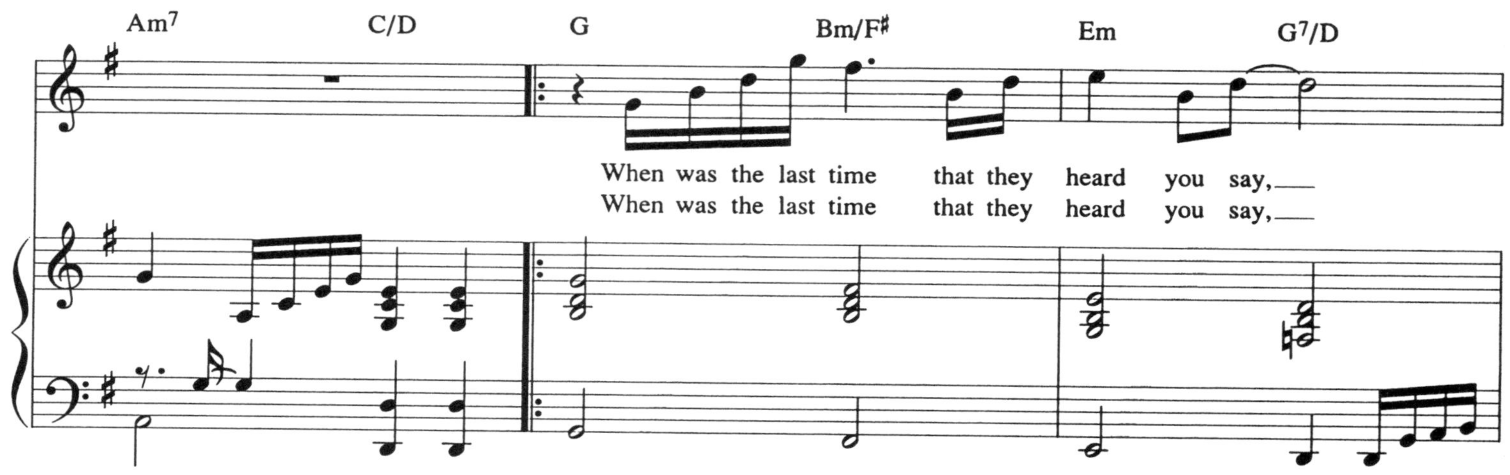
Am7
C/D
G
Bm/F♯
Em
G7/D
When was the last time that they heard you say,
When was the last time that they heard you say,

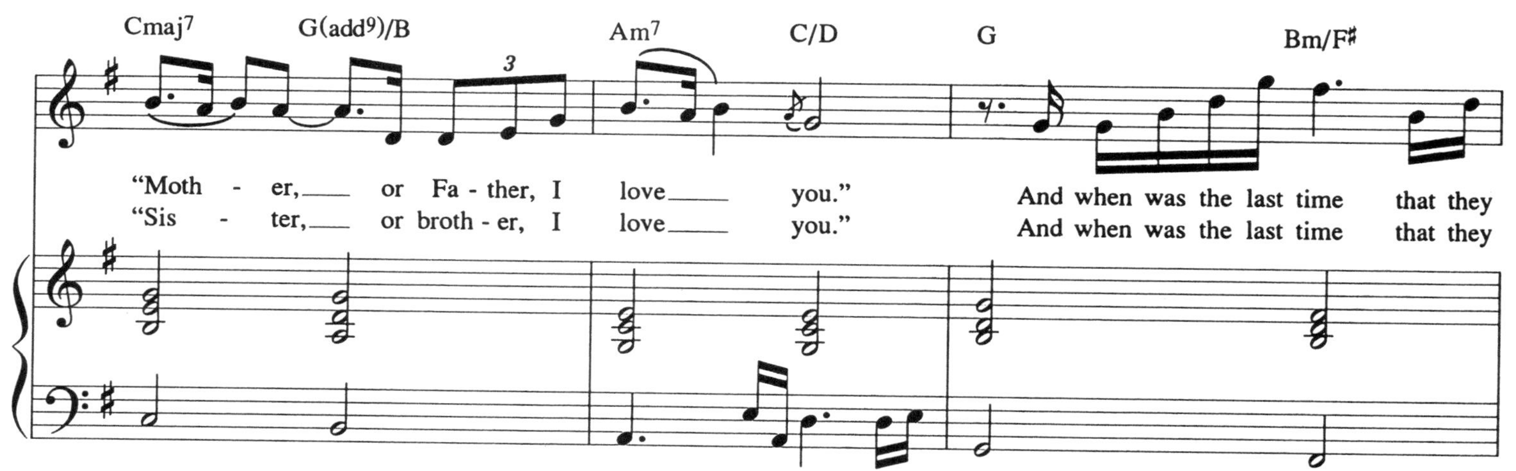
Cmaj7
G(add9)/B
Am7
C/D
G
Bm/F♯
3
"Moth - er, or Fa - ther, I love you."
"Sis - ter, or broth - er, I love you."
And when was the last time that they
And when was the last time that they

Em G7/D Cmaj7 G(add9)/B Am7 C/D
heard you say, "Daugh - ter, or son, I love you."
heard you say, "Dar - ling, or best friend, I love you." The
Em G/F
Ones you say you cher - ish ev - ery day
ones for whom you give your ver - y life
C/G B/A
can in - stant - ly be tak - en a - way.
could be tak - en in the twink - ling of an eye.
E/B C♯m7
Then you'd say, "I know this can't be true," when you
Through your tears, you'd ask, "Why did you go?" Know - ing

Am7sus
1.
C/D
nev - er took the time to sim - ply tell them, "I love you."
you didn't al - ways show just how much
2.
C/D
Am7 Bm7 D/E
you love them so.
These three words,
G Am7
sweet and sim - ple,
Bm7 D/E
these three words,
G Am7
short and kind.

Am7 Bm7 D/E
G Am7
These three words always kin-
dles an aching heart to smile in-side.
C/D
Esus E
Am7
I know a fam-i-ly who has-n't a cent to their name, and yet the
F♯sus F♯
Bm7
joy and love they have be-tween them, they al-ways claim. And when one's

Em7
A
Dmaj7
Bm7
called from life, the sur - vived mourn the lost and will nev - er be the same. Yet they re -
Em7
A7
C/D
D/E
C♯m7
E/F♯
joice in know - ing they gave them their all. These three words,
A
Bm7
sweet and sim -
C♯m7
E/F♯
- ple, these three words,

A
Bm7
C♯m7
E/F♯
short and kind.
These three words
always kindles an aching heart
to smile inside.
These three words,
Repeat and fade

THIS OLD HEART OF MINE
(Is Weak For You)

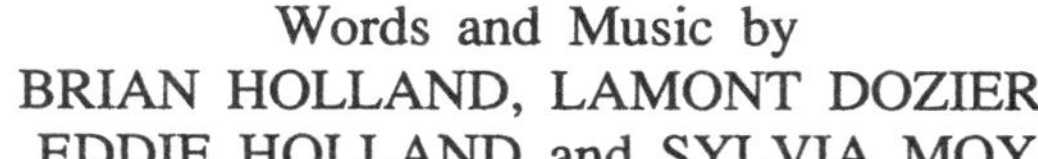
Words and Music by
BRIAN HOLLAND, LAMONT DOZIER,
EDDIE HOLLAND and SYLVIA MOY

Rock ♩ = 116

1. A C♯m7 D A/C♯ Bm7 Bm7/E

2. D A/C♯ Bm7 Bm7/E

mf

with pedal

1,3. This old heart

𝄋 *Verse:*

A C♯m7 D D/E A C♯m7

of mine been broke a thou - sand times. Each time you break a - way, I fear you've gone to stay. Lone-ly nights that come, mem-o - ries that flow, bring-ing you back

D
C♯m
Bm7
a - gain, hurt-ing me more and more.
May - be it's

E
C♯m7
F♯m
E/F♯
my mis - take to show this love that I feel in - side;

Bm7
E
Bm7
A/C♯
'cause each day that pass - es by you got me nev - er know-ing if I'm

Chorus:
To Coda
D
D/E
E
A
C♯m7
com-ing or go - ing, 'cause
1,3. I love you.
2,4. I love you.
Yes, I
This old

D A/C♯ Bm7 D/E E A
do, this old heart. I love you.
heart is weak for you.

C♯m7 D C♯m7 1. Bm7 D/E E
Yes, I do, yes, I do.
This old heart, weak for

A C♯m7 D A/C♯ Bm7 D/E D.S.
2. I try hard

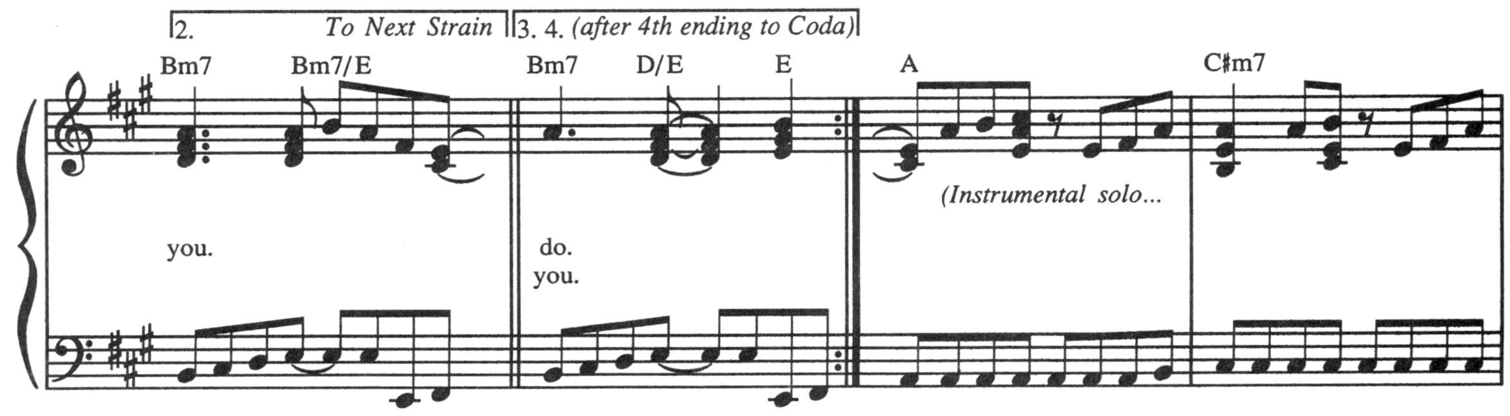
2. To Next Strain
3. 4. (after 4th ending to Coda)
Bm7 Bm7/E Bm7 D/E E A C♯m7
you. do.
you.
(Instrumental solo...

Verse 2:

I try hard to hide my hurt inside.
This old heart of mine always keeps me cryin'.
The way you treat me leaves me incomplete,
You're here for the day, gone for the week.

But, if you leave me a hundred times, a hundred times I'll take you back.
I'm yours whenever you want me.
I'm not too proud to shout it, tell the world about it, 'cause I love you.

(To Chorus 2:)

TOUCH ME (ALL NIGHT LONG)

Words and Music by
GREGORY CARMICHAEL and PATRICK ADAMS

Abmaj7
4fr.
Bb(addC)
3fr.
Cm7
3fr.
Fm7
We're start - ing it o - ver, we're mak - ing way for des - ti - ny.
The more that I see you, the more I know that love be - longs.
Bb(addC)
3fr.
Cm7
3fr.
Abmaj7
4fr.
Bb(addC)
3fr.
Cm7
3fr.
A time to turn o - ver, a
With you in my mind, boy, I
Fm7
Bb(addC)
3fr.
Cm7
3fr.
Abmaj7
4fr.
bet - ter life for you and me. A new re - cre - a -
would - n't know what's right from wrong. Cos love will take o -
Bb(addC)
3fr.
Cm7
3fr.
Fm7
Bb(addC)
3fr.
Cm7
3fr.
tion to chan - nel all the en - er - gy.
ver and leave you out of sight and mind.

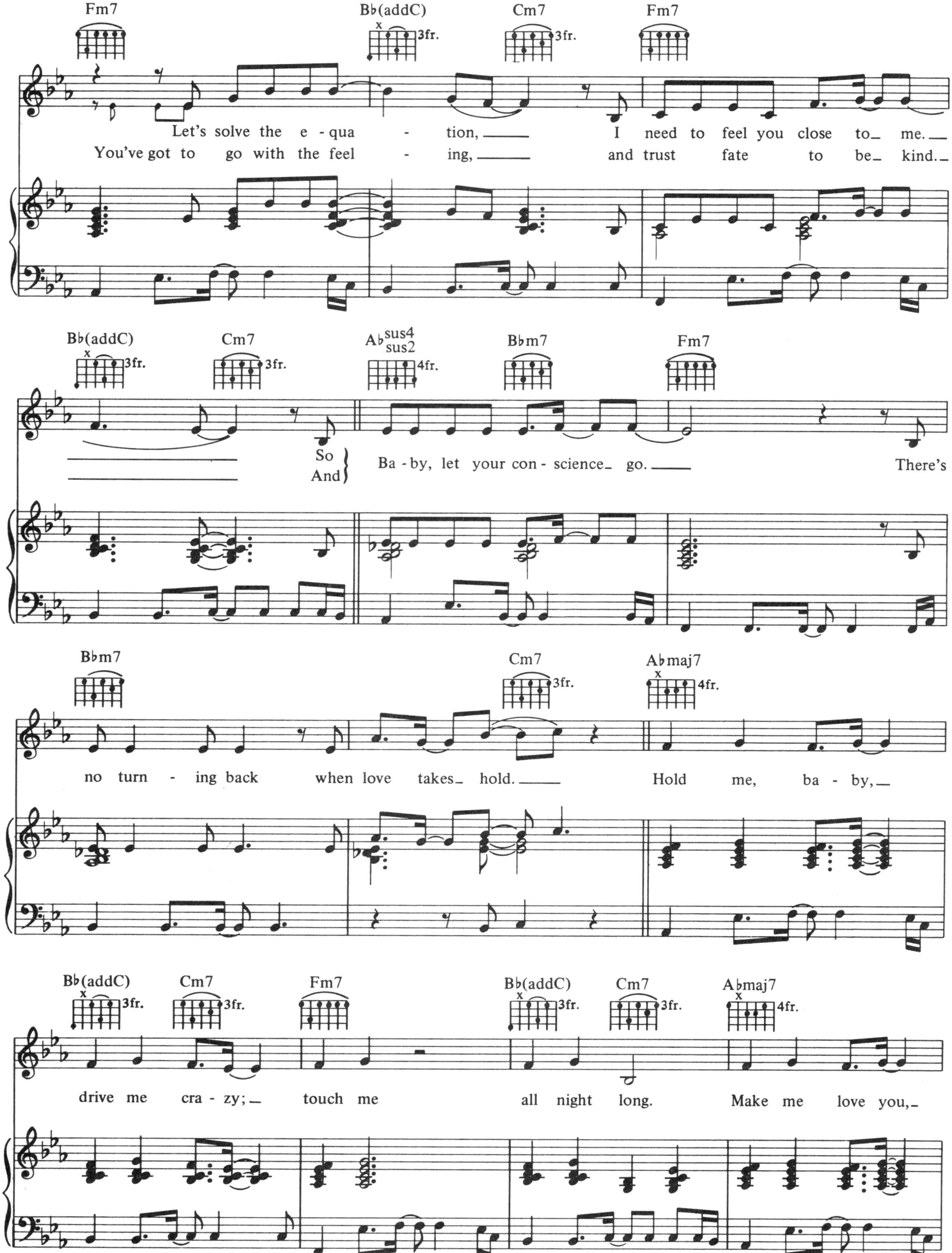

Fm7
Bb(addC)
3fr.
Cm7
3fr.
Fm7
Let's solve the e-qua - tion, I need to feel you close to me.
You've got to go with the feel - ing, and trust fate to be-kind.
Bb(addC)
3fr.
Cm7
3fr.
Ab sus4 sus2
4fr.
Bbm7
Fm7
So
And
Ba-by, let your con-science go. There's
Bbm7
Cm7
3fr.
Abmaj7
4fr.
no turn - ing back when love takes hold. Hold me, ba - by,
Bb(addC)
3fr.
Cm7
3fr.
Fm7
Bb(addC)
3fr.
Cm7
3fr.
Abmaj7
4fr.
drive me cra-zy; touch me all night long. Make me love you,

1.
B♭(addC)
Cm7
Fm7
A♭maj7
3fr.
4fr.
kiss and hug you; touch me...
all night long.
2.
No chord
Oh.
And

Ab sus4 sus2
4fr.
Bbm7
Fm7
Bbm7
ba - by, let your con - science go.
There's no turn - ing back when
Cm7
3fr.
Repeat and fade
Abmaj7
4fr.
Bb(addC)
3fr.
Cm7
3fr.
love takes hold.
Hold me, ba - by, drive me cra - zy;
Fm7
Bb(addC)
3fr.
Cm7
3fr.
Abmaj7
4fr.
touch me all night long.
Make me love you,
Bb(addC)
3fr.
Cm7
3fr.
Fm7
Bb(addC)
3fr.
Cm7
3fr.
kiss and hug you; touch me all night long.

TRUE COMPANION

Words and Music by
MARC COHN

D A E A
when it comes to love, I'm just an-oth-er fool. Yes, I'll
E A D A E A
climb a moun-tain, I'm gon-na swim the sea.
D A E A D A
There ain't no act of God, girl, could keep you
E A D A Bm/F# F#m
safe from me, My arms are reach-ing out,

Bm/F♯
F♯m
A
E9sus/A
A
E9sus/A
out a - cross this can - yon.
D
A
E
A
D
A
I'm ask - ing you to be my true com - pan - ion,
true
E
A
D
A
E
A
com - pan - ion,
true com - pan - ion.
To Coda
1.
D
A
E
A
D
A

D.S. 𝄋
2.
E
D
E
A
D
A
true com - pan - ion.
cresc.
ff
E
A
D
A
E
D
D
A
E
A
D
A
dim.
E
D
D.S. 𝄋 al Coda

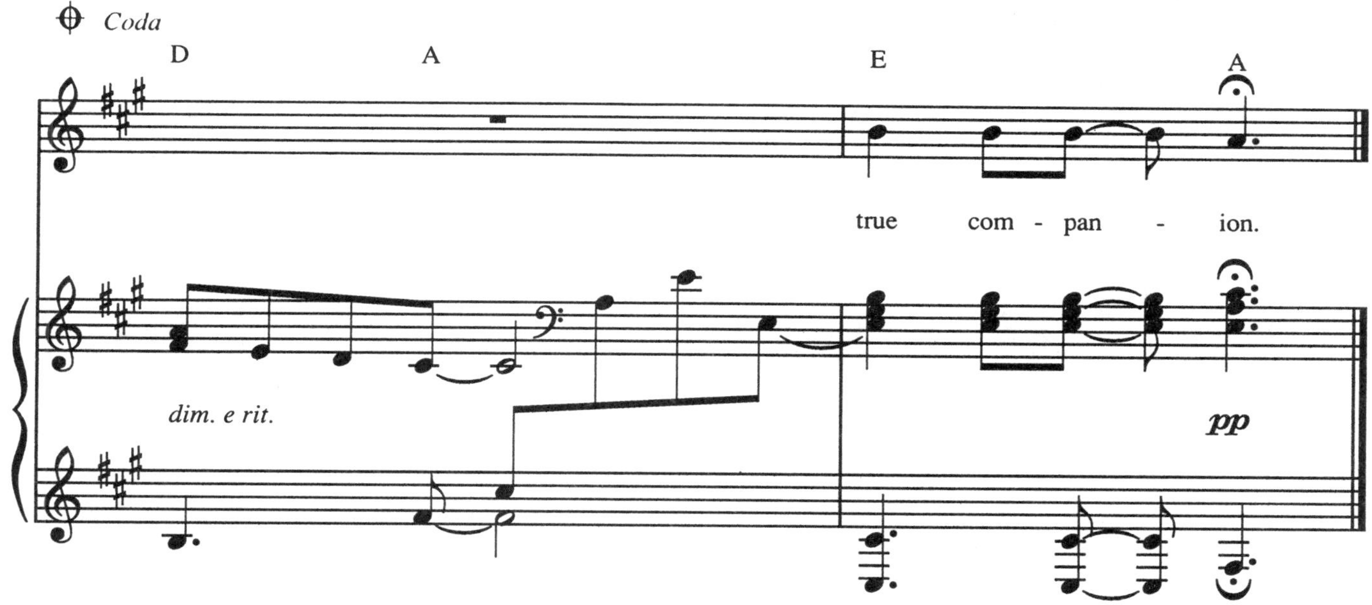

Verse 2:
So don't you dare and try to walk away;
I've got my heart set on our wedding day.
I've got this vision of a girl in white,
Made my decision that it's you all right.
And when I take your hand,
I'll watch my heart set sail.
I'll take my trembling fingers
And I'll lift up your veil.
Then I'll take you home,
And with wild abandon
Make love to you just like a true companion.
You are my true companion.
I got a true companion,
Woah, a true companion.

Verse 3:
When the years have done irreparable harm,
I can see us walking slowly arm in arm,
Just like that couple on the corner do,
'Cause girl I will always be in love with you.
And when I look in your eyes,
I'll still see that spark,
Until the shadows fall,
Until the room grows dark.
Then when I leave this earth,
I'll be with the angels standin';
I'll be out there waiting for my true companion,
Just for my true companion.
True companion,
True companion.

TRY A LITTLE TENDERNESS

Words and Music by
HARRY WOODS, JIMMY CAMPBELL
and REG. CONNELLY

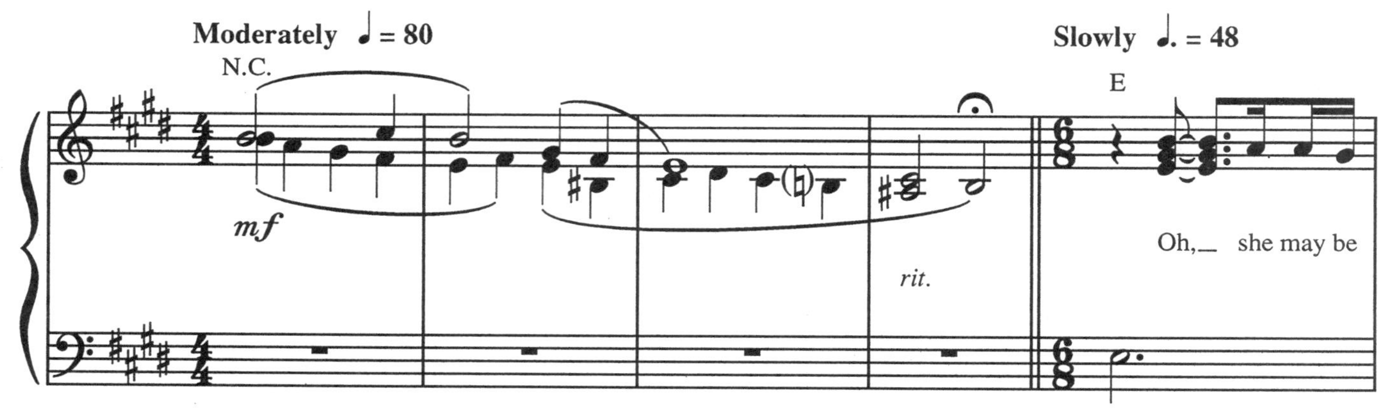

Moderately ♩ = 102
F♯m7
B7
E
C♯m
F♯m
You know she's wait - ing, just an -
B7
E
D
tic - i - pat - in' the things that she nev - er, nev - er, nev -
C♯7
F♯m
er, nev - er pos-sess-es, yeah.
But while she's there wait - ing,
3
B7
E
A
E
try a lit-tle ten-der - ness.
That's all you got-ta do.
E7
A
G♯7
It's not just sen-ti - men-tal, no.
3
3

C♯m F♯7
She had her grief and her care, yeah.

A G♯
But for soft words we all spoke so gen - tle, it makes it eas -

F♯7 F♯m7 B B+
- i - er, eas - i - er to bear, yeah.

E C♯m7 F♯m B
You won't re-gret it, no, no. Young girls, they nev-er for-get it.

E D
Love is their on - ly hap-pi - ness. But it's all

F#m7
B7
so eas - y,
all you got - ta
do is try a lit - tle

E/G#
C#
ten-der - ness,
yeah.

F#m7 E/G# A A#dim7 B B# C# D D#
Squeeze her, tease her, nev-er leave her, you got to, you got to, you got to, you got to try a lit-tle

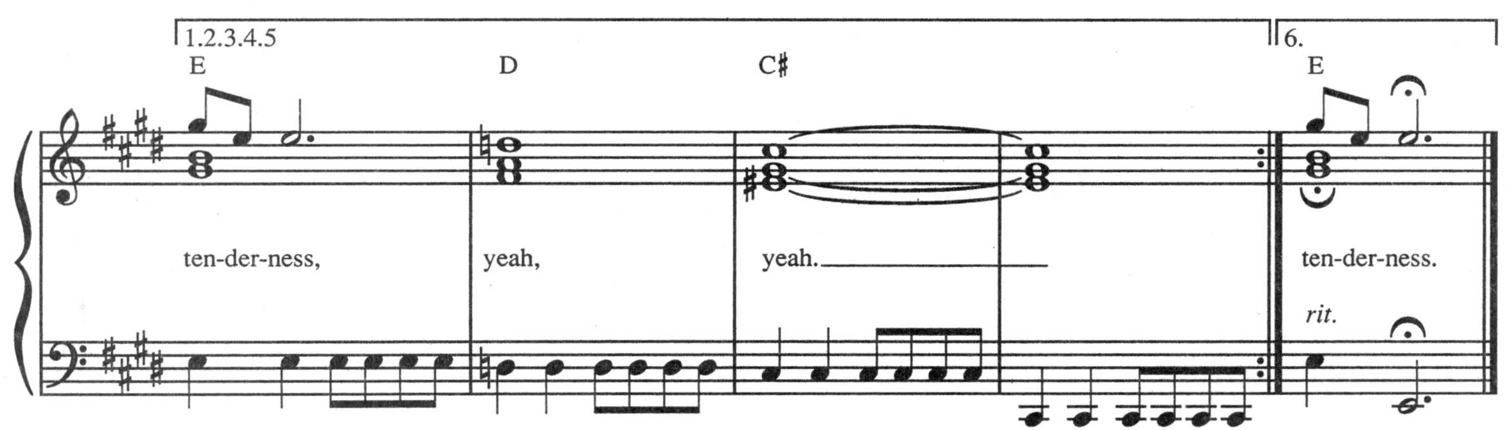
1.2.3.4.5
6.
E D C# E
ten-der-ness, yeah, yeah.
ten-der-ness.
rit.

U CAN'T TOUCH THIS

Words and Music by
RICK JAMES, ALONZO MILLER
and M.C. HAMMER

G
Am
D
Am
G
Am
su-per-dope home boy from the "Oak" town. And I'm
known
as such, and
this is a beat, uh,
U can't touch.
D
Am
G
Am
D
Am
I told U
home boy,
U can't touch this.
Yeah, that's how we're livin'
G
Am
D
Am
G
Am
and U know,
U can't touch this.
Look in my eyes,
man,
U can't touch this.
1. 2.
3. 4. 5. 6.
D
Am
G
Am
G
Am
Here, let me bust
the funky lyrics,
U can't touch this.
Break it down.
Bridge:
D7
Oh,
oh.

Verse 2:

Fresh new kicks and pants.
U got it like that now U know U wanna dance.
So, move out of your seat and get a fly girl and
catch this beat - while it's rollin'.
Hold on, pump a little bit
and let them know it's going on like that.
Like that cold on a mission, so fall on back.
Let 'em know that you're too much
and this is a beat U can't touch.

Chorus 2:

Yo! I told U,
U can't touch this.
Why U standin' there man?
U can't touch this.
Yo, sound the bells, school is in sucker,
U can't touch this.

Verse 3:

Give me a song, or rhythm
making 'em sweat. That's what I'm giving 'em.
Now they know U talk about the Hammer,
you're talking about a show that's hyped.
And tight singers are sweating so pass them a wipe,
or a tape to learn; what it is going to take
in the "90's" to burn the charts.
Legit. Either work hard or U might as well quit.
(To Chorus)

Verse 4:

Go with the flow. It is said
that if U can't groove to this, then U probably are dead.
So wave, your hands in the air.
Bust a few moves. Run your fingers through your hair.
This is it for a winner,
dance to this an you're gonna get thinner.
Move. Slide your rump. Just for a minute, let's all do the bump.
Bump, bump.
(To Chorus)

Verse 5:

Everytime U see me, the Hammer's just so hyped.
I'm dope on the floor. And I'm magic on the mic.
Now why would I ever stop doing this?
When others making records that just don't hit.
I've toured around the world from London to the Bay.
It's Hammer, go Hammer, M.C. Hammer, yo Hammer,
and the rest can go and play.
(To Chorus)

UNTIL YOU COME BACK TO ME
(That's What I'm Gonna Do)

Words and Music by
STEVIE WONDER, MORRIS BROADNAX
and CLARENCE PAUL

Moderate shuffle ♩ = 88
Amaj7
C/D
Gmaj7
mf

Verse:
Amaj7
C/D
1. Though you don't
call an - y - more,
I sit and wait

Gmaj7
Amaj7
in vain.
I guess I'll
rap on your door, (your door)

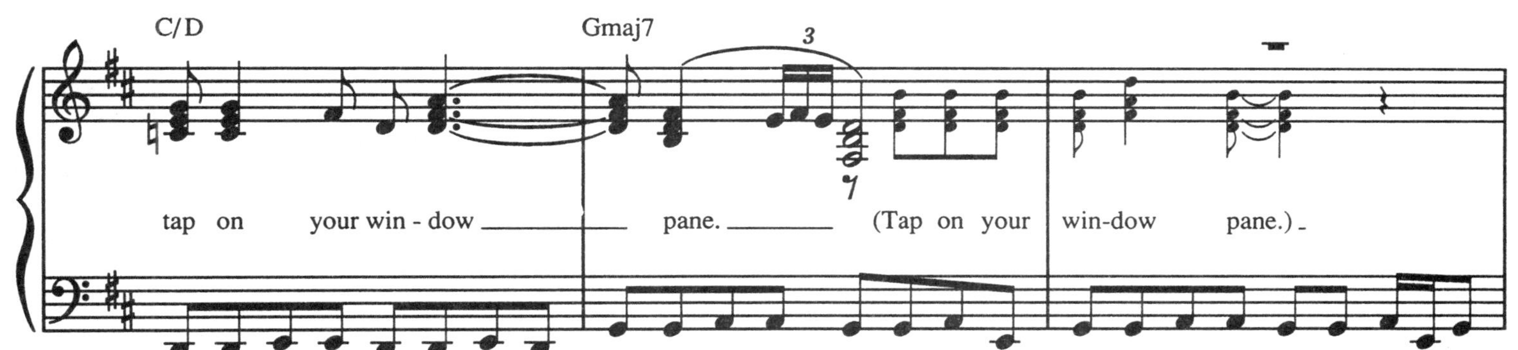
C/D
Gmaj7
3
tap on your win - dow
pane.
(Tap on your
win-dow pane.)

Em7
A7
I want to tell you ba - by, the chang - es I've been go - ing through
F#m7(♭5)
B7(♭9)
miss - ing you. Lis - ten you.
Chorus:
Em7
A11
Dmaj7
To Coda
Til you come back to me, that's what I'm gon - na do.
1.
D.S.
2.
To Next Strain
3. 4.
(4th time To Coda)
Dm7/G
G13
2. Why did you
Bridge:
Dm7
G7
Liv - ing for you my dear is like liv - ing in a world

Verse 2:
Why did you have to decide
You had to set me free?
I'm going to swallow my pride, (my pride)
And beg you to please see me.
(Baby won't you see me?)
I'm going to walk by myself
Just to prove that my love is true;
All for you baby.
(To Chorus:)

Verse 3:
Although your phone you ignore,
Somehow I must, somehow I must,
How I must explain.
I'm gonna rap on your door,
Tap on your window pane.
(Tap on your window pane.)
I'm gonnna camp on your steps
Until I get through to you;
I've got to change your view, baby.
(To Chorus:)

WALKING IN MEMPHIS

Words and Music by
MARC COHN

*chord symbols in parentheses indicate implied harmony

(Am)
(F)
(G)
(C)
(Am)
(F)
Del - ta Blues_ in the mid-dle of the pour - ing rain.___
(G)
(C)
(Am)
(F)
(G)
(C)
W.________ C. Han - dy, won't you look down o - ver me?_
(dou - ble u____)
(Am)
(F)
(G)
(C)
(Am)
(F)
_ Yeah,__ I got a first class___ tick - et, but I'm as
Chorus:
(G)
C
Am
F
G
C
blue as a boy__ can be.____ Then I'm walk-ing in Mem - phis,

**implied harmony with no bass

(G7sus)
(C/G)
(G7sus)
to the gates of Grace - land,
then I watched him walk_ right through._
(C/G)
F2
G7sus
C
Am
_ Now, se - cu - ri - ty, they did not_ see him.
They just
F2
G7sus
C
Am
F2
G7sus
hov - ered 'round his_ tomb._
But there's a pret - ty lit - tle thing_ wait -
C
Am
F
N.C.
C
3
3
ing for the King,_ down in the Jun - gle_Room.
When I was walk - ing in Mem -

Chorus:
F G C Am F G C
- phis, I was walk-ing with my feet ten feet off of Beale.
Am F G C Am
Walk-ing in Mem - phis, but do I real - ly
F G C7sus C7 C7sus C7
feel the way I feel? They've got
mp
dim.
mp
Bridge:
C7sus C7 C7sus C7
cat-fish on the ta - ble. They've got

C7sus
C7
C7sus
C7
gos - pel in the air.
And Rev - er - end Green
Rubato - vocal ad lib.
E7
F7
F♯dim7
be glad to see you when you have - n't got a
Rubato
G7 C/G G7 N.C.
(F)
(G)
(C)
prayer.
But boy you got a prayer in Mem - phis...
a tempo
a tempo
(Am)
(F)
(G)
(C)
(Am)
(F)
Now,

Verse:
(G) (C) (Am) (F) (G) (C)
Mu - ri - el plays pi - a - no ev - ery Fri - day at the Hol - ly - wood.
(Am) (F) (G) (C) (Am) (F)
3
And they brought me down to see her, and they
(G) (C) (Am) F2 G7sus C
asked me if I would do a lit - tle num -
mf
cresc.
mf
Am7 F2 G7sus C Am7
- ber. And I sang with all my might. She said,

F2
G7sus
C
Am7
F2
3
N.C.
"Tell_ me, are you a Christ - ian, child?"_ And I___ said, "Ma'am, I am_______
cresc.
f
Chorus:
C
F
G
C
Am
to-night." Walk-ing in Mem - phis, I was walk-ing with my
F
G
C
Am
F
G
C
feet ten feet___ off of Beale.___ Walk-ing in Mem - phis,
1.
Am
F
C/E
Dm
C
Am
but do I real - ly feel the way__ I feel?___ Walk - ing in Mem -

2.
F G Csus (G) (C) (Am) (F)
feel the way I feel?
(G) (C) (Am) (F) (G) (C)
Put on my blue
(Am) (F) (G) (C) (Am) (F)
suede shoes and I board-ed the plane. Touched down
(G) (C) (Am) (F) (G) (C)
in the land of the Del - ta Blues in the mid-dle of the pour - ing rain.
dim.

(Am)
(F)
(G)
(C)
Am
— Touched down in the land of the Del - ta Blues in the
mp
rit.
mp
rit.
F
G
(F)
(G)
(C)
(Am)
(F)
mid-dle of the pour - ing rain.
a tempo
a tempo
(G)
(C)
(Am)
(F)
(G)
(C)
(Am)
F
G
C
dim. e rit.
p

THE WAY YOU DO THE THINGS YOU DO

Chorus:
A♭
E♭
D♭
per - fume.
school book.
Well you could have
been an - y-thing that you wan-ted to, I can

E♭
D♭
N.C.
To Coda
A♭
D♭/A♭
tell.
The way you do the things you
do.
The way you do the things you

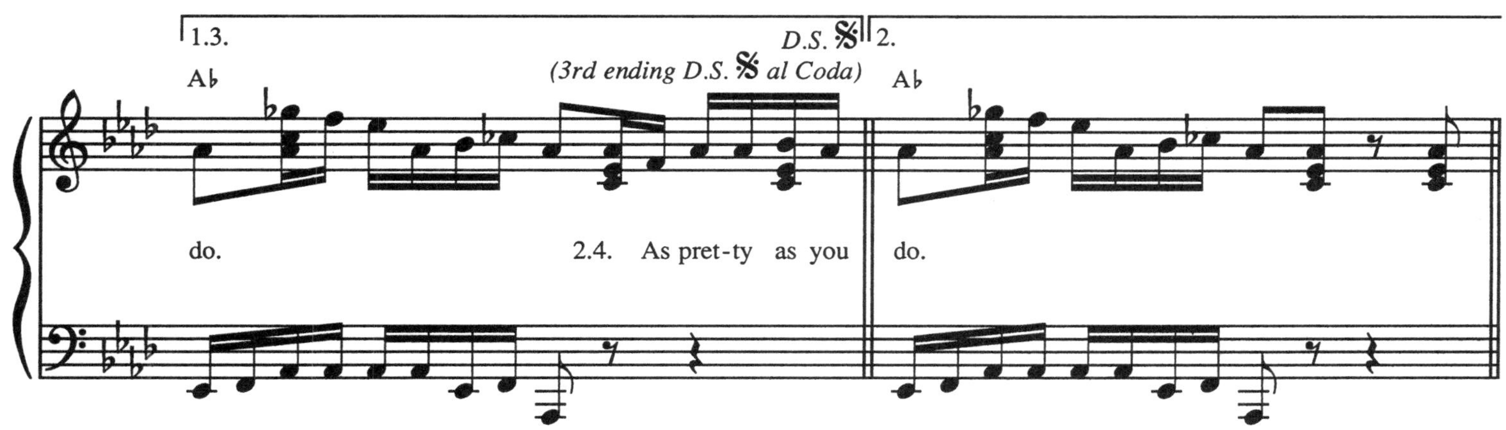
1.3.
D.S.
(3rd ending D.S. al Coda)
2.
A♭
do.
2.4. As pret-ty as you
A♭
do.

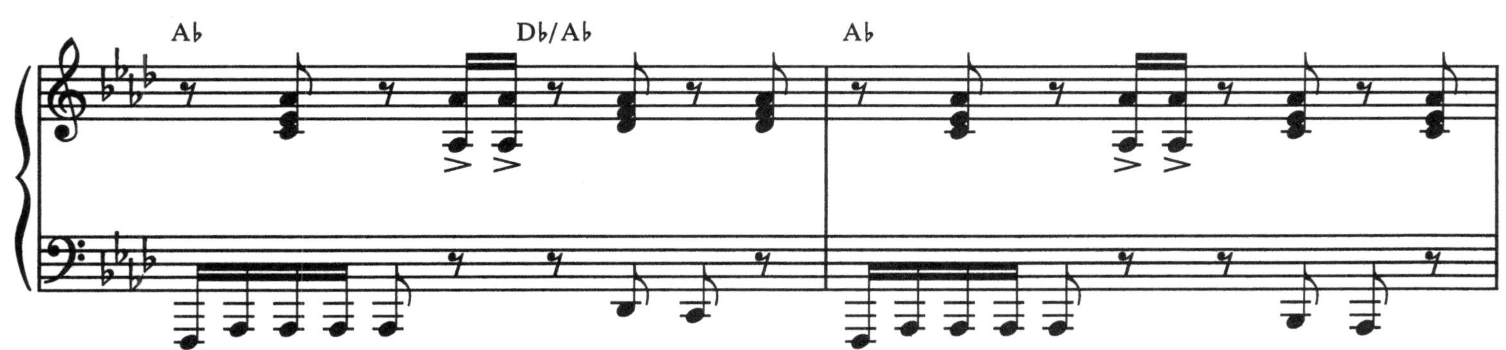
A♭
D♭/A♭
A♭

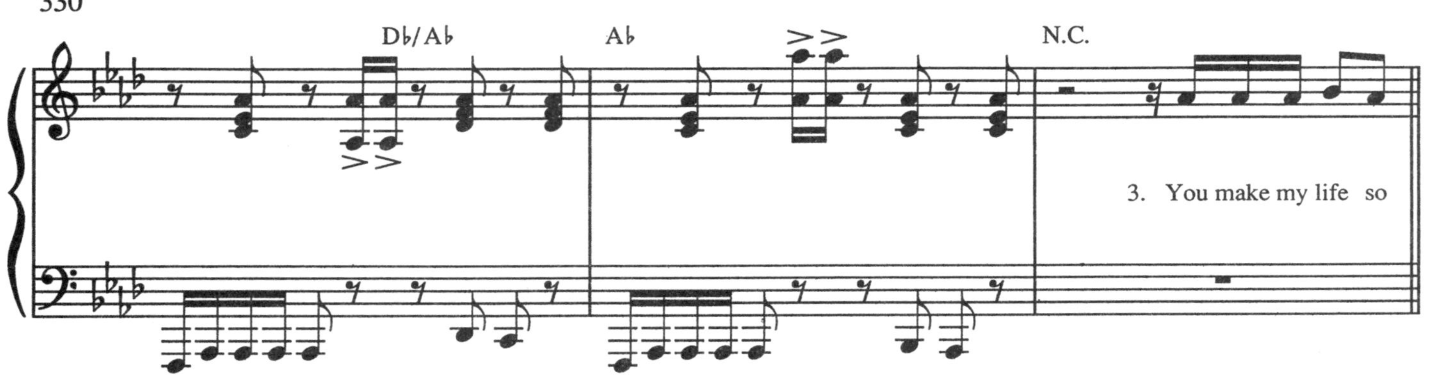
Db/Ab
Ab
N.C.
3. You make my life so

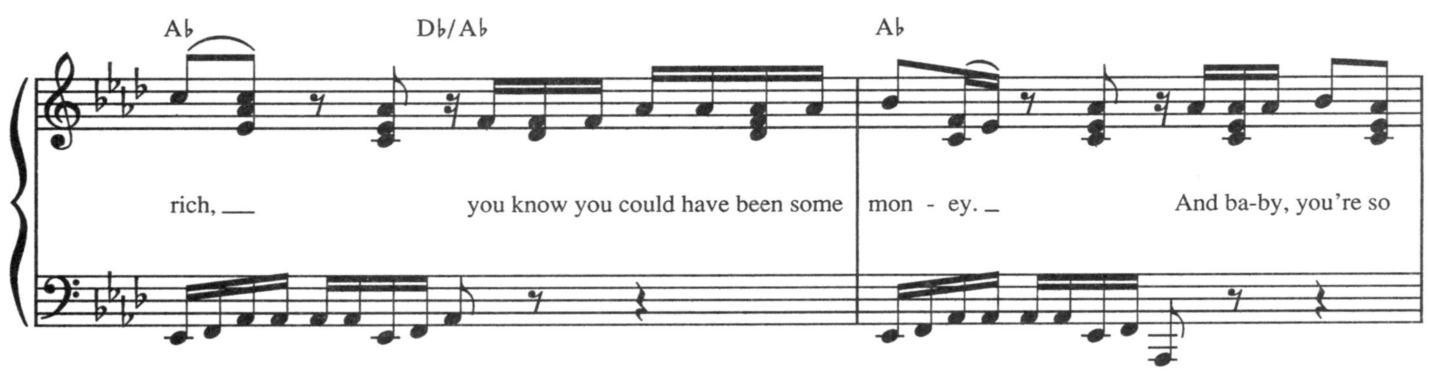
Ab
Db/Ab
Ab
rich, you know you could have been some
mon - ey.
And ba-by, you're so

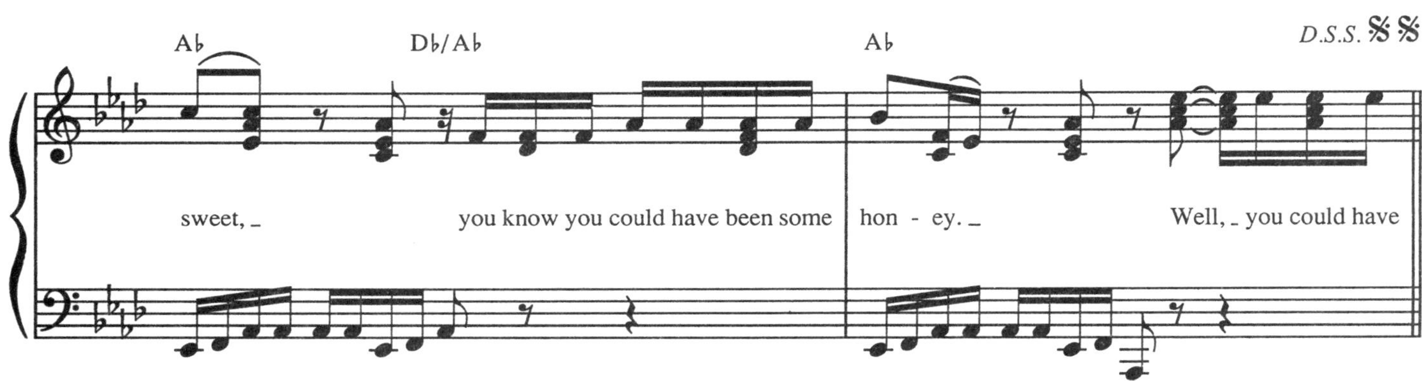
Ab
Db/Ab
Ab
D.S.S.
sweet, you know you could have been some
hon - ey.
Well, you could have

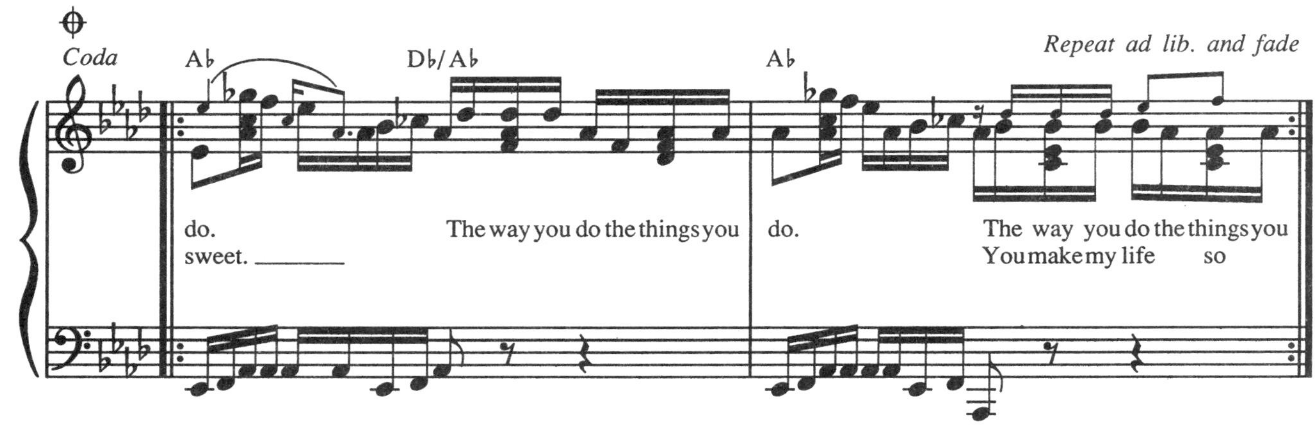
Coda
Ab
Db/Ab
Ab
Repeat ad lib. and fade
do. The way you do the things you
sweet.
do. The way you do the things you
You make my life so

WHAT BECOMES OF THE BROKEN-HEARTED

Words and Music by
JAMES DEAN, PAUL RISER
and WILLIAM WEATHERSPOON

Chorus:
F♯m
C♯7/G♯
G7(♯11)
B
filled with sad - ness
and con - fu - sion.
What be-comes of the
D♯m/A♯
G♯m
E
bro - ken-heart - ed
who had love that's
now de - part - ed?
B
D♯m/A♯
G♯m
B/F♯
D♯7
E/B
F♯m7/C♯
B
I know I've got to find
some kind of peace of mind.
Help me, please.
A
C♯m
F♯m
2. The roots of love grow
all a - round,
but for me they come
D
A
D♯dim7
tum - bl - in' down.
Ev - ery day, heart - aches
grow a lit - tle stron - ger,

Verse 3:
I walk in shadows, searching for light,
Cold and alone, no comfort in sight.
Hoping and praying for someone who cares,
Always movin', but goin' nowhere.
(To Chorus:)

Verse 4:
Instrumental solo
(To Verse 5:)

Verse 5:
I'm searching though I don't succeed, no.
For someone's love, there's a growing need.
All is lost, there's no place for beginnning,
And all that's left is an unhappy ending.
(To Chorus:)

WHEN SOMETHING IS WRONG WITH MY BABY

Moderately slow

Words and Music by
ISAAC HAYES and
DAVID PORTER

Em Fm — A7 B♭7

She: We've been through so much to - geth - er.

Em Fm — F7 G♭7

We stand as one, that's what makes it bet - ter.

C/G D♭/A♭ — Dm7 E♭m7

f

Both: When some - thing is wrong with my ba - by,

C/G D♭/A♭ — F G♭ — 1. C D♭ — F/G G♭/A♭ — G A♭ — 2. C D♭ — N.C.

some - thing is wrong with me. me.

Additional Lyrics

2. *He:* Just what she means to me now,
Oh, you just wouldn't understand.
People can say that she's no good,
But ah, she's my woman and I know I'm her man.
She: And if he's got a problem,
Oh, I know I got to help him solve 'em.
Both: When something is wrong with my baby,
Something is wrong with me.

YER SO BAD

Words and Music by
TOM PETTY and
JEFF LYNNE

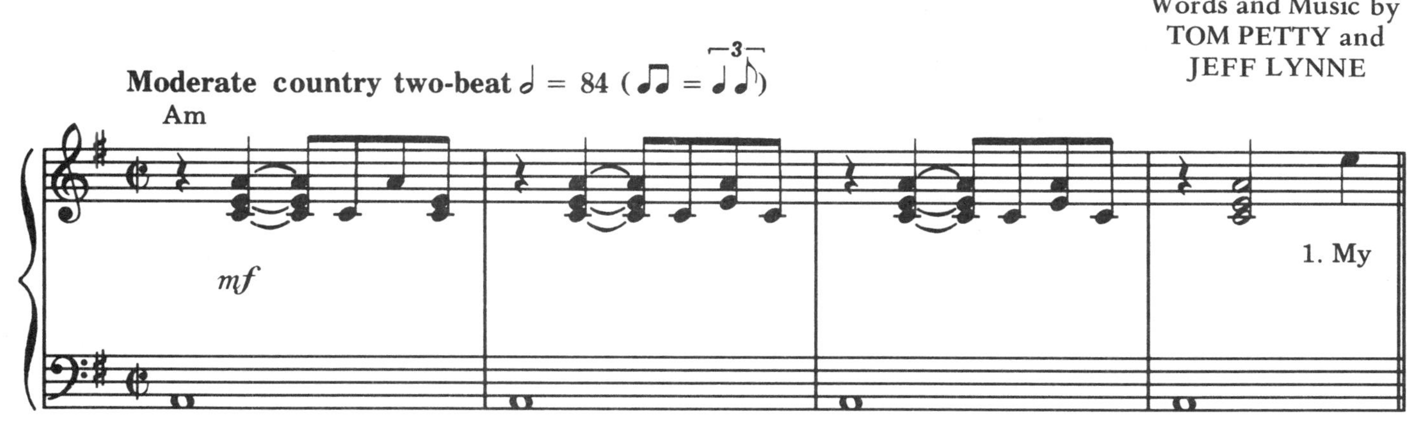
Moderate country two-beat ♩ = 84
Am
mf
1. My

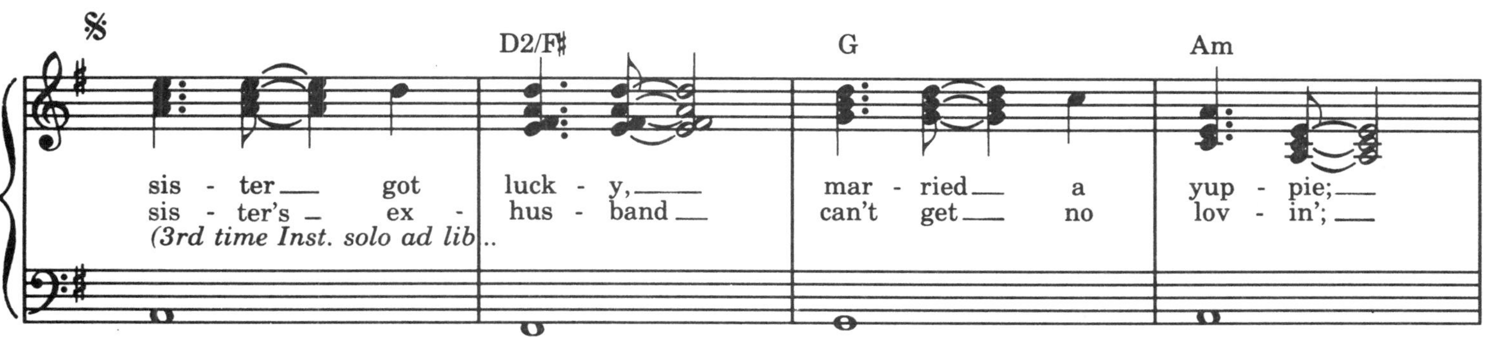
D2/F♯
G
Am
sis - ter got luck - y, mar - ried a yup - pie;
sis - ter's ex - hus - band can't get no lov - in';
(3rd time Inst. solo ad lib..

D2/F♯
G
took him for all he was worth.
walks 'round dog faced and hurt.

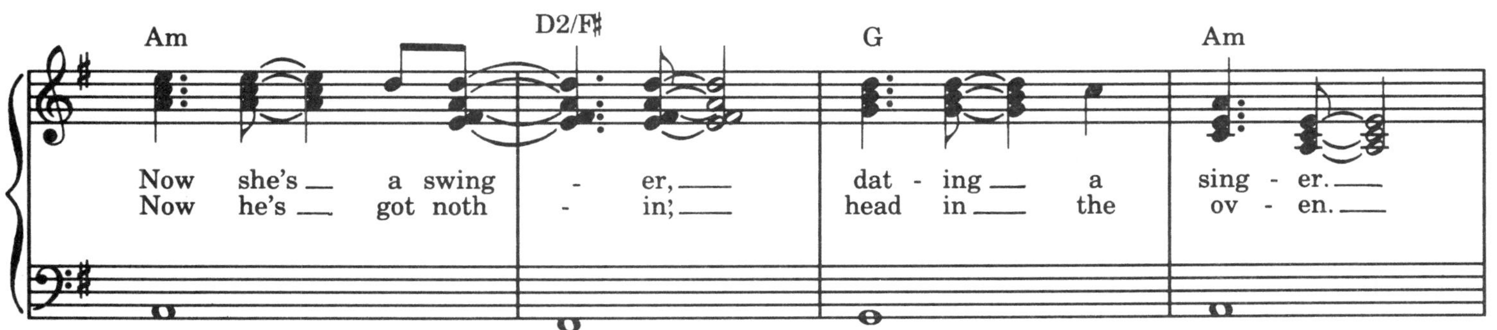
Am
D2/F♯
G
Am
Now she's a swing - er, dat - ing a sing - er.
Now he's got noth - in'; head in the ov - en.

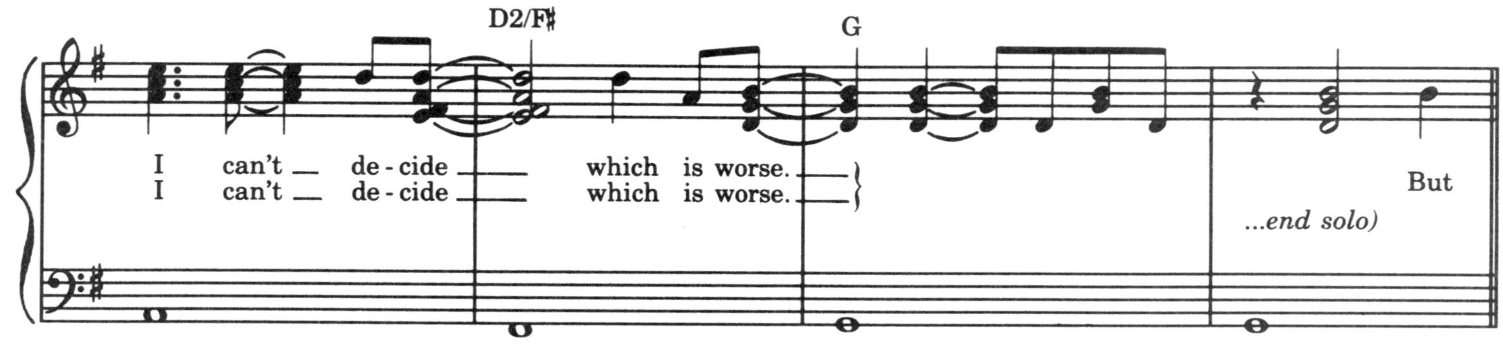
D2/F♯
G
I can't de-cide which is worse.
I can't de-cide which is worse.
But
...end solo)

Em
C
G
D
Em
C
not me ba - by. I've got you to

G
D
Chorus:
G
D
C
save me. Oh, yer so bad;

G
D
C
best thing I ev-er had. In a

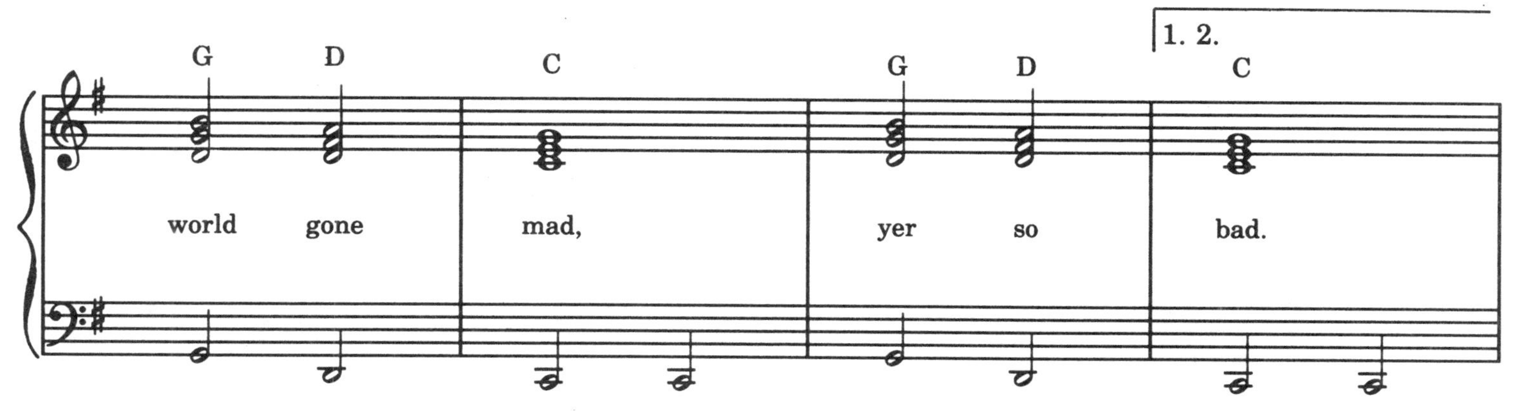
1. 2.
G
D
C
G
D
C
world gone mad, yer so bad.

D
D. S.
3.
C
2. My bad.

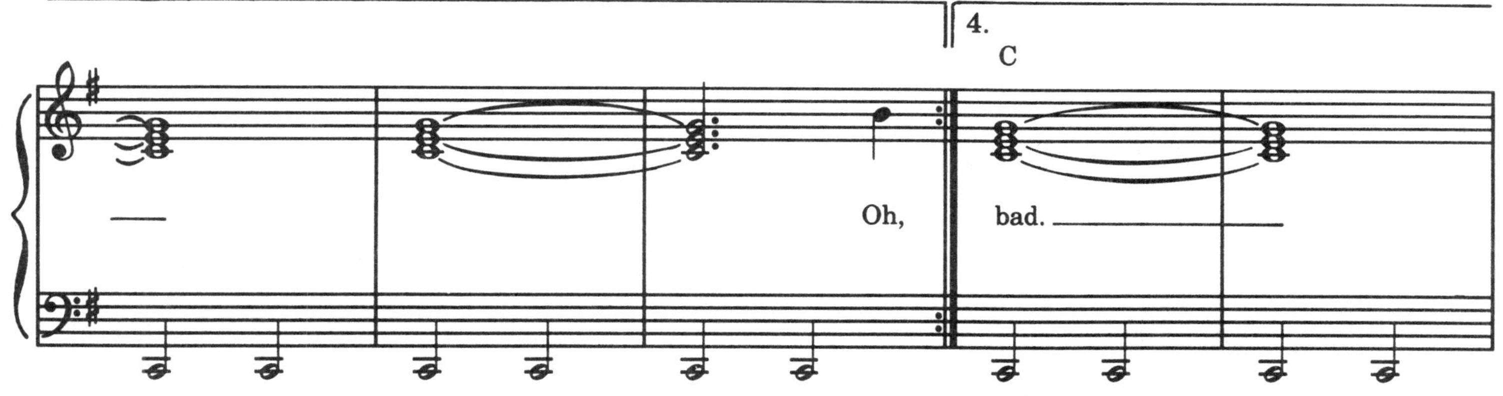
4.
C
Oh, bad.

D
G
C
G

MY GIRL

Words and Music by
WILLIAM "SMOKEY" ROBINSON
and RONALD WHITE

Moderate rock ♩ = 108

N.C.

mp

mf

Verse:

C F

1. I've got sun - shine on a cloud - y

C F C F

day. When it's cold out - side, I've got the

Chorus:

C F 𝄋 C Dm F G

month of May. I guess you say,

C Dm F G C

what can make me feel this way? My girl. *(My girl, my girl.)* Talk-ing 'bout

To Coda Φ *Verse:*

Dm C/G G7 N.C. Dm G7 C F

my girl. My Girl! 2. I've got so much hon - ey the bees en-vy

C F C

me. I've got a sweet-er song

D.S. 𝄋 *al Coda*

F C F

than the birds in the tree. Well,

Φ *Coda*

C/D G7/D N.C. Dm7 G7 N.C.

My girl!

C
F
C
F
Dm
G
G/F
Em
A
3. I don't_
D
need no___ mon - ey,___
G
for - tune or
D
fame._
G
I got
D
all___ the rich - es, ba - by

G D G

one man can claim. Well,

D Em G A D Em

I guess you say, what can make me

G A D

feel this way? My girl. *(My girl, my girl.)* Talk-ing 'bout

Em D/A A7 G F♯m A/E Dmaj7

my girl. My girl! Talk-ing 'bout my girl.

Em7 A G F♯m A/E

Repeat ad lib. and fade

Talk-ing 'bout

A WORLD OF OUR OWN
(From RETURN TO THE BLUE LAGOON)

Words and Music by
BARRY MANN, BERNARD JACKSON
and CYNTHIA WEIL

C D G Cmaj7 D/F♯ G Am7
geth - er.
ev - er.
So, just close your eyes and let me take you there, to
G/B C(2) Bm7 G/B
some-where on - ly dream-er's ev - er go.
It won't be
Am D7/F♯ G/B C G/B
just a fan - ta - sy, oh no, if you be - lieve with me, the
Am7 Am7/D G(2) G
two of us all a - lone in a world of our own.
A world of our
cresc.
f
Chorus:
Bm7 Em7 Am7 C/D D/C
own where we know we be - long. A world of our

Bm7
Em7
Am7
C/D
B/D♯
own
where
love this sure and strong can nev - er die
Em7
Em/D
To Coda
1.
C(2)
C/D
and
lov - ers nev - er say
"Good-bye".
G(2)
D.S.
2.
C(2)
C/D
dim.
mf
lov-ers nev - er say
"Good-bye".
G(2)
Bridge:
Bm7
So,
wrap your arms a - round me
and we'll

C(2)
C
Bm7
leave it all__ be - hind._ We'll go where no - one else__ will ev - er find__
C
D
Am
D/F♯
— us.
Instrumental solo . . .
G/B
C
Am7
G/B
We can make it come___ true_ just by lov-ing each oth-er,___ the
. . . end solo
C
C/D
G(2)
G
D.S.S. al Coda
two of us__ all a - lone__ in a world all__ our own.__ A world all our
Coda
C
C/D
G(2)
you and I__ won't ev - er say__ "Good-bye."___
rit.
dim.
mp
dim.
p

IF YOU GO

Words and Music by
JON SECADA and
MIGUEL A. MOREJON

G(2) A Bm7

as I go, baby, without taking you

G(2) A

along for a ride.

Bridge 1:

Gmaj9 A Gmaj9

Tried to find myself, tried to find the truth, get out from this shell.

A Gmaj9 A Gmaj9

Girl, I'm almost there to show you how much I real-

cresc.

Chorus:

A D A

ly care. If you go, say, "Goodbye." There'll be some-

mf

Em
Bm
A/C#
D
- thing miss - ing in my life. 'Cause you know that
Bm7
Cmaj7
1.
Gmaj7
A
D.S.
all I real - ly want is you.
(is you.)
2.
Gmaj7
A
Bridge 3:
Bm7
Gmaj9
Tried to find my - self, tried to find the truth,
A
Gmaj7
get out from this shell. Girl, I'm al - most there,
A
Gmaj7
A
N.C.
so let me show you, so let me show you. If you go,

Verse 2:
Sorry, if you felt misled,
But I know what I feel, I know what I said, baby.
God, I hope you believe, believe in all that we can be,
The future in us together in love.

Bridge 2:
You're the reason I'm strong.
Don't you think I don't know
This is where I belong?
Give me the time
To say that you're mine, to say that you're mine.
(To Chorus:)

WHEN THE NIGHT COMES

Lyrics and Music by
BRYAN ADAMS, JIM VALLANCE
& DIANE WARREN

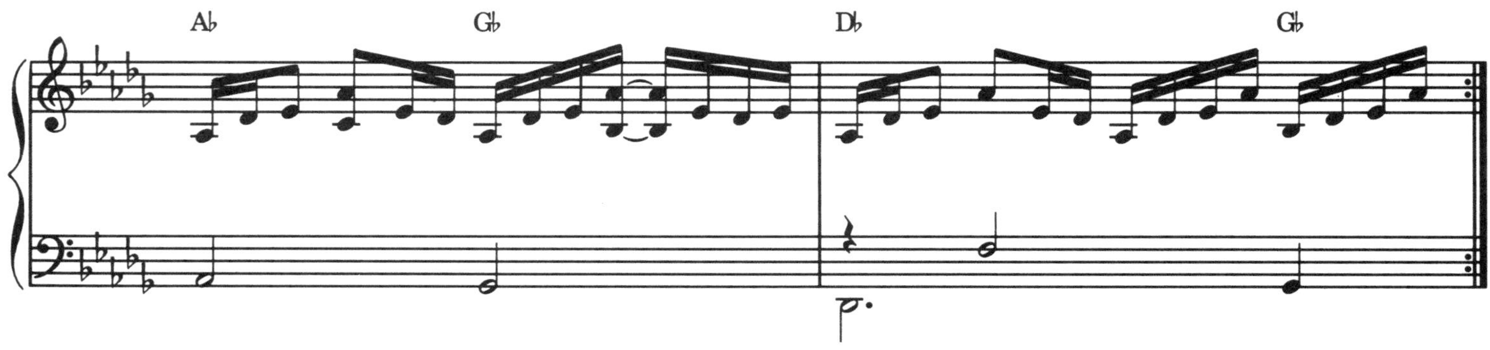

A♭
G♭
D♭
G♭
But for now, there's some-thing out there call-ing me.
So, take me down that lone-some road. Point me east and let me go.
This suit-case weighs me down with mem-o-ries. I just
cresc.
mf
D♭/E♭
Chorus:
wan-na be the one you run to, I just wan-na be the one you come to. I just
wan-na be there with some - one when the night comes. Let's

A♭
G♭
D♭
D♭/E♭
put all our cares be-hind us, and
go where they'll nev-er find us. I just
A♭
G♭
1.
D♭
wan-na be there be-side you when the
night comes, when the night comes.
D.S. 𝄋
A♭
G♭
D♭
G♭
A♭
G♭
D♭
G♭
dim.
mp
2.
To Next Strain
3.
Repeat ad lib. and fade
D♭
D♭
night comes, when the night comes.
cresc.
night comes, when the night comes. I just

Bridge:

B♭m D♭ B♭m

f

I know there'll be a time for you and I, just take my hand and run a - way.

D♭ E♭m

Pick up all the piec - es of this shat - tered dream, we're gon - na make it ours some - day.

B♭m G♭

That's when we're com - in' back, com - in' back to stay.

A♭

D.S. 𝄋

Verse 2:
Two spirits in the night,
We could leave before the morning light.
When there's nothin' left to lose,
There's nothin' left to fear.
So meet me on the edge of town.
Won't keep you waitin', I'll be 'round.
Then, you and I, we'll just roll right outa here.
To Chorus:

Verse 3: (Instrumental Solo)
To Chorus:

LOVE SNEAKIN' UP ON YOU

Words and Music by
TOM SNOW and
JIMMY SCOTT

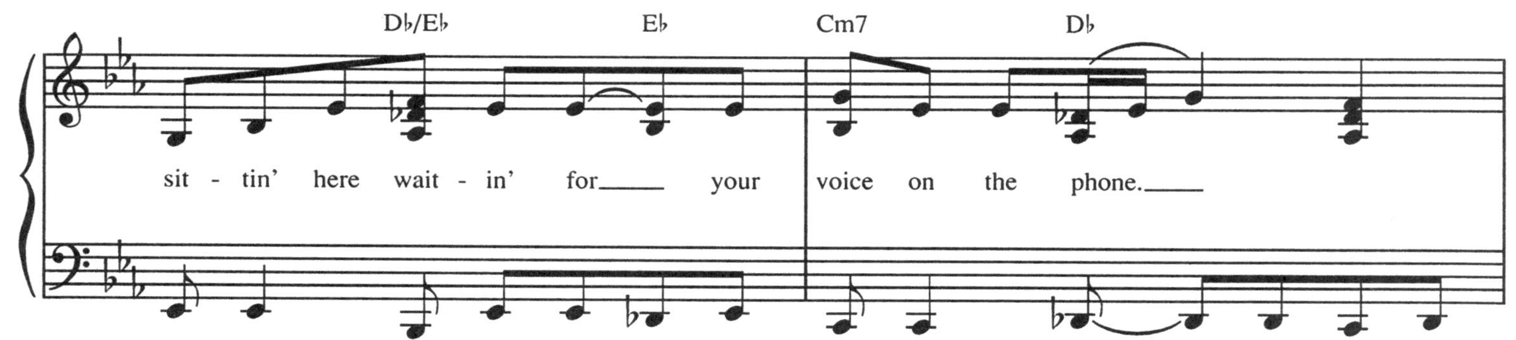

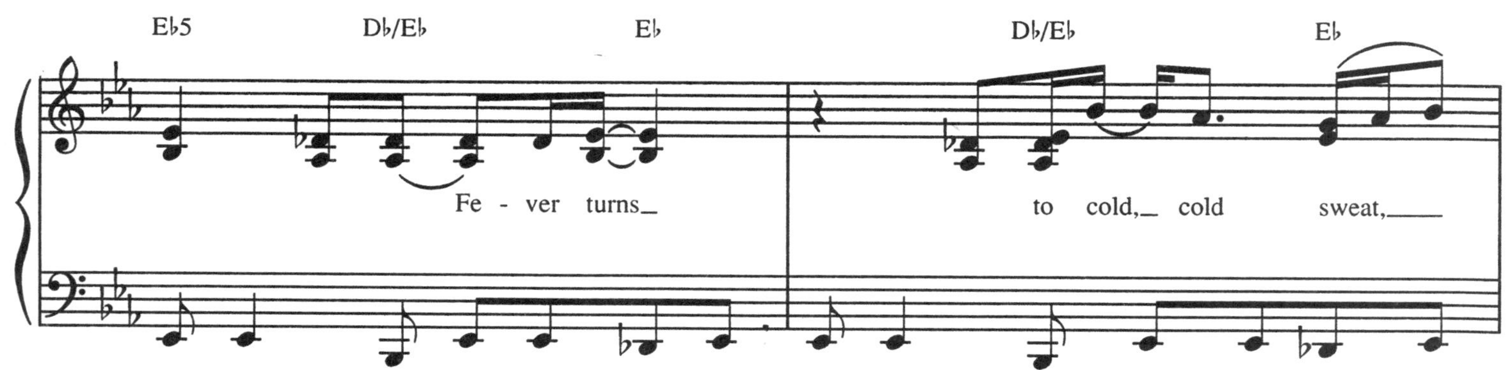

Db/Eb
Eb
Cm7
Db
think - in' a - bout things we ain't done yet.
Bridge:
G7
Tell me now, I've got to know, do you feel the same?
Bb7
Do you just light up at the men - tion of my name? Yeah.
Chorus:
Db/Eb
Eb
Db/Eb
Eb
Don't wor - ry, ba - by, it ain't noth - in' new.
Cm7
Db2
That's just love sneak - in' up on you. If your

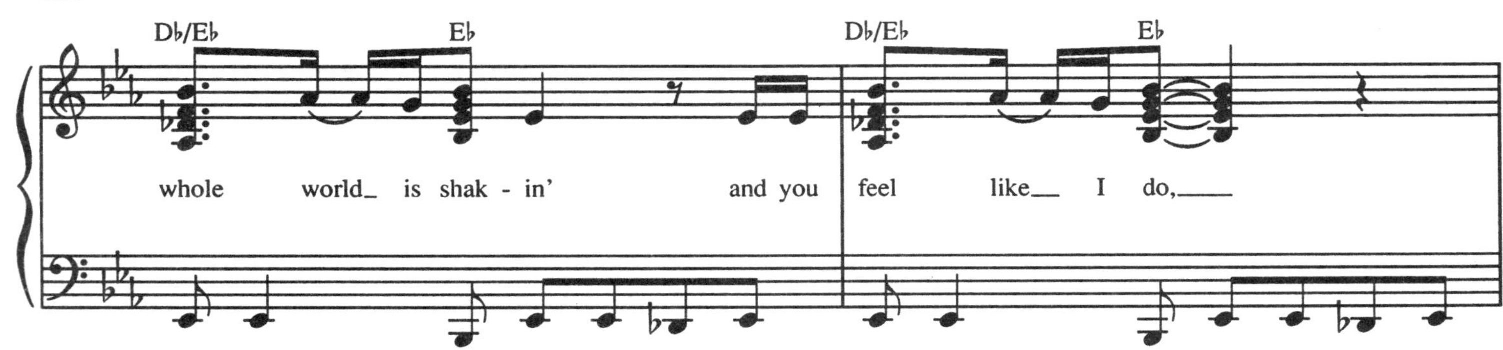

D♭/E♭
E♭
D♭/E♭
E♭
whole world_ is shak - in' and you feel like__ I do,____

1.
Cm7
D♭2
that's just love____ sneak - in' up on you.____

D.S. 𝄋
2.
To next strain
E♭5
D♭2
up on you.__

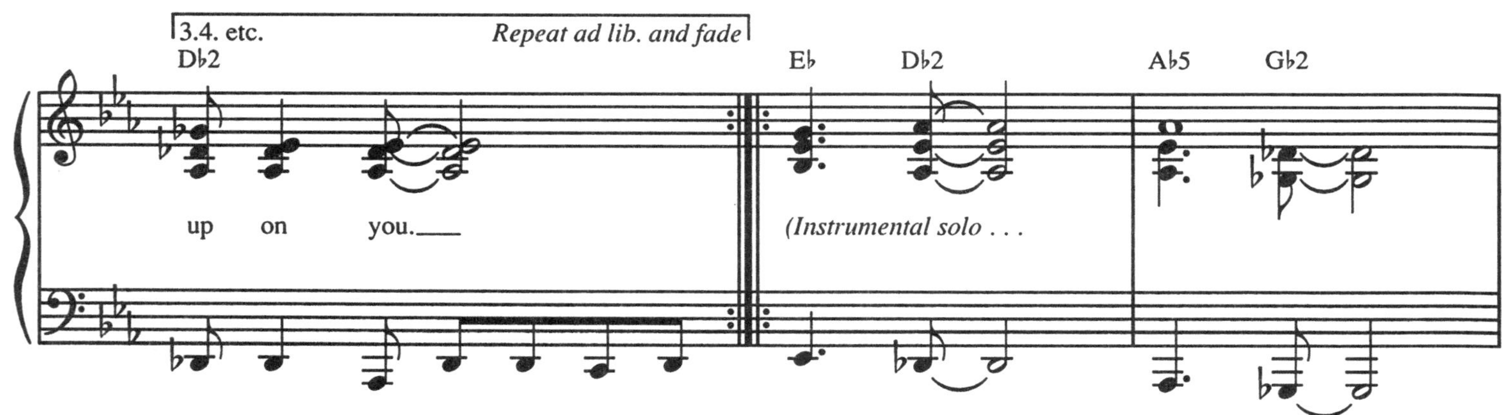

3.4. etc.
Repeat ad lib. and fade
D♭2
E♭
D♭2
A♭5
G♭2
up on you.____
(Instrumental solo . . .

Verse 2:
Nowhere on earth for your heart to hide
Once love comes sneakin' up on your blind side.
And you might as well try to stop the rain
Or stand in the tracks of a runaway train.

Bridge 2:
You just can't fight it when a thing's meant to be.
So, come on, let's finish what you started with me.
(To Chorus:)

I APOLOGIZE

Words and Music by ANITA BAKER,
BARRY J. EASTMOND & GORDON CHAMBERS

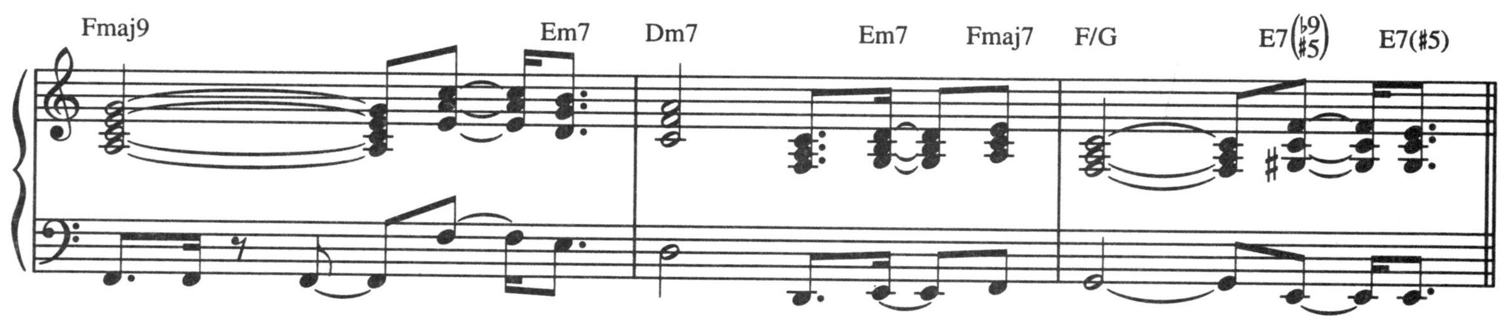

*Recorded Key: B major
**Vocal sung one octave lower than written.

G/A
Am
just the oth - er night we had a
G/A
Am
hor - ri - ble fight. I ad -
Dm7
mit that I, I was out
F
G
of con - trol, oh but I
G/A
Am7
still love my man with my
G/B
C
bod - y and soul. Well,
Fmaj7
the road gets rough, you say
E7(♭9 ♯5)
E7(♯5)
things you should not say.
Dm7
I nev - er meant to treat my
Dm7/G
ba - by that way. I a-pol-o-gize,
Chorus:
Am9
C9
woh, be - lieve me I do. I
Fmaj7
E7(♯5)
a-pol-o-gize
Am9
C13
hon -

Fmaj7
E7(♭9 ♯5)
Am9
C13
- est and true. Be-cause I
know I was wrong and so I

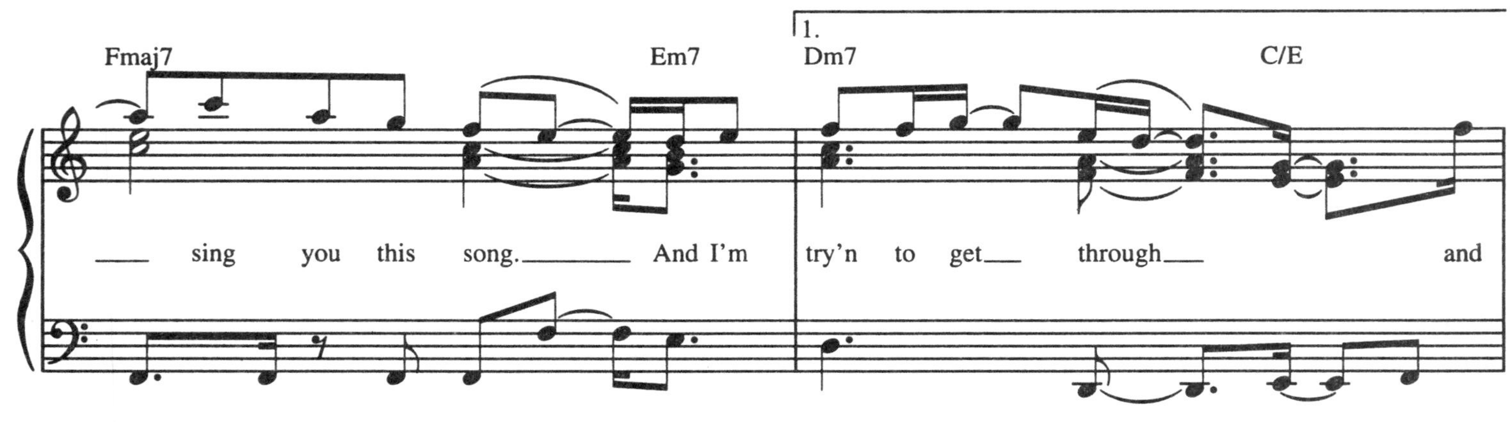
Fmaj7
Em7
1.
Dm7
C/E
sing you this song. And I'm
try'n to get through and

Dm7/G
E7(♯5)
2.
Dm7
C/E
make it up to you, yeah.
gon - na get through to you and I'll

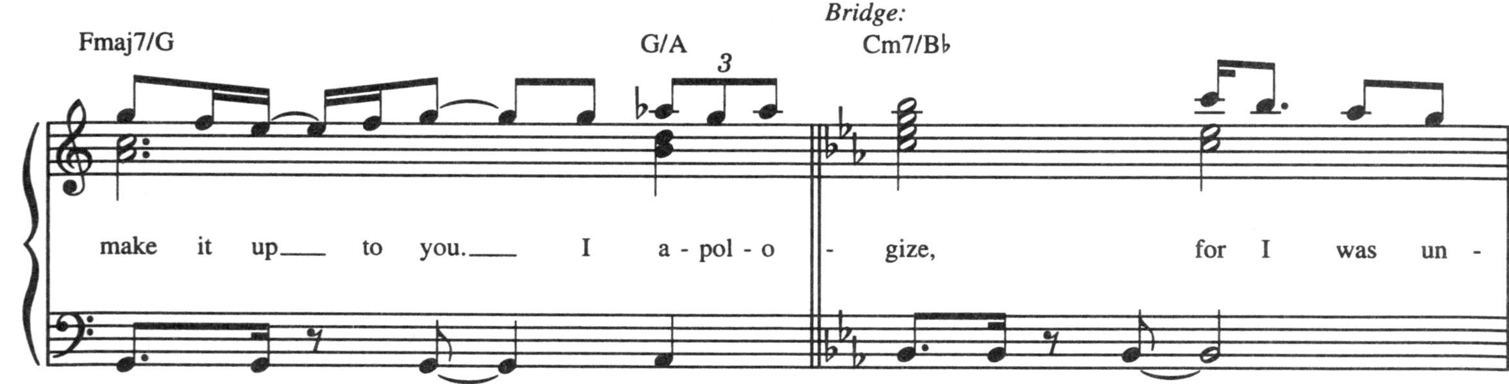
Fmaj7/G
G/A
3
Bridge:
Cm7/B♭
make it up to you. I a - pol - o
- gize, for I was un -

B♭/C
Cm7/B♭
kind___ and I wish that I___ could_ roll back in time,_

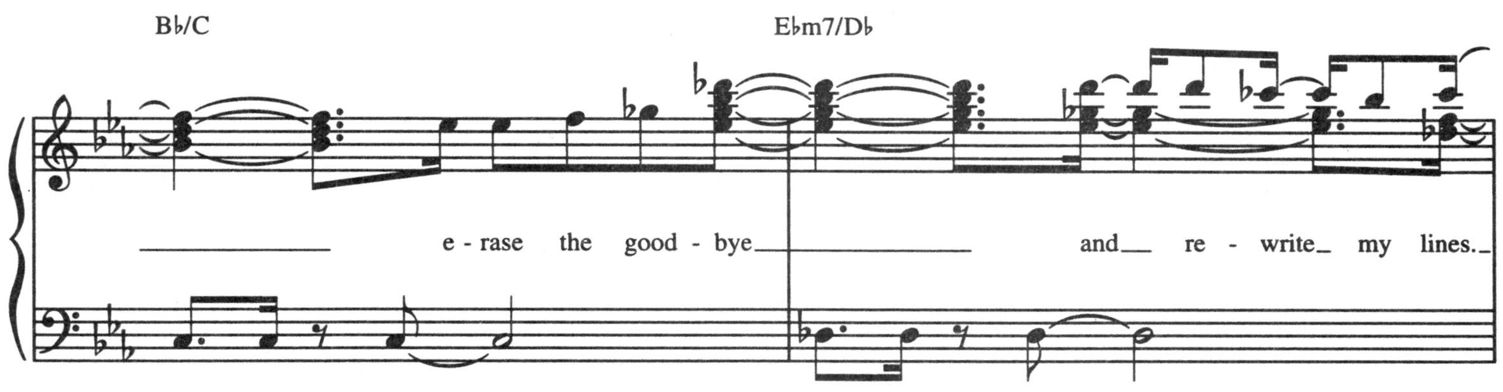
B♭/C
E♭m7/D♭
___ e - rase the good - bye___ and_ re - write_ my lines._

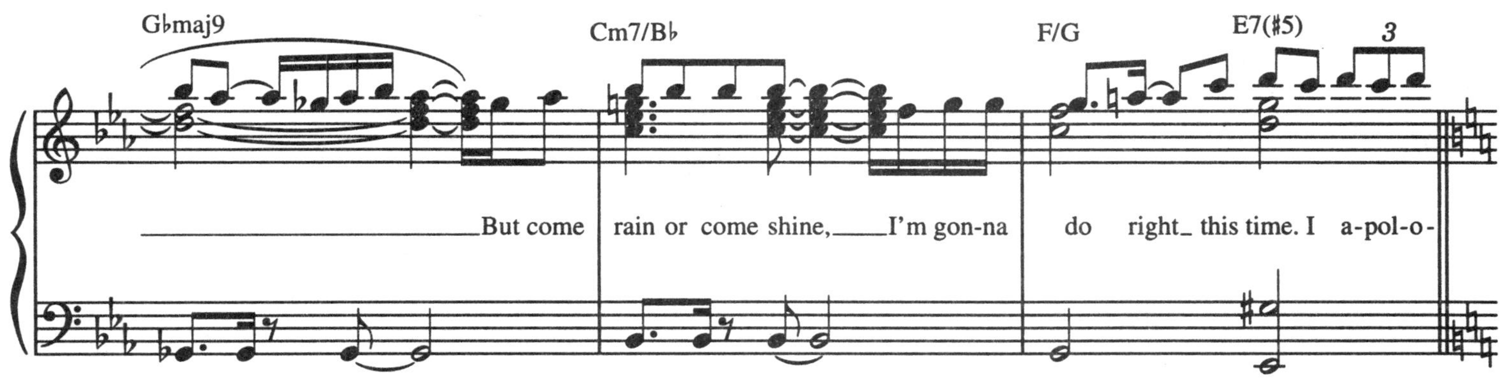
G♭maj9
Cm7/B♭
F/G
E7(♯5)
3
___But come rain or come shine,___I'm gon-na do right_ this time. I a-pol-o-

Am9
C7
Fmaj7
E7(♯5)
gize,___ woh, be - lieve me,_ I do._ I a - pol - o - gize_

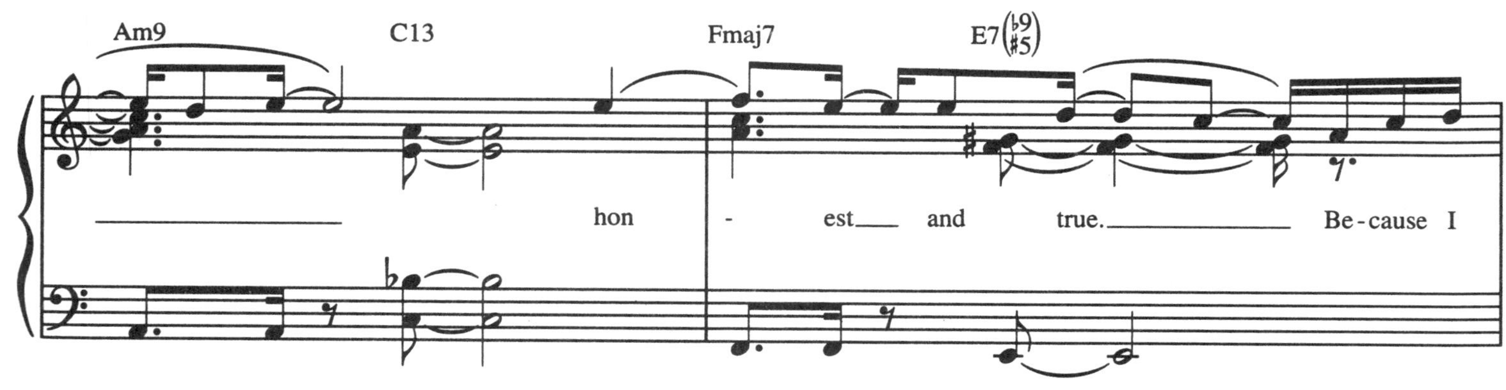

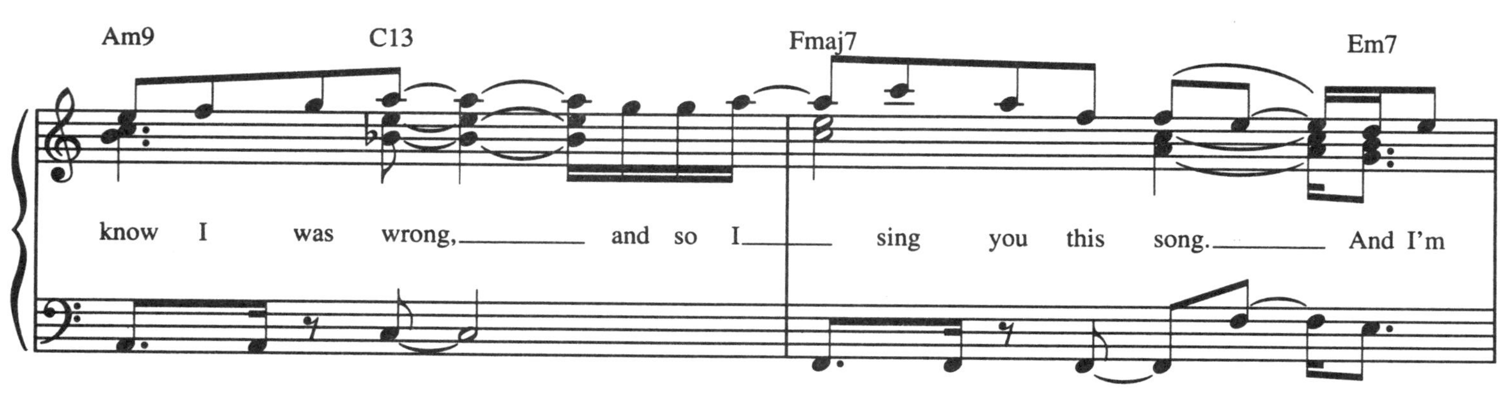

Verse 2:
Operator, it was like a bad dream.
And Lord, you should have heard the way he shouted
And the way that I screamed.
Oh, I regret it 'cause I was unfair.
I took it all out on him
Just because he was there.
When the road gets rough
You say things you should not say.
I never meant to treat my baby that way. *(To Chorus:)*

YOU'RE THE VOICE

Lyrics and Music by
ANDY QUNTA & CHRIS THOMPSON &
MAGGIE RYDER & KEITH REID

Rock ♩=84
N.C.
mf
1.
2.
E♭/F
Gm/F
E♭/F
Verse:
F
1. We have
the chance
to turn
the pag - es
2. This
time
we know
we all
can stand
to -
mf
mf

o - ver.
geth - er,
We can
with the
write what we wan-na write,
pow-er to be pow-er-ful,
we got-ta make ends meet be-fore we get much
be - liev - ing we can make it
old - er.
bet - ter.

B♭ C/B♭ B♭ C/B♭ B♭
We're all some-one's daugh-ter,
B♭ C/B♭ B♭ C F B♭ C/B♭ B♭ C/B♭
we're all some-one's son. How long can we look at each oth-er
B♭ C/B♭ B♭ C
1. To Next Strain
down the bar-rel of a gun?
cresc.
2. 3.
cresc.

Chorus:
F
f You're the voice, try and un - der-stand _ it. Make a noise and make _ it clear. _
f
E♭
B♭/D
E♭
Oh, _ oh. _
F
We're not gon-na sit in si - lence. We're not gon-na live with fear. _
To Coda
1.
D.S.
E♭
B♭/D
E♭
Oh, _ oh. _
dim.

2.
To Next Strain
3. 4. 5. (after 5th ending to Coda)
B♭/D
E♭
B♭/D
E♭
B♭
(Instrumental solo...
A♭
1.
E♭/G
A♭
2.
E♭/G
A♭
D.S.S.
...end solo)
Coda
B♭/D
E♭
N.C.
dim.
mf dim.
mp
dim.
p

Showstoppers

100 or more titles in each volume of this Best-Selling Series!

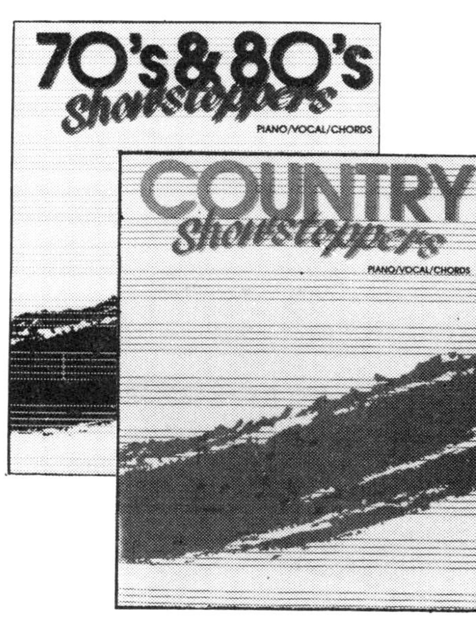

Piano/Vocal/Chords:

20's, 30's, & 40's SHOWSTOPPERS
(F2865SMX)

100 nostalgic favorites include: Chattanooga Choo Choo • Pennsylvania 6-5000 • Blue Moon • Moonglow • My Blue Heaven • Ain't Misbehavin' • That Old Black Magic and more.

50's & 60's SHOWSTOPPERS
(F2864SMB)

Bop back to a simpler time and enjoy: Aquarius/Let the Sunshine In • (Sittin' On) The Dock of the Bay • Hey, Good Lookin' • Sunny • Johnny Angel and more.

70's & 80's SHOWSTOPPERS
P/V/C (F2863SME)
Easy Piano (F2863P2X)

100 pop songs from two decades. Titles include: Anything for You • Blue Bayou • Hungry Eyes • I Wanna Dance with Somebody (Who Loves Me) • If You Say My Eyes Are Beautiful • I'll Never Love This Way Again • Isn't She Lovely • Old Time Rock & Roll • When the Night Comes.

BIG NOTE PIANO SHOWSTOPPERS
Vol. 1 (F2871P3C) Vol. 2 (F2918P3A)

Easy-to-read big note arrangements of 100 popular tunes include: Do You Want to Know a Secret? • If Ever You're in My Arms Again • Moon River • Over the Rainbow • Singin' in the Rain • You Light Up My Life • Theme from *Love Story*.

BROADWAY SHOWSTOPPERS
(F2878SMB)

100 great show tunes include: Ain't Misbehavin' • Almost Like Being in Love • Consider Yourself • Give My Regards to Broadway • Good Morning Starshine • Mood Indigo • Send in the Clowns • Tomorrow.

CHRISTMAS SHOWSTOPPERS
P/V/C (F2868SMA)
Easy Piano (F2924P2X)
Big Note (F2925P3X)

100 favorite holiday songs including: Sleigh Ride • Silver Bells • Deck the Halls • Have Yourself a Merry Little Christmas • Here Comes Santa Claus • Little Drummer Boy • Let It Snow! Let It Snow! Let It Snow!

CLASSICAL PIANO SHOWSTOPPERS
(F2872P9X)

100 classical intermediate piano solos include: Arioso • Bridal Chorus (from *Lohengrin)* • Clair de Lune • Fifth Symphony (Theme) • Minuet in G • Moonlight Sonata (1st Movement) • Polovetsian Dance (from *Prince Igor)* • The Swan • Wedding March (from *A Midsummer Night's Dream)*.

COUNTRY SHOWSTOPPERS
(F2902SMC)

A fine collection of 101 favorite country classics and standards including: Cold, Cold Heart • For the Good Times • I'm So Lonesome I Could Cry • There's a Tear in My Beer • Young Country and more.

EASY GUITAR SHOWSTOPPERS
(F2934EGA)

100 guitar arrangements of new chart hits, old favorites, classics and solid gold songs. Includes melody, chords and lyrics for songs like: Didn't We • Love Theme from *St. Elmo's Fire* (For Just a Moment) • Out Here on My Own • Please Mr. Postman • Proud Mary • The Way He Makes Me Feel • With You I'm Born Again • You're the Inspiration.

EASY LISTENING SHOWSTOPPERS
(F3069SMX)

85 easy listening songs including popular favorites, standards, TV and movie selections like: After All (Love Theme from *Chances Are)* • From a Distance • The Greatest Love of All • Here We Are • Theme from *Ice Castles* (Through the Eyes of Love) • The Vows Go Unbroken (Always True to You) • You Are So Beautiful.

EASY ORGAN SHOWSTOPPERS
(F2873EOB)

100 great current hits and timeless standards in easy arrangements for organ include: After the Lovin' • Always and Forever • Come Saturday Morning • I Just Called to Say I Love You • Isn't She Lovely • On the Wings of Love • Up Where We Belong • You Light Up My Life.

EASY PIANO SHOWSTOPPERS
Vol. 1 (F2875P2D) Vol. 2 (F2912P2C)

100 easy piano arrangements of familiar songs include: Alfie • Baby Elephant Walk • Classical Gas • Don't Cry Out Loud • Colour My World • The Pink Panther • I Honestly Love You.

JAZZ SHOWSTOPPERS
(F2953SMX)

101 standard jazz tunes including: Misty • Elmer's Tune • Birth of the Blues • It Don't Mean a Thing (If It Ain't Got That Swing).

MOVIE SHOWSTOPPERS
(F2866SMC)

100 songs from memorable motion pictures include Axel F • Up Where We Belong • Speak Softly Love (from *The Godfather)* • The Entertainer • Fame • Nine to Five • Nobody Does It Better.

POPULAR PIANO SHOWSTOPPERS
(F2876P9B)

100 popular intermediate piano solos include: Baby Elephant Walk • Gonna Fly Now (Theme from *Rocky)* • The Hill Street Blues Theme • Love Is a Many-Splendored Thing • (Love Theme from) *Romeo and Juliet* • Separate Lives (Love Theme from *White Nights)* • The Shadow of Your Smile • Theme from *The Apartment* • Theme from *New York, New York*.

RAGTIME SHOWSTOPPERS
(F2867SMX)

These 100 original classic rags by Scott Joplin, James Scott, Joseph Lamb and other ragtime composers include: Maple Leaf Rag • The Entertainer • Kansas City Rag • Ma Rag Time Baby • The St. Louis Rag • World's Fair Rag and many others.

ROMANTIC SHOWSTOPPERS
(F2870SMC)

101 beautiful songs including: After All (Love Theme from *Chances Are)* • Here and Now • I Can't Stop Loving You • If You Say My Eyes Are Beautiful • The Vows Go Unbroken (Always True to You) • You Got It.

TELEVISION SHOWSTOPPERS
(F2874SMC)

103 TV themes including: Another World • Dear John • Hall or Nothing (The Arsenio Hall Show) • Star Trek -The Next Generation (Main Title) • Theme from "Cheers" (Where Everybody Knows Your Name).

Piano/Vocal/Chords Editions

Featuring more than than 400 great titles spanning over 100 years of popular music songwriting.

Volume 1
THE GREATEST SONGS OF 1890-1920
Piano/Vocal/Chords (THL1001B)

Volume 2
THE GREATEST SONGS OF 1920-1940
Piano/Vocal/Chords (THL1002C)

Volume 3
THE GREATEST SONGS OF 1940-1960
Piano/Vocal/Chords (THL1003B)

Volume 4
THE GREATEST SONGS OF 1960-1975
Piano/Vocal/Chords (THL1004C)

Volume 5
THE GREATEST SONGS OF 1975-1990
Piano/Vocal/Chords (THL1005B)

Volume 6
THE GREAT SONGS & CAROLS OF CHRISTMAS
Piano/Vocal/Chords (THL1006C)

Volume 7
THE GREAT SONGS & THEMES OF THE MOVIES
Piano/Vocal/Chords (THL1007A)

Volume 8
THE GREAT SONGS OF BROADWAY
Piano/Vocal/Chords (THL1008B)

Volume 9
THE GREAT SONGS OF COUNTRY MUSIC
Piano/Vocal/Chords (THL1009A)

Volume 10
THE GREAT THEMES & PIECES OF CLASSICAL MUSIC
Piano Solo (THL1010A)

also available:
HOME LIBRARY COMPREHENSIVE INDEX
(CATTHL)
A complete listing of all the song titles used throughout the various volumes and editions of this ten volume series. Adjacent to each song title is the number of the volume(s) which contains the song.

For your free copy of this important reference, please write to:
NEW HOME LIBRARY SERIES COMPREHENSIVE INDEX,
P.O. Box 4340, Hialeah, FL 33014-4340

The Book of *Golden* Series

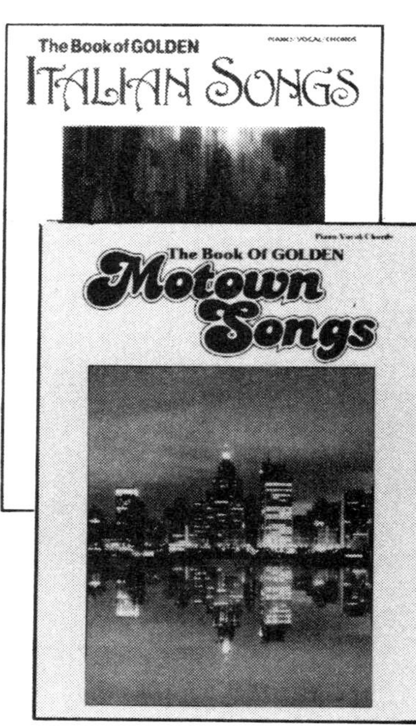

THE BOOK OF GOLDEN ALL-TIME FAVORITES
(F2939SMX) Piano/Vocal/Chords

THE BOOK OF GOLDEN BIG BAND FAVORITES
(F3172SMX) Piano/Vocal/Chords

THE BOOK OF GOLDEN BROADWAY
(F2986SMX) Piano/Vocal/Chords

THE NEW BOOK OF GOLDEN CHRISTMAS
(F2478SMB) Piano/Vocal/Chords
(F2478EOX) Easy Organ
(F2478COX) Chord Organ

THE BOOK OF GOLDEN COUNTRY MUSIC
(F2926SMA) Piano/Vocal/Chords

THE BOOK OF GOLDEN HAWAIIAN SONGS
(F3113SMX) Piano/Vocal/Chords

THE BOOK OF GOLDEN IRISH SONGS
(F3212SMX) Piano/Vocal/Chords

THE BOOK OF GOLDEN ITALIAN SONGS
(F2907SMX) Piano/Vocal/Chords

THE BOOK OF GOLDEN JAZZ
(F3012SMX) Piano/Vocal/Chords

THE NEW BOOK OF GOLDEN LATIN SONGS
(F3049SMX) Piano/Vocal/Chords

THE NEW BOOK OF GOLDEN LOVE SONGS
(F2415SOX) Organ

THE BOOK OF GOLDEN MOTOWN SONGS
(F3144SMX) Piano/Vocal/Chords

THE NEW BOOK OF GOLDEN MOVIE THEMES, Volume 1
(F2810SMX) Piano/Vocal/Chords

THE NEW BOOK OF GOLDEN MOVIE THEMES, Volume 2
(F2811SMX) Piano/Vocal/Chords

THE BOOK OF GOLDEN POPULAR FAVORITES
(F2233SMX) Piano/Vocal/Chords

THE BOOK OF GOLDEN POPULAR PIANO SOLOS
(F3193P9X) Intermediate/
Advanced Piano

THE BOOK OF GOLDEN ROCK 'N' ROLL
(F2830SMB) Piano/Vocal/Chords

THE NEW BOOK OF GOLDEN WEDDING SONGS
(F2265SMA) Piano/Vocal/Chords